Contents

ROME AT WAR

Kate Gilliver, Adrian Goldsworthy
& Michael Whitby
Foreword by Steven Saylor

ROME AT WAR

Kate Gilliver, Adrian Goldsworthy
& Michael Whitby
Foreword by **Steven Saylor**

First published in Great Britain in 2005 by Osprey Publishing,
Midland House, West Way, Botley, Oxford OX2 0PH, UK

443 Park Avenue South, New York, NY 10016, USA

Email: info@ospreypublishing.com

Previously published as Essential Histories 43: *Caesar's Gallic Wars
58–50 BC*, Essential Histories 42: *Caesar's Civil War 49–44 BC*,
and Essential Histories 21: *Rome at War AD 293–696*

Every attempt has been made by the publisher to secure the
appropriate permissions for material reproduced in this book.
If there has been any oversight we will be happy to rectify
the situation and written submission should be made to
the Publishers.

CIP data for this publication is available from the British Library

ISBN 1 84176 856 1

Editor: Ruth Sheppard
Design: Ken Vail Graphic Design, Cambridge, UK
Cartography by The Map Studio
Index by Alison Worthington
Originated by PPS Grasmere, Leeds, UK
Printed and bound in China by L. Rex Printing Company Ltd.

05 06 07 08 09   10 9 8 7 6 5 4 3 2 1

For a catalogue of all books published by Osprey Publishing
please contact:

Osprey Direct UK, PO Box 140,
Wellingborough, Northants, NN8 2FA, UK.
Email: info@ospreydirect.co.uk

Osprey Direct USA, 2427 Bond Street,
University Park, IL 60466, USA
E-mail: info@ospreydirectusa.com

www.ospreypublishing.com

Caesar's legacy and its twilight
by Steven Saylor

'Julius Caesar stood before a statue of Alexander the Great and wept,' Gore Vidal tells us, 'for Alexander at 29 had conquered the world and at 32 was dead, while Caesar, a late starter of 33, had not yet subverted even his own state.'

In due course, Caesar would become a conqueror himself, then a revolutionary, and finally dictator for life of the Roman world. His achievements would more than match those of Alexander, but at the age of 56 he would nonetheless feel compelled to follow in Alexander's footsteps and head eastward in pursuit of further conquests. For better or worse, his campaign against the Parthians never got past the planning stages, thanks to the assassins who abruptly ended all Caesar's ambitions on the Ides of March, 44 BC.

Like Alexander, Caesar conquered the world but never had the chance to rule it; he can be assessed as a general, but not as a king. And like Alexander, Caesar would cast a long shadow across those who followed, all the way from Augustus, the founder of empire, to the rulers who oversaw the Empire's dismantlement and gradual eclipse. Seven centuries after Caesar, emperors who no longer ruled from Rome but from Constantinople, who no longer issued orders in Latin but in Greek, who no longer sacrificed to Jupiter but instead shared the body of Christ, and whom we would call Byzantine rather than Roman, would nonetheless declare themselves the heirs of Caesar and do their best to emulate him.

Caesar was a tireless self-promoter as well as a bold and skilful general, and thanks to his propagandistic memoirs we know a great deal about his campaigns against the Gauls. We must assume that most contemporary Romans approved of Caesar's actions in Gaul, even when those actions amounted to what we would call atrocities. Consider the massacre of the Usipi and Tencteri, the details of which we know from Caesar's own cold-blooded account: 'Because they had brought all their possessions with them when they had abandoned their homes and crossed the Rhine, there were also many women and children, and they began to flee in all directions. Caesar ordered the cavalry to hunt them down.' No mercy was shown, as Kate Gilliver reminds us in her study of Caesar's Gallic Wars in Part I, and the result was a bloody slaughter of non-combatants. Undoubtedly many citizens back in Rome proudly applauded such a result, however, some expressed dismay at Caesar's conduct; Cato demanded that Caesar should be tried for war crimes, and his intransigence on the matter was one of the issues that eventually led to civil war. Of course, Cato was no less a politician than Caesar, and it may be, as Gilliver asserts, that the concern of those wishing to prosecute Caesar 'was aimed more at destroying Caesar's reputation than exacting justice.'

Historians who lived a century ago, looking back on Napoleon from a safe distance and unable to imagine what awaited the world with Hitler and Stalin, tended to be a bit starry-eyed in their assessment of Caesar. Nowadays, historians feel obliged to come to grips with the human suffering of the Gallic Wars, where, as Adrian Goldsworthy notes, Caesar and his legions fought 'with extreme brutality, some sources claiming that over a million people had been killed in less than a decade.' Of course, genocide was not the actual goal of Caesar's campaign; survivors were valuable as slaves, and the sale of humans made Caesar a very wealthy man.

His successes in Gaul also put Caesar in a position to make his next move: a war against Rome itself, or more precisely, against his rivals in the ruling class. The complicated events that led to the Roman Civil War have seldom been so concisely laid out as in Goldsworthy's evaluation in Part II. Equally cogent is his assessment of the two ways of viewing Caesar and his legacy. In between, the course of battles from Spain to Egypt, and the interplay of personalities still vivid across the centuries – Cato, Clodius, Cicero, Caesar, Pompey, Cleopatra, Antony and the rest – make for one of the most fascinating epochs in all of human history.

The chaos of civil war was eventually replaced by the Pax Romana of the Empire, which reached its height under Hadrian and the Antonines, two centuries after Caesar; but then, to borrow from the historian Cassius Dio, 'a realm of gold' turned 'to one of iron and rust'. The era of which Michael Whitby writes in Part III finds the ship which Caesar launched to be overloaded, springing one leak after another, encircled by sharks, and sailing dangerously close to the rocks.

The emperors and generals of this era would surely have emulated Caesar – and, looking east, Alexander – if they could have, but most of their energy was consumed with putting down palace intrigues, snuffing out treacherous kinfolk, fretting about taxation, bracing for barbarian invasions, and keeping up with the Persians – the rival 'superpower' of the day. Justinian and his general Belisarius enjoyed the satisfaction of reconquest, but those who came before and after learned to live with disaster as a daily occurrence; no wonder apocalyptic religion took such a firm hold on the popular imagination. The emperor Heraclius, who should be better known, lost an empire, then regained it, then lost it again to the sudden and overwhelming rise of Islam, which dismembered the enfeebled Roman Empire for good and put an end forever to the dreams of any would-be Caesars.

Whitby's task – to give coherence to a tumultuous era of lowered expectations – is more problematic than that of Gilliver and Goldsworthy, and the sources upon which he must draw are more scattered and obscure. Nonetheless, this era of decline and fall, which so inspired Gibbon, casts its own spell – not the sun-drenched allure of the Classical World with its godlike mortals emulating the conduct of all-too-human gods, but the more mysterious, shadowy, ethereal fascination of the Byzantines, who charted a path away from earthly glory toward an invisible empire which they declared to be divine.

Chronology

390 BC	Gallic sack of Rome.
154 BC	Marseilles, a Greek city, requests help from Rome after threats from Gallic tribes.
122 BC	Alliance formed between Rome and Aedui tribe; Rome campaigns against Allobroges tribe.
121 BC	A Roman army 30,000 strong defeats a combined force of Arverni and Allobroges reportedly 200,000 strong; the Allobroges are incorporated within Roman territory; the Via Domitia road is built across southern France, linking Italy and Spain.
118 BC	Roman colony of Narbo (Narbonne) is founded.
113–101 BC	Invasions of Gaul and Italy by Cimbri and Teutones (Germanic tribes).
106 BC	Birth of Cnaeus Pompey and Marcus Tullius Cicero.
105 BC	Romans suffer massive defeat at Arausio at the hands of migrating German tribes.
104–100 BC	Caius Marius elected to five successive consulships to deal with German threat.
100 BC	Birth of Julius Caesar.
91–89 BC	The Social War, a widespread rebellion of Rome's Italian allies, defeated only after heavy Roman losses; Roman citizenship is extended to nearly all the peoples of Italy.
88 BC	Marius attempts to take the eastern command away from Lucius Cornelius Sulla; Sulla marches with his army on Rome, the first time any Roman commander has done this.

87 BC	Marius and his ally Cinna seize power in Rome, massacring their opponents; Marius dies of natural causes.
83–80 BC	Sulla lands in Italy and is joined by Pompey; Sulla defeats his opponents and wins the civil war; Sulla becomes dictator, publishes the proscriptions, and attempts to reform the state, rebuilding the Senate's authority.
79 BC	Sulla retires.
78 BC	One of the consuls, Lepidus, stages a coup; the Senate uses Pompey to defeat him.
73–71 BC	An escaped gladiator called Spartacus rebels and forms a huge army of slaves; he defeats successive Roman armies and devastates much of Italy before he is finally defeated by Marcus Licinius Crassus.
71 BC	Rivalry between Aedui and Arverni leads to the Sequani, Arvernian allies, hiring German mercenaries and together they defeat the Aedui.
71 BC	Pompey and Crassus camp with their armies outside Rome and demand the right to stand for election to the consulship.
70 BC	Consulship of Pompey and Crassus.
67 BC	Pompey given extraordinary command against the pirates.
66 & 62 BC	Allobroges revolt, mainly because of poor Roman administration.
66 BC	Pompey given extraordinary command against Mithridates of Pontus.

63 BC	The consul Cicero defeats the attempted coup of Catiline.
62 BC	Pompey returns from the east but fails to secure land for his veterans or the ratification of his Eastern Settlement.
61 BC	Caesar becomes propraetorian governor of Further Spain.
61 BC	Aedui request help from Rome; Rome declines to assist but the Senate formally confirms Roman support for them. The Helvetii prepare to migrate to western France.
60 BC	Caesar returns and forms the 'first triumvirate' with Pompey and Crassus.
59 BC	Consulship of Caesar and Bibulus; Caesar is appointed governor of northern Italy (Cisalpine Gaul) and Dalmatia for five years; Southern France (Transalpine Gaul) is added to Caesar's jurisdiction after the sudden death of the governor.
58 BC	Clodius forces Cicero into exile. Caesar takes up his governorship; in late June he defeats the migrating Helvetii at Bibracte and orders them home; in mid-September Caesar defeats Ariovistus.
57 BC	Serious rioting in Rome; Pompey called upon to supervise corn supply. Caesar campaigns against the Belgae; late in the year, Galba is defeated in the Alps.
56 BC	Crisis in the triumvirate averted by meeting of Pompey, Crassus and Caesar at Luca; Caesar's command is extended for a further five years. Roman naval defeat of Veneti; Roman legate Sabinus defeats tribes of Normandy; Roman legate Crassus reduces Aquitania (south-west France); The Menapii and Morini (Belgian coast and Rhine delta)

	successfully resist Roman incursions.
55 BC	Second consulship of Pompey and Crassus. German tribes cross the Rhine and are massacred by Caesar; the Romans bridge the Rhine. First Roman invasion of Britain.
54 BC	Serious rioting in Rome; death of Julia. Crassus invades Parthia. Morini submit to Rome, possibly intimidated by the presence of the Roman fleet in the English Channel; attacks on Roman winter camps in Gaul. Second Roman invasion of Britain.
53 BC	Crassus is defeated and killed by Parthians at Carrhae. Caesar leads punitive campaigns against Belgic tribes.
52 BC	Milo's gang kills Clodius. Gallic revolt: siege of Alesia; surrender of Vercingetorix.
51 BC	Repeated attacks on Caesar's position in the Senate; Pompey passes law requiring a five-year interval between holding a magistracy and being appointed to a province. Cicero sent to Cilicia. Gallic revolt: Blockade and surrender of Uxellodunum (in Lot, south-west France).
50 BC	Curio acts on Caesar's behalf in the Senate; Cato and other prominent senators struggle to ensure that Caesar will not be permitted to stand for the consulship without laying down his command; Pompey's position unclear for much of the year. Minor Roman campaigns in central Gaul.
49 BC	The tribunes flee from Rome; Caesar crosses the Rubicon and civil war begins; Pompey

chased out of Italy, and sails with most of his troops from Brundisium to Macedonia; Caesar defeats Afranius and Petreius in Spain; Curio defeated and killed in Africa.

48 BC Caesar crosses to Macedonia; prolonged stalemate at Dyrrachium eventually broken when Caesar retreats; Pompey brought to battle at Pharsalus and utterly defeated; Pompey flees to Egypt and is murdered; Caesar pursues him and is besieged in Alexandria; beginning of affair between Caesar and Cleopatra.

47 BC Caesar is able to break the siege of Alexandria after reinforcements arrive, and defeats the Egyptian army; later in the year he moves to Asia and defeats Pharnaces at Zela; Caesar returns to Rome and prepares to campaign against the Pompeian army mustering in Africa under Scipio, Cato and Juba.

46 BC African war ended by Caesar's victory at Thapsus; Cato and Juba commit suicide, and Scipio is drowned; Caesar returns to Rome and celebrates triumphs, but departs for Spain in the autumn.

45 BC Spanish War ended by Caesar's victory at Munda; Labienus, Pompey's eldest son, killed; Caesar returns to Rome and establishes dictatorship.

44 BC Caesar is planning major Parthian expedition; he is murdered on 15 March by a conspiracy led by Brutus and Cassius; Octavian arrives in Rome and rallies support from Caesar's veterans; Antony given command in Cisalpine Gaul.

43 BC Octavian initially fights Antony on the Senate's behalf, but later in the year they, with Lepidus, form the Second Triumvirate; they capture Rome and reintroduce the proscriptions, executing large numbers of prominent Romans, including Cicero.

42 BC Brutus and Cassius defeated at Philippi.

41 BC Antony visits Cleopatra in Alexandria and their affair becomes publicly known.

40 BC Antony marries Octavia.

40–36 BC Antony's Parthian War.

38 BC Sextus Pompeius wins naval victories over Octavian.

37 BC Antony publicly 'marries' Cleopatra.

36 BC Sextus Pompeius defeated at Naulochus near Sicily.

32 BC Octavia openly divorced by Antony; open civil war between Antony and Octavian.

31 BC Octavian defeats Antony at Actium; Antony and Cleopatra escape, but commit suicide; Octavian becomes undisputed master of the Roman world.

27 BC Octavian takes name Augustus and restores Republic; provinces shared between Senate and Augustus.

27–24 BC Campaigns in Gaul and Spain.

20 BC Parthians return captured Roman standards.

12–9 BC Campaigns in Balkans.

12 BC–AD 6 Campaigns in Germany.

AD 6–9 Suppression of provincial revolts.

AD 9 Varian disaster in the Teutoberger forest in Germany.

AD 14 Death of Augustus; legions revolt in Pannonia and on Rhine.

AD 17–24 Campaigns against Tacfarinas in Africa.

AD 40–44 Conquest of Mauretania.

AD 43 Claudius begins invasion of Britain.

AD 58–63 Campaigns against Parthia.

AD 61	Revolt of Boudicca in Britain.
AD 66	Start of Jewish Revolt.
AD 68–9	The Year of the Four Emperors: civil war breaks out after suicide of Nero.
AD 69	Victory of Vespasian ends civil war.
AD 70	Capture of Jerusalem and destruction of Temple.
AD 83–97	Domitian campaigns against Dacians on Danube and Chatti on Rhine.
AD 98	Accession of Trajan.
AD 101–6	Dacian Wars.
AD 106	Annexation of Arabia.
AD 113–17	Campaigns against Parthians.
AD 115–17	Jewish revolt.
AD 117	Accession of Hadrian; evacuation of eastern conquests.
AD 122–6	Construction of Hadrian's Wall in north Britain.
AD 132–5	Bar Kochva revolt in Judaea.
AD 142	Construction of Antonine Wall in north Britain.
AD 161	Accession of Marcus Aurelius; Parthians invade Syria and Armenia.
AD 162–6	Lucius Verus campaigns against Parthians.
AD 166	German tribes cross upper Danube.
AD 167–80	German wars of Marcus Aurelius.
AD 180	Accession of Commodus; peace with Quadi and Marcomanni.
AD 192	Assassination of Commodus.
AD 192–3	Year of the Five Emperors: civil war.
AD 193	Septimius Severus defeats Pescennius Niger in East.
AD 194–5	Severus campaigns against Parthians.
AD 197	Severus defeats Clodius Albinus in Gaul.
AD 197–200	Further campaigns of Severus against Parthians.
AD 208–11	Severus campaigns with sons Caracalla and Geta in north Britain.
AD 211	Accession of Caracalla.
AD 213–14	Caracalla campaigns on Danube.
AD 215–17	Caracalla campaigns in East.
AD 217	Assassination of Caracalla.
AD 222	Accession of Severus Alexander.
AD 226	Sassanid Ardashir overthrows Parthian dynasty.
AD 231–2	Severus Alexander campaigns against Sassanids.
AD 234–5	Severus Alexander campaigns against German tribes.
AD 235	Murder of Severus Alexander by troops.
AD 243/4	Gordian defeated by Shapur I of Persia.
AD 251	Death of Decius in battle against Goths.
AD 260	Defeat and capture of Valerian by Persians. Franks invade Gaul; Alamanni invade Italy; revolts in Balkans.
AD 261–68	Odaenathus of Palmyra takes control of eastern provinces.
AD 262–67	Goths invade Asia Minor.
AD 271	Aurelian withdraws Romans from Dacia. Circuit of walls built for Rome.
AD 272	Aurelian defeats Palmyra.
AD 275	Murder of Aurelian.
AD 284	Accession of Diocletian.
AD 293	Tetrarchy: Diocletian appoints Maximian as co-Augustus and Constantius and Galerius as Caesars.
AD 305	Abdication of Diocletian and Maximian.
AD 312	Constantine captures Rome after battle of Milvian Bridge.
AD 324	Constantine defeats Licinius and becomes sole emperor.
AD 337	Death of Constantine at start of campaign against Persia.
AD 353	Constantius II defeats usurper Magnentius and reunifies Empire.
AD 355	Julian co-opted by Constantius as Caesar.
AD 357	Julian defeats Alamanni at Strasburg.

AD 361	Death of Constantius.
AD 363	Julian's invasion of Persia and death.
AD 376	Goths cross the Danube.
AD 378	Defeat and death of Valens at Adrianople (Edirne).
AD 382	Theodosius settles Goths in Balkans as federates.
AD 394	Theodosius defeats usurper Eugenius and reunifies Empire.
AD 395	Death of Theodosius; Empire divided between Arcadius and Honorius.
AD 406	German tribes breach Rhine frontier.
AD 408	Stilicho executed.
AD 410	Sack of Rome by Alaric and Visigoths.
AD 418	Establishment of Visigoths in Aquitania.
AD 429	Vandals cross into Africa.
AD 445	Attila becomes sole ruler of Huns.
AD 451	Attila invades Gaul; defeated at Catalaunian Plains (near Troyes).
AD 453	Death of Attila.
AD 455	Vandals sack Rome.
AD 476	Odoacer deposes Romulus Augustulus, the last western emperor.
AD 493	Theoderic captures Ravenna and kills Odoacer.
AD 502	Kavadh invades eastern provinces and captures Amida (Diyarbakir).
AD 505	Truce on eastern frontier; construction of Dara starts.
AD 507	Clovis and Franks defeat Visigoths at Vouillé.
AD 527	Renewed warfare in east. Accession of Justinian.
AD 532	'Endless Peace' with Persia.
AD 533	Belisarius defeats Vandals and recovers Africa.
AD 540	Belisarius enters Ravenna and ends Ostrogothic kingdom. Khusro I invades eastern provinces and captures Antioch.
AD 542	Arrival of bubonic plague.
AD 546	Totila recaptures Rome.
AD 552	Narses defeats and kills Totila at Busta Gallorum.
AD 562	Fifty Years Peace with Persia.
AD 568	Lombards invade Italy.
AD 572	Justin II launches new war on eastern frontier.
AD 578/9	Avar invasions of Balkans start.
AD 586/7	Slav raids reach Athens and Corinth.
AD 591	Termination of war with Persia.
AD 602	Revolt of Balkan army and overthrow of Maurice.
AD 610	Heraclius captures Constantinople and kills Phocas.
AD 614	Persians capture Jerusalem.
AD 622	Muhammad leaves Medina (*Hijra*).
AD 626	Avars besiege Constantinople, with Persian support.
AD 627	Heraclius defeats Persians at Nineveh.
AD 632	Death of Muhammad.
AD 636	Arabs defeat Romans at River Yarmuk.
AD 638	Arabs capture Jerusalem.
AD 639	Arabs attack Egypt.
AD 642	Arabs capture Alexandria.
AD 651	Death of Yazdgard III, last Sassanid ruler.
AD 661	Mu'awiyah becomes Caliph at Damascus.

Introduction

The Roman Republic and its growing problems

Although originally a monarchy, Rome had become a republic near the end of the sixth century BC. Such political revolutions were commonplace in the city-states of the ancient world, but after this Rome proved remarkably stable, free from the often violent internal disputes that constantly beset other communities. Gradually at first, the Romans expanded their territory, and by the beginning of the third century BC they controlled virtually all of the Italian peninsula. Conflict with Carthage, which began in 265 BC and continued sporadically until that city was utterly destroyed in 146 BC, resulted in the acquisition of overseas provinces. By this time Rome dominated the entire Mediterranean world, having defeated with ease the successor kingdoms which had emerged from the break-up of Alexander the Great's empire.

Roman expansion continued, and time and time again her legions were successful in foreign wars, never losing a conflict even if they sometimes suffered defeat in individual battles. Yet, the stability and unity of purpose which had so characterised Roman political life for centuries began to break down.

The Roman republican system was intended to prevent any individual or group within the state from gaining overwhelming and permanent power. The Republic's senior executive officers or magistrates, the most senior of whom were the two consuls, held power (*imperium*) for a single year, after which they returned to civilian life. A mixture of custom and law prevented any individual being elected to the same office in successive years, or at a young age, and in fact it was rare for the consulship to be held more than twice by any man. Former magistrates, and the pick of the wealthiest citizens in the state formed the Senate, a permanent council which advised the magistrates and also supervised much of the business of government, for instance, despatching and receiving embassies. The Senate also chose the province (which at this period still meant sphere of responsibility and only gradually was acquiring fixed geographical associations) to be allocated to each magistrate, and could extend the *imperium* of a man within the same province for several years.

Roman politics was fiercely competitive, as senators pursued a career that brought them both civil and military responsibilities, sometimes simultaneously. It was very rare for men standing for election to advocate any specific policies, and there was nothing in any way equivalent to modern political parties within the Senate. Each aristocrat instead tried to represent himself as a capable man, ready to cope with whatever task the Republic required of him, be it leading an army or building an aqueduct. Men paraded their past achievements and – since often before election they personally had done little – the achievements of past generations of their family. Vast sums of money were lavished on the electorate, especially in the form of games, gladiator shows, feasts and the building of great monuments. This gave great advantages to a small core of established and exceptionally wealthy families who as a result tended to dominate the senior magistracies. In the first century there were eight praetorships (senior magistracies of lower ranking than consulships), and even more of the less senior posts, but still only ever two consulships. This meant that the majority of the 600 senators would never achieve this office. The higher magistracies and most of all

The Via Sacra runs through the heart of Rome, at this point passing through the Forum. This route was followed by the triumphal processions honouring successful generals. (AKG Berlin)

the consulship offered the opportunity for the greatest responsibilities and therefore allowed men to achieve the greatest glory, which enhanced their family name for the future. The consuls commanded in the most important wars, and in Rome military glory always counted for more than any other achievement. The victor in a great war was also likely to profit from it financially, taking a large share of the booty and the profits from the mass enslavement of captured enemies. Each senator strove to serve the Republic in a greater capacity than all his contemporaries. The propaganda of the Roman élite is filled with superlatives, each man striving to achieve bigger and better deeds than anyone else, and special credit was attached to being the first person to perform an act or defeat a new enemy.

Aristocratic competition worked to the Republic's advantage for many generations, for it provided a constant supply of magistrates eager to win glory on the state's behalf.

However, in the late second century BC the system began to break down. Rome had expanded rapidly, but the huge profits of conquest had not been distributed evenly, so a few families benefited enormously. The gap between the richest and poorest in the Senate widened, and the most wealthy were able to spend lavishly to promote their own and their family's electoral success. It became increasingly expensive to pursue a political career, a burden felt as much by members of very old but now modestly wealthy families as by those outside the political élite. Such men could only succeed by borrowing vast sums of money, hoping to repay these debts once they achieved the highest offices. The risk of failure, which would thus bring financial as well as political ruin, could make such men desperate. At the same time men from the richest and most prestigious families saw opportunities to have even more distinguished careers than their ancestors by flouting convention and trying to build up massive blocks of supporters. Both types were inclined to act as *populares*, an abusive term employed by critics to signify men who appealed to the poorer citizens for support by promising them entertainment, subsidised or free food, or grants of land. The *popularis* was an outsider, operating beyond the bounds of and with methods unattractive to the well-established senators. It was a very risky style of politics, but one which potentially offered great opportunities. In 133 BC a radical tribune – the ten tribunes of the plebs were magistrates without military responsibilities who were supposed to protect the interests of the people – from one of the most prestigious families, Tiberius Sempronius Gracchus, was lynched by a mob of senators when he tried to gain re-election to a second year of office. In 121 BC, his brother Caius, who pursued an even more radical agenda, was killed by his

opponents in something that came close to open fighting in the very centre of Rome. Yet a small number of men began to have previously unimaginable electoral success, as many of the old precedents restricting careers were broken. From 104 to 100 BC, a successful general named Caius Marius was elected to five successive consulships.

In the same period the conversion of the Roman army into a professional force fundamentally altered its relationship with the rest of society. Until this time the legions had been militia forces, all citizens who possessed a certain property qualification being obliged to serve when called upon by the Republic. The wealthiest, able to provide themselves with a horse and the necessary equipment, served as cavalry, the moderately well off as heavy infantry, the poorer as light infantry and the poorest rarely served at all. In a real sense the army represented a cross-section of Roman society under arms. For these men service in the army was not a career but a duty to the Republic. As men of property – most were farmers – they easily returned to civilian life after each period of service. However, as the Empire expanded, wars tended to last longer and be fought further away, while there was a growing need for permanent garrisons to protect conquered territory. A decade of service in a garrison in one of the Spanish provinces could well mean ruination for the owner of a small farm. Service became increasingly unpopular and the eventual solution was to turn to men willing to make the army their profession. A soldier's pay was low, the conditions of his service extremely harsh, and a military career tended only to be attractive to the poorest citizens, who in the past had not been obliged to serve. Such men proved excellent soldiers, but when the war ended and their legion was disbanded they had nothing to return to in civilian life. The Senate refused to acknowledge this change, maintaining that military service was a duty requiring no formal reward, and made no provision to provide for discharged soldiers. Individual commanders began to demand land for their veteran soldiers, wanting to settle them in colonies on conquered territory. Soldiers started to become more loyal to generals who offered such rewards than to the Republic which neglected them.

The rise of the professional army was probably the most important of the problems besetting the Republic with which the Senate failed to deal, but it was by no means the only one. Italy's economy and society had been profoundly changed by Roman expansion and the influx of huge numbers of slaves. The population of Rome itself had swollen to 1,000,000 by the end of the 1st century BC, a high proportion of them without steady employment. *Popularis* politicians who tried to address the problems of dispossessed farmers or the urban or rural poor were sure of winning support. All of these factors produced a dangerous instability. In 88 the consul Lucius Cornelius Sulla led his legions to seize power in Rome when Marius tried to seize the command allocated to him. Civil war followed, leading to Sulla eventually becoming dictator for more than a year. After this, stability never really returned to the Republic for more than very brief periods, as attempted coups, political violence and civil war followed each other with monotonous regularity. Sulla was a member of an old aristocratic family that had fallen on hard times, and had to use extreme methods to achieve the distinguished position within the Republic that he felt his birth warranted. There were several other men from similar backgrounds who acted in a similar way, and the most successful of these was Caius Julius Caesar, probably the most famous Roman of all.

Julius Caesar

As dictator, Julius Caesar paved the way for the establishment of the Roman Empire under his great-nephew Augustus, more infamously had a love affair with Cleopatra of Egypt, and even invented the leap year, before being assassinated by friends and colleagues who had previously supported him. But before his dictatorship he had

conquered a vast area of Europe in an incredibly short time. The provinces of Gaul invaded by Caesar (Aquitania, Gallia Belgica and Gallia Lugdunensis) relate to modern-day France, Belgium, Luxembourg and Germany to the west of the Rhine, an area of over 300,000 square miles. The political map of much of modern Europe can be traced back to Julius Caesar's nine years of campaigning. During his battles in Gaul, Caesar also became the first Roman to cross the Rhine at the head of an army, and to cross the Channel to Britain, an island that contemporaries considered a mysterious, frightful and possibly even mythical place.

There is only one detailed account surviving of this extraordinary war, and that is by Caesar himself. As well as being a great (and exceptionally fortunate) general and an inspirational leader of men, Caesar was an astute politician fully aware of the importance of self-presentation; in today's terms, he was his own, extremely able spin-doctor. Caesar's *De Bello Gallico* (*Gallic War*) is the most detailed eye-witness account of war that survives from the Greek or Roman world. He wrote up his *Commentaries* annually and had them published in Rome every year. Everyone in the capital was hungry for news of events in Gaul and there was great excitement at the progress of the war. Caesar made sure they got a one-sided version of events that stressed the magnitude of the Roman victories (and his part in them), and underplayed the size and significance of the reverses. The historical reconstruction of the conquest of Gaul must be accomplished using this one extremely biased source, a few brief descriptions in other works of literature written by Romans, and limited archaeological evidence. There is nothing that presents the motives, aims or feelings of the Gauls, except Caesar's interpretation of them, for they had no tradition of recording their history.

The conquest of Gaul took place amid cultural and political change in both Gaul and Rome. By the mid-1st century BC, parts of Gaul were starting to become urbanised and 'Romanised' as they adopted some of the customs of the inhabitants of the

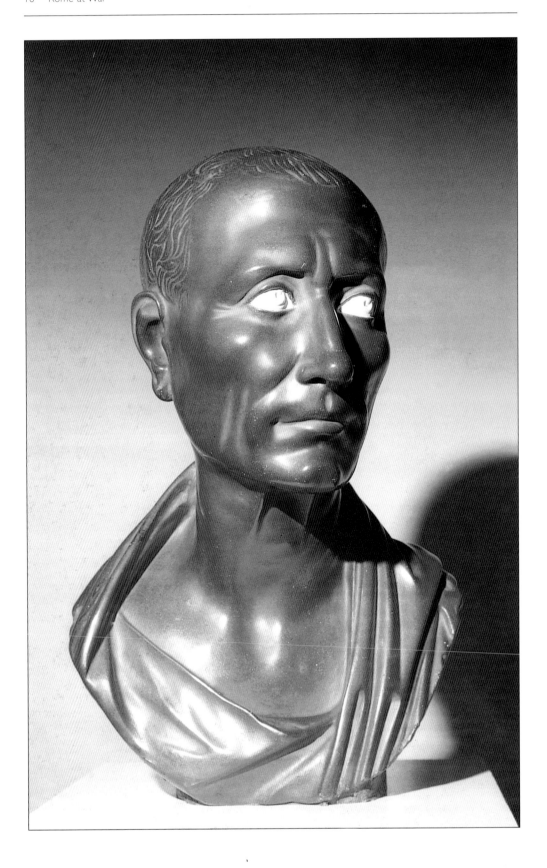

neighbouring Roman province of Transalpine Gaul in southern France. Roman traders were very active in Gaul, particularly in the southern and central areas, and they too helped to spread their own culture, exchanging 'luxury' goods such as wine in return for grain, iron, hides and slaves. Some of the Gallic tribes were developing more centralised forms of organisation, and towns were beginning to grow. Ironically, this helped to make the Roman conquest, when it came, more straightforward: while some of the more 'Romanised' tribes such as the Aedui allied themselves to the invaders, some of those who resisted were easier to conquer because they were centralised and had clear centres of occupation and wealth. The tribes with few key occupation centres often had more mobile wealth and resources, and could more easily avoid conquest simply by evading the Romans.

Rome itself was sliding towards civil war; military success and loyal soldiers were now prerequisites for becoming a leading figure in the power games, and consequently huge areas of the Mediterranean were being swiftly conquered by ambitious Romans. Most recently, Pompey, lately returned from the East after a magnificent tour of conquest had set new standards for others to emulate. When Julius Caesar engineered for himself the governorship of Cisalpine Gaul (northern Italy) and Dalmatia in 59 BC, there was no doubt that he would conduct campaigns to enhance his military reputation and political future. When the governorship of Transalpine Gaul (southern France) was added to his command and the Helvetii in Switzerland began a huge migration westwards, Caesar decided to campaign in Gaul.

Over the next few years the Romans made rapid conquests throughout Gaul. The task was made easier by the inability of the Gallic tribes to unite to form a combined resistance to the invaders. Indeed, some tribes supported the Romans, and the Romans themselves played one tribe off against another, exploiting the territorial ambitions of different Gallic tribes and even political divisions within tribes. Few Gallic armies were capable of resisting the disciplined and well-equipped Roman legions, and Caesar was able to draw on an increasingly large and experienced army, as well as allies from Gaul and occasionally Germany to supply him with cavalry in particular. Within three years of leading his army into Gaul, Caesar was able to pronounce that the whole province was conquered and lead his army into Germany and across the Channel to Britain, expeditions that provoked shocked admiration back in Rome.

Gaul may have been conquered, but the Gauls were not. The last years of Caesar's command were spent dealing with sporadic revolts across the province, which were followed, in 52 BC, by a major uprising. Finally the Gauls had found a leader who could unite them: Vercingetorix. The year 52 BC was make or break for both sides: the Gauls pursued a guerrilla campaign of hit-and-run tactics and a scorched-earth policy, while the Romans utilised more sophisticated engineering skills; it also saw two huge-scale sieges of hill forts at Avaricum (Bourges) and Alesia (Alise-Ste-Reine, near Dijon). It was at Alesia that the whole war in Gaul came to a climax, and when the army raised to relieve the besieged Gauls was repulsed, the revolt was effectively over. The relieving army dissolved and Vercingetorix surrendered. Although it was not until the reign of the first emperor, Augustus, that Gaul was properly pacified (and even after that there are indications of the occasional rumble into the mid-1st century AD), the Gauls were never able to unite effectively again. Gaul became several Roman provinces, evolving after five centuries into the Frankish kingdoms and eventually becoming France.

OPPOSITE Portrait bust of Caius Julius Caesar, (c. 102–44) the Roman politician and general who conquered Gaul in the mid-1st century BC. (Ancient Art and Architecture)

In this 19th-century oil painting the Gallic chief Vercingetorix throws down his arms at the feet of the victorious Caesar. Plutarch's description of events goes on to say that Vercingetorix dismounted and took off his armour before seating himself before Caesar in silence, until Caesar had him taken away under guard. After his surrender, Vercingetorix was kept for six years, before being displayed at Caesar's triumph, and then ritually strangled. (Musée Croatier)

Part I

Caesar's Gallic Wars
58–50 BC

This frieze from the headquarters building of the
legionary fortress at Mainz in Germany dates to
over a century after the Gallic Wars, but gives a good
idea of the classic fighting stance of the legionary –
crouching slightly to gain the maximum protection
from his shield, with his left leg advanced and sword
thrust underarm.
(AKG Berlin/Erich Lessing)

Building an empire

Romans and Gauls had been clashing for centuries before the conquest of Gaul in the 1st century BC, but for long periods they had also experienced comparative peace as neighbours or near neighbours. Celtic or Gallic tribes (as the Greek writers called them) migrated into northern Italy during the late 5th and early 4th centuries BC, with some tribes settling, particularly around the fertile Po valley. The first major encounter between Rome and these Celtic tribes of what is known as the La Tène culture came in the early 4th century BC. They penetrated south into Etruria and Latium (Toscana and Lazio) where the invaders captured and sacked some of the largest cities, including the important Etruscan centre of Veii only a few miles north of Rome. In 390 BC Rome's field forces were defeated, and the poorly defended city captured by the Gauls. Only the citadel held out: according to tradition, when the Gauls tried to scale it in a surprise night attack, the guard dogs failed to bark and it was only the honking of geese (kept on the Capitol because they were sacred to Jupiter) that awoke the guards. The guards then repelled the attack. The story may not be true, but after sacking Rome, or being paid off by the Romans, the Gauls withdrew. They were defeated shortly afterwards by Camillus, the great Roman general who is traditionally credited with making fundamental changes to the Roman army in order to deal with this new Gallic threat. The sacking of Rome was never forgotten, and Romans remained haunted by a kind of collective inbred fear of hordes of barbarians returning to destroy the city. The sack, along with the long subsequent history of violent encounters between the two cultures, formed part of the background to Caesar's conquest of Gaul.

During the 150 years after the sack, Rome was gradually able to establish superiority over much of the Italian peninsula, ejecting several of the Gallic tribes from lands to the north of Rome. Between the First and Second Punic Wars (during the 3rd century BC) this conquest of Italy extended to the north as a coalition of Gallic tribes from northern Italy and across the Alps moved south, only to suffer a devastating defeat at Telamon in 225 BC which broke Gallic resistance in Italy. In the following five years much of the territory beyond the Po was incorporated as the province of Cisalpine Gaul, and Roman colonies were founded at Piacenza and Cremona. The final reduction of this new province had to wait until after the Second Punic War and the repulse of the Carthaginian raiding forces under Hannibal. After the first big Roman defeat at the hands of Hannibal at the Trebia in 218 BC, Gallic mercenaries flocked to join Hannibal and served with him through much of the Italian campaign. But after defeating Carthage, Rome turned back to north Italy and punished the tribes who had fought against them. The whole of Italy as far north as the Alps was incorporated as Roman territory and further colonies were created at Bologna and Parma. By the mid-2nd century BC Rome was ready to move into France, having secured her occupation of the whole of Cisalpine Gaul.

The excuse came in 154 BC when the Greek city of Marseilles requested help from Rome against raids from Liguria. The Roman response included the establishment of a small veteran settlement at Aix en Provence, which irritated the powerful Allobroges tribe nearby, on whose territory it was founded. They and their allies, including the Arverni, were defeated in a series of campaigns fought by Domitius Ahenobarbus and Fabius Maximus. Fabius inflicted an appalling defeat on the Gauls in 121 BC, claiming the

quite extraordinary (and highly unlikely) casualty figures of 120,000 Gallic dead to only 15 Roman. The new province of Transalpine Gaul was created, which the Romans frequently referred to as simply 'The Province', from which modern Provence gets its name. As in Cisalpine Gaul, colonies were founded, at Nîmes and Toulouse, and a road was built, the Via Domitia, linking Italy with Spain. As well as leading to the creation of another province, the campaign to assist Marseilles also brought Rome into alliance with the Aedui, a Gallic tribe of modern Burgundy who were also allied to Marseilles. The existence of the new province and a formal alliance with the Aedui provided Rome with opportunities for further intervention in Gaul and the affairs of the Gallic tribes, but any further expansion was brought to a sudden stop by the arrival in southern Gaul of the Cimbri and Teutones. These migrating Germanic tribes offered serious resistance to Rome, defeating

LEFT Hellenistic and Roman art regularly illustrated Celts and Gauls being defeated in battle or, as in this case, committing suicide after a defeat. The heroically nude Gaul holds his dead wife whom he may have just killed himself, to prevent her falling into enemy hands. (AKG London/A. Lorenzini)

BELOW Detail from the Altar of Domitius Ahenobarbus, a 1st-century BC relief illustrating the taking of a census which included details of the military liability of every citizen. The two soldiers represent the link between citizen status and military service. (Ancient Art and Architecture)

successive consular armies in the late 2nd century BC. They were eventually beaten by Marius (a great Roman general and consul), but as with the Gallic sack of 390 BC, the experience left scars on the Roman psyche. Future Roman attacks and campaigns against Germanic tribes could be passed off as retribution for the defeats and casualties of the 2nd-century incursions.

By the 1st century BC many of the tribes in Gaul were becoming urbanised, particularly those in the south where they came under the cultural influence of Marseilles and then, with the establishment of the province of Transalpine Gaul, Rome. Although Caesar uses the word *oppidum* to describe hill forts, he also uses it for defended settlements that were not on hills. Some of these could have been described as towns even by Romans who might have regarded Gaul and nearly everything about it and its inhabitants as barbaric. Avaricum (Bourges) had an open space which Caesar called a forum and may have had civic buildings; it had a huge defensive wall and its inhabitants regarded it as the most beautiful city in Gaul. Cenabum (Orleans) had a series of narrow streets which may well have had some kind of plan to them: Gallic towns were starting to adopt the grid plans of Mediterranean cities. Evidence of coin manufacture at important *oppida* suggests that they may have been tribal capitals, indicating some degree of political centralisation; Bibracte, for example, seems

to have been the 'capital' of the Aedui, who were a fairly centralised tribe although plagued by factions. Other tribes that lacked this degree of centralisation might have been considered culturally backward by the Romans, but this added to their military reputation: Caesar considered the Belgae to be the bravest warriors of the Gauls because they were furthest removed from Roman influence. Their lack of centralisation also meant that they could be harder to conquer, as Caesar was to find when fighting tribes like the Veneti and Menapii who had no single centre of occupation and wealth.

One of the main reasons for the Greek and Roman influence on the Gallic tribes was trade. Marseilles was a significant centre of trade, and though Gallic tribes and Rome regularly fought each other, that did not prevent a huge amount of trade taking place between them well before the conquest under Caesar. Romans imported raw materials from Gaul, including iron, grain, hides and, particularly, slaves, the source of the latter being regular inter-tribal warfare that took place between both Gallic and Germanic tribes. In exchange, the Gauls (or at least the Gallic elite) received luxury goods and foods, and enormous amounts of wine. Wine had become a key symbol of wealth, status and 'civilisation', though the historian Diodorus Siculus says that the Gauls drank it neat, rather than diluted with water in the Roman style. Hence, although they were adopting the 'civilised' customs of the Mediterranean, Diodorus makes it clear that they were still barbarians because they did not know how to drink it properly. He goes on to say that wine had become such a valuable commodity that the exchange rate for an amphora of wine was one slave, although there were certainly plenty of slaves around. There must have been many Roman merchants already in Gaul before

A modern archaeological dig on the site of Bibracte, the chief *oppidum* of the Aeduan people who were supporters of Rome. Bibracte was a useful supply point for Roman armies throughout the Gallic War. (Ancient Art and Architecture)

Caesar's campaigns, including a community of citizens at Cenabum. Some of them were of high status and belonged to the Roman 'equestrian' order, the influential class immediately below senatorial rank, itself a prime source of new senators. They might expect to benefit from the opportunities conquest would bring, especially if they provided assistance in the form of intelligence and supplies for the Roman army.

Many of the tribes that had come under greater influence from the Greek and Roman cultures to the south were ruled by oligarchies with annually appointed magistrates. The spreading centralisation and tendency towards urbanisation made such tribes easier targets for Rome, and internal factions within them helped the Romans too. In the mid-1st century BC the Aedui were divided between a pro-Roman faction under Diviciacus, and those who opposed the Romans led by his brother Dumnorix. Dumnorix held a monopoly over the wine trade on the Saône, a tributary of the Rhône, and probably resisted the growing Roman influence for economic as well as political reasons. His influence came from his wealth and his position as a druid: druids held high social status in Celtic society which could bring them political influence. According to the account by Caesar, Dumnorix was attempting to increase his power-base within the Aedui not just because he was opposed to the tribe's pro-Roman stance, but because he was keen to seize power and make himself king. It was important for Rome that the Aedui remained a united and powerful ally of Rome among the Celtic tribes of Gaul, and the squabbling between the two brothers must have given Rome cause for concern.

But the Aedui were coming under pressure from other tribes in Gaul in the 1st century BC. They were a powerful tribe with other lesser tribes under their protection and they had a long-standing rivalry with their neighbours, the Arverni. This rivalry came to a head in 71 BC when the Arverni attacked, along with their allies the Sequani, and German mercenaries from the Suebi whom the Sequani had rather foolishly invited in.

A silver coin of the Aeduan leader, Dumnorix. The coin shows an Aeduan warrior with a boar standard. Whilst the Aedui were allied to Rome, there were anti-Roman elements within the tribe led by the aristocratic druid Dumnorix, who Caesar referred to as 'a man of boundless daring'. (AKG Berlin)

Once the Aedui were defeated the German mercenaries under their king Ariovistus turned on their erstwhile allies and seized much of the Sequanian territory. These events had several consequences. Rome failed to assist her ally, the Aedui, which must have damaged her reputation among the Gallic tribes, and Germans were now settling in Gaul near the territory of the Helvetii. This must have seriously worried the Helvetii who had already been forced

into Switzerland by earlier migrations of Germanic tribes and they prepared to evacuate their homelands and migrate themselves, to western France.

In 61 BC the Roman senate had confirmed its support for the Aedui, but still failed to act. Romans were expecting some kind of involvement with Gaul in 60 BC though, perhaps military support for the Aedui. Probably because of concern about the huge migration which was obviously about to take place, preparations were made in Rome, including the holding of a levy. During his consulship in 59 BC Julius Caesar had bought off the Suebic king Ariovistus by diplomatic gifts and the title of Friend of the Roman People. It was not an unusual move

A barge being pulled upriver by manpower. Many of Gaul's rivers were navigable and provided excellent trade routes, and supply and communication conduits for the invading Roman army. Gaulish leaders were keen to import luxury goods, such as wine, in return for raw materials such as iron, grain and slaves. (AISA)

for a leading politician to make alliances with kings outside the Roman empire, especially kings of neighbouring territories who might supply additional troops for a campaign. During his year as Consul, Caesar also engineered for himself the appointment as governor of Cisalpine Gaul and Illyricum (the Adriatic coast of Dalmatia); when at the end of the year the governor of Transalpine Gaul suddenly died, Caesar was given that command as well. The forces under his command consisted of one legion based in Transalpine Gaul and three more legions that were in garrison at Aquileia in north-east Italy, based there because of the potential threats from Ariovistus and the Helvetii to the north and the Dacians to the north-east. Caesar may have been planning a campaign against Illyricum initially, but the late addition of Transalpine Gaul to his command opened up a better option.

Caesar was an ambitious politician and in order to dominate politics as a senator in

Rome in the 1st century BC, it helped to be extremely wealthy (to bribe the electorate), and to have a great military reputation. Of his two allies and rivals, Marcus Crassus was fabulously rich, and Pompey was both wealthy and Rome's leading general after conquering much of Spain and Turkey. On his appointment as governor of Cisalpine and Transalpine Gaul, Caesar was pretty much broke and had had little opportunity to establish himself as an able general. Conquest of a new province would allow him both to enrich himself and impress the public in Rome with his military ability. There was no doubt at all that Caesar would campaign somewhere and conquer a new province, either on the eastern Adriatic coast or in Gaul. It just happened that there were two convenient pretexts for launching operations in Gaul: the Helvetii began their migration just as Caesar was taking over command, and there was still the matter of Rome's previous failure to support their allies the Aedui. If they requested assistance, particularly against the German King Ariovistus, Caesar could justifiably intervene. At the start of 58 BC the new governor of Cisalpine and Transalpine Gaul was still in Rome when news arrived of the movement of the Helvetian tribes.

Discipline vs. spectacle

The Roman army that campaigned in Gaul in the 1st century BC was to all intents and purposes a professional one, with many soldiers in the legions regarding their military service as a career. The soldiers were equipped, trained and paid by the state, often serving for many years at a stretch. The Gallic armies were completely different. Gallic warfare was based on the values of a warrior society; while the elite warriors may have been able to spend time raiding neighbouring tribes and may have possessed high quality arms and armour, tribes were unable to maintain armies for long because of the lack of any organised supply system and the need for many of those fighting to return to their fields. The Roman conquest of Gaul was a clash between two cultures employing very different methods of waging war.

The Romans

The Roman army was made up of two types of troops: the legions, comprising Roman citizens and auxiliaries, and non-Romans who fought alongside Roman generals

because of treaty obligations or out of choice. When Caesar started his governorship he had four legions assigned to his command, but he immediately began recruiting more, mainly from northern Italy, and possibly not being too strict about the citizen status of his recruits, since much of the population of Cisalpine Gaul did not have full Roman citizenship.

In the Imperial period a legion was usually commanded by a legate who was a senator or equestrian, but in the late Republic the legion had no permanent commander. Instead, the provincial governor appointed senators from his staff to command one or more legions. These might be legates of quite senior status (Caesar's most experienced legate, Labienus, had held the important magistracy of Praetor), or they might be much younger men like Publius Crassus who was just beginning his senatorial career. Each legion had six

The Roman legion was arranged into 10 cohorts of six centuries. The cohort of c. 480 men was a key tactical unit in the Roman army and provided great flexibility as one or more cohorts could be detached from a legion for tactical purposes.

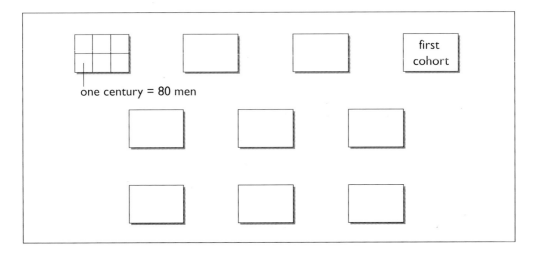

one century = 80 men

first cohort

military tribunes who were usually equestrians or the sons of senators gaining military experience before starting their own political careers. The most important officers within the legion were the centurions, and there were 60 in each legion. Appointed for their bravery and experience, these men were responsible for the training of their centuries and the day-to-day running of the legion whether on campaign or in winter quarters. The senior centurions of each legion (the *primi ordines*) regularly attended Caesar's councils of war and would have contributed to strategic discussions; they were the backbone of the legion.

Legionaries were uniformed at state expense, and were well equipped for their military roles. Each legionary, with his mail coat and bronze or iron helmet, was armed as well as the most wealthy and successful Celtic warriors and this must have given

A Montefortino-style helmet. Although this example dates from the 2nd century BC, with its cheek guards and ample dome, it is fairly typical of the kind of helmets issued to soldiers in the late Republic.

them a huge psychological advantage when facing the Gauls. The large shield or *scutum* provided additional protection. The legionary's principal weapons were the *pilum* (javelin) and short sword, the *gladius*.

Recruitment to the legions was based on a mixture of conscription and volunteering, the only qualification for service being citizenship, at least in theory. Recruits were supposed to be at least 17, although the majority were in their early 20s when they joined up. Roman ideology preferred recruits from rural backgrounds rather than from towns and cities with their softening and corrupting influences, but Caesar probably experienced little difficulty in raising troops for his campaigns in Gaul because there had previously been little wide-scale recruitment in Cisalpine Gaul. The legionaries signed up for military service of no fixed length, although they could expect to be discharged with a grant of land on which to settle after five years or so continuous service. Military pay was not especially good, but there were plenty of opportunities for enrichment, particularly on a lucrative campaign like Caesar's conquest of Gaul with the likelihood of generous amounts of booty.

While the legions were armed and equipped uniformly, and were principally heavy infantry, the variation in type of forces a successful army needed was provided by 'auxiliary' units raised from other provinces of the Roman empire or from neighbouring states and tribes friendly to Rome. It was up to the provincial governor to maintain friendly relationships established by his predecessors with local tribes, such as the treaty of friendship between Rome and the Aedui. Caesar was so successful in his early campaigns in Gaul and his military prestige so great that he was able to attract auxiliary units from the Germans as well as support from Gallic tribes, who provided him with another source of cavalry that was particularly valuable when the loyalty of the Aedui wavered in 52 BC. Auxiliaries used their own fighting techniques, they were not trained in the Roman style of fighting, and were commanded by their own officers,

This 1st century BC stone relief from Estepa, Seville, depicts two different dressed and equipped Roman soldiers. They both carry large shields, and the one on the left has his sword drawn for action. The right-hand figure appears to be wearing mail armour and greaves on his legs.
(Ancient Art and Architecture)

usually members of the ruling elite of the tribe or state from which they were recruited.

Auxiliaries provided the Roman army's main cavalry force. The cavalry Caesar employed in Gaul, consisting mainly of Gallic or Germanic elites, was not always reliable or effective, and sometimes they lacked discipline, particularly early on in the campaigns. Its drubbing by the Nervian cavalry in 57 BC was probably the most serious setback it suffered, and by the end of the campaigns the cavalry was a powerful force that contributed to Caesar's victory in the Civil War. The German cavalry sometimes worked in concert with light infantry which allowed the holding of terrain in addition to the useful mobility of cavalry.

The Celtic-style saddle allowed Caesar's cavalry to be as effective as later stirruped cavalry, despite the absence of stirrups. Cavalry troops might vary considerably in their equipment, since they equipped themselves, but a wealthy cavalryman might have a mail shirt and helmet, an oval or hexagonal shield which was more manoeuvrable on horseback than a rectangular one, a spear and a long sword, which was ideal for running down those fleeing from battle, one of the principal roles of the cavalry.

The Roman army in Gaul included slingers from the Balearics and archers from Crete and Numidia who provided lightly armed mobile troops to increase the firepower of the army, particularly at a distance or in a siege. Their role is rarely commented upon, but they added an important degree of flexibility to the Roman army. Additional infantry was provided by Gallic tribes in the same way as cavalry, and would have consisted of groups of warriors from tribes who were allied to Rome like the

TOP Detail of the Altar of Domitius Ahenobarbus showing two legionaries and a cavalryman. Each legion included a small cavalry force, but the majority of the Roman army's cavalry was provided by allied tribes under treaty obligations. (Ancient Art and Architecture)

ABOVE Detail from Trajan's Column. Roman casualties are treated by their comrades on the battlefield. Considerable effort was taken to assist the convalescence of sick and wounded soldiers so that they could be returned to active service in their units quickly. (Ancient Art and Architecture)

Aedui or Remi who surrendered to Caesar following his invasion. The wealthiest of these warriors were probably armed and equipped in a way very similar to the Roman legionaries, but the Gauls placed greater emphasis on individual prowess and prominent displays of courage in battle, rather than the discipline and training of the legions.

Logistical support was generally well organised, with a supply system usually reliant on shuttling provisions from a supply base to the campaigning army. The army made use of Gaul's navigable rivers to move supplies around, but the poor road system and the speed of Caesar's movements led to difficulties. Although Caesar could call on his Gallic allies and later the subjected tribes for supplies, his movements and the direction of the campaign were often heavily influenced by logistical demands. An understanding of this lay behind the Gallic scorched-earth policy in the revolt of 52 BC. When the legions were in winter quarters, Caesar ensured they were garrisoned in the territories of recently conquered tribes to serve the dual purpose of ensuring a strong military presence in newly reduced territory, and punishing those who resisted Rome by forcing them to feed the occupying army, a penalty that could have affected a tribe's ability to support its own population. The winter allowed troops time to recover from the often exhaustive campaigning that Caesar demanded of his armies, in particular those who were sick or had been wounded in fighting. Roman imperial armies had medics attached to them, and this may have been the case in the late Republic, too. In the aftermath of pitched battle Roman armies usually paused, sometimes for several days, so the dead could be buried and the wounded treated. The wounded would later be escorted to a base, probably a supply base, to recuperate before rejoining their units.

Gauls, Britons and Germans

In the 1st century BC Celtic tribes employed different methods of warfare. Although prowess in combat remained important for the tribal elite, in some tribes, particularly in southern and central Gaul, other means were becoming available to gain and maintain status. The Aeduan aristocrat Dumnorix fought as a cavalryman to display his elite warrior status, but he also held a monopoly over the wine trade, which enhanced his wealth and therefore his position within Celtic society. Encouraged by the impact of Mediterranean culture on Gallic society, the Romans interpreted this shift in emphasis as a demoralising factor.

Caesar perceived the Belgae as the bravest of the Gauls 'because they are furthest away from the culture and civilisation of Provence, and are least often visited by merchants importing degenerate luxury goods, and also because they are nearest to the Germans who live across the Rhine and with whom they are continuously at war'.

Sculpture of an aristocratic warrior from Vachères in France, 1st century BC. Wearing a torque round his neck, he may represent a Gaul who fought against the Romans, or perhaps a Gallic officer in a Roman auxiliary unit. He is equipped in the Roman style, with mail shirt, large shield and sword. (Ancient Art and Architecture)

The Battersea shield, found in the Thames at London. This bronze shield may just have been for ceremonial purposes, but is the same design as the wooden versions used in battle. The Celtic shield, like the Roman *scutum*, provided good protection to the infantryman. (Ancient Art and Architecture)

In most Gallic tribes, raiding neighbours was the warrior's principal means of acquiring wealth and position, and tribes sought to extend their influence over smaller neighbours. The bravest tribes, and therefore the most secure, were those with wide influence and many dependent tribes. Tribes might form alliances with neighbours or even, in the case of the Sequani, the Germans, in order to increase their own military prowess. Gallic war bands consisted of groups of warriors belonging to an elite class, following their chieftain and concentrating on raiding; larger-scale armies of the kind faced by the Romans in Gaul were probably less common, and may have included peasants, the dependent farmers who would not normally have been involved in regular warfare. If Caesar really did face an army of 50,000 Helvetii and their allies, it probably included tribesmen of all status, but we hear no details of them or how they were armed and equipped. The warriors equipped themselves according to their wealth and status: the braver and more successful, the more likely they were to be able to adorn themselves with beautifully decorated and high quality equipment.

Only the wealthiest warriors would have possessed mail coats, but such aristocrats could have been equipped in a way very similar to a Roman legionary, with the mail armour providing reasonably good protection from the slashing blows of the long Celtic swords, a bronze or iron helmet, sword and shield. Helmets, like mail coats, were probably very rare and worn only by the wealthiest warriors, but stylistically they were very similar to some Roman helmets; indeed the *coolus* helmet which evolved into one of the main helmets of the Roman imperial army was originally a Gallic design. Gallic warriors carried spears and swords, the latter considerably longer than the Roman *gladius*. They were designed primarily for slashing rather than stabbing, and pointed to a fighting technique that required plenty of room for the individual to wield his long weapon. Though the Greek historian Polybius claims these long swords had a tendency to bend on impact, many were made of high quality iron and they were extremely effective weapons. The Gallic elongated rectangular shield was probably made of hide or wood like the Roman *scutum*. Some shields may not have been particularly thick or strong, which may explain why Caesar reports that the Roman *pila* were able to pierce several of them simultaneously; the bronze shields that survive from antiquity may have been for decorative or ceremonial

Celtic infantry and cavalry on the Gundestrup Cauldron. The warriors have distinctive animal motifs on their helmets which would have made them stand out on the battlefield, and they are accompanied into battle by the carnyx, a long trumpet-like instrument made of bronze. (Ancient Art and Architecture)

purposes and not actually for use in battle. Given that the majority of warriors probably lacked body armour, and indeed some may have chosen to fight without armour to stress their courage and military prowess, the shield was a vital piece of protective equipment. When their shields were put out of action by the Roman *pila*, the Helvetii became dangerously exposed to the Roman attack.

Celtic cavalry, manned by the wealthiest warriors, was particularly effective and scored significant victories against Caesar's more numerous auxiliary cavalry in the first couple of campaigning seasons. The lack of stirrups was no bar to powerful cavalry: the design of the Celtic saddle provided its rider with a secure mount from which to throw spears, thrust with a spear or slash with a sword and implement shock tactics. Some German cavalry may have used these saddles as well, but the horsemanship of the cavalrymen and their co-operation with the light infantry who regularly worked alongside the German cavalry was clearly impressive and indicative of at least some training, which we hear little about in any sources. The Celtic tribes in Britain were still using chariots, something that had gone out of fashion on the Continent, but their speed and agility caused the Roman infantry serious difficulties. The chariots served as battlefield 'taxis' for the wealthiest nobles, dropping them off at the fighting and then collecting them up again if they were injured or needed to withdraw from the battle.

Firepower was available in the form of slingers and archers, although these men were probably not members of the warrior class, as this form of warfare was not really regarded as 'heroic'. Slingers were sometimes involved in open warfare (such as the Gallic ambush of a Roman column in 54 BC), but more often in the defence of hill forts, along with archers. In preparation for the general revolt of 52 BC, Vercingetorix called up all the archers of Gaul; they were probably Gauls of the lower classes, but were vital to the success of the strategy of the revolt.

Very little is known about the organisation of Gallic armies and their workings in pitched battle, although they seem to have relied heavily on the

Images of fighting were common in ancient Rome including, as in this case, on sarcophagi. This late 2nd-century AD sarcophagus from Rome has a stylised depiction of battle between Romans and barbarians that portrays the confusion and urgency of pitched battle. (Museo Nazionale Romano)

effectiveness of infantry and cavalry charges at the start of battle to break the enemy lines. Pitched battle, even at a small scale, provided one of the best opportunities to display military prowess and so was an important way of making war, but not all Gallic tribes were so keen on meeting the enemy in the open, especially when that enemy was as powerful as Rome, so the strategies of the tribes varied. While some

stronger tribes and coalitions like the Nervii were eager to meet the Romans in pitched battle, others like the tribes of Aquitania in south-western Gaul relied more on hit-and-run tactics and attacking the invaders' supply lines as Vercingetorix planned to do during the revolt of 52 BC. Some of the coastal tribes who possessed mobile wealth (usually in the form of cattle) were able to withdraw into marshlands and

avoid direct conflict with the Romans, like the Menapii and Morini of the Channel coast. The Veneti, whose wealth was founded on trade and whose military strength was maritime, based their strategy around defence of hill forts situated on coastal promontories, simply moving by sea to another when one was about to be captured by the Romans. Different tribes, then, had the military capacity to adapt their strategies to deal with the new threat of Rome, and some of these variations were quite successful in impeding Roman progress. Hit-and-run tactics and the avoidance of pitched battle may also have been preferred by Gallic tribes, or necessitated by the absence of the kind of logistical support that Roman armies could depend upon. Large Gallic armies could not remain in existence for very long and unless a decisive engagement quickly occurred, such an army would usually have to disband because of lack of supplies. The Belgic army in 57 BC, which combined many different tribes, was forced to dissipate for this reason when a decisive engagement with Caesar was not forthcoming.

The professional Roman army had many advantages over the armies of the Gallic warrior societies and it was not surprising that several tribes quickly went over to Rome, or that under the leadership of such an effective general as Caesar, the conquest of Gaul was completed remarkably quickly.

Gallic flair and Roman discipline

Gallic and Roman fighting styles were the complete antithesis of each other. For both cultures, victory in pitched battle was the ultimate accolade for a warrior or soldier, and also for tribal chieftains and Roman generals. To show courage on the battlefield was expected; to die in battle was glorious. By the mid-1st century BC, when Caesar began his conquest of Gaul, Romans and Gauls had been fighting each other on and off for centuries. In their literature the Romans betrayed both a fear of their

barbarian neighbours, and a sneaking admiration for the way they fought. Gauls were perceived as much larger than Romans (they are portrayed as being of almost giant stature in some accounts); certainly they probably were generally a little taller than the average Italian legionary, and the Romans seem to have been rather defensive about being shorter than their adversaries. Nonetheless, the style of fighting they employed was perfect for fighting Gauls. Indeed, the organisation of legions into maniples (120-man units), and the introduction of the large *scutum* and short *gladius* as the principal weapons of legionary hand-to-hand combat may have been inspired by conflicts with the Gauls in the 4th century BC.

The Gallic fighting style allowed the warrior to display himself on the battlefield, either through fighting naked or by wearing elaborately decorated armour, and he showed off his valour by fighting as an individual. The warrior's long sword required him to have a fair amount of space around him on the battlefield in order to operate properly. The Celtic sword was essentially a slashing weapon and in the hands of a tall Gallic warrior with a long reach, could be a deadly blade, particularly against shorter opposition with short swords. But the Gallic warriors fought as individuals; though training and especially experience must have provided them with some understanding of tactics, and commands could have been communicated on the battlefield through musical instruments, they did not possess the same degree of training to fight as a unit that Roman soldiers did. When forced to

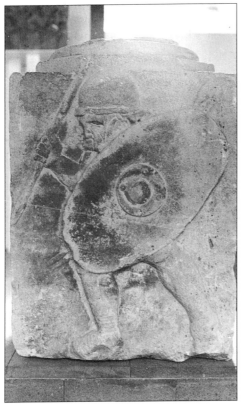

TOP Marble bust of Caius Julius Caesar. It was said that he was particularly pleased when given the right to wear a laurel wreath on public occasions, as it covered his thinning hair. (Museo Nazionale Archaeologico, Naples/AKG Berlin)

LEFT Column base from Mainz, Germany. An auxiliary soldier in action. Unlike the legionaries, he is armed with an oval shield and spears instead of a *pilum* (javelin) and short sword. Auxiliary troops on the Rhine would have been raised from nearby provinces, including Gaul. (Landesmuseum, Mainz)

retreat, they could not always maintain ranks and withdraw in good order, something that required considerable training and absolute trust in one's fellow soldiers. This made them vulnerable to outflanking manoeuvres and to cavalry attacks on retreating warriors. Lack of space to swing their swords could also cause havoc in the Gallic ranks. When forced together, Gallic warriors could not use their swords properly, and this made them vulnerable to an enemy who could operate at very close quarters with deadly efficiency.

The Roman legionary's equipment did not make him reliant on his neighbour's shield for protection in combat as in a Greek phalanx formation, as he fought as an individual, but he was dependent on the strength of his unit. If his comrades in his century, cohort or legion gave way, he would eventually become exposed to attack on the flank or rear. The might of the Roman army lay in the strength of its formations, and that was based on unit morale, discipline and training. These can clearly be seen when Caesar's legions came under sudden attack by the Nervii in the second season of campaigning. The legionaries did not even need their officers to give them orders: they automatically dropped their entrenching tools, picked up their weapons, and formed a battle line. Their training ensured that even though they were not with their own units and the men they normally fought with, they were resourceful enough to create an effective line of battle. Roman soldiers were not automatons in a 'military machine': they were trained to think and use their initiative as well as follow orders. The

training and discipline instilled in the soldiers meant that Roman units could move over battlefields in formation and even retreat while maintaining a defensive formation, an invaluable technique in warfare for minimising casualties.

In combat with their taller Gallic opponents with their slashing swords, they threw their *pila* and then moved in very close for hand-to-hand combat. The large *scutum* protected most of the legionary's front and left side, his short *gladius* was ideal for stabbing in close-quarter fighting, and he could even punch at the enemy with the metal boss of his shield. If the legionaries moved in close enough, they could literally cramp the style of their Gallic opponents while still giving themselves the small amount of room they needed to operate effectively. The short *gladius* was a brutally efficient tool for killing: a short stab at the torso or especially the belly of his opponent, who may well have been fighting without armour, and he would have been killed or badly injured with damage to internal organs and serious bleeding. Though Roman soldiers were trained to stab with their swords, that did not stop them from slashing with them, and the fine quality and perfect weighting of the *gladius* meant that they could easily hack off limbs. The average Roman legionary may have been shorter in stature than his Gallic opponent, but his equipment meant he was not at a disadvantage. Moreover, the tactics and fighting style employed in pitched battle against Celtic opponents turned it into an advantage. Usually, in pitched battle Roman discipline triumphed over Gallic flair.

The migration of the Helvetii

On 28 March 58 BC the Celtic tribe of the Helvetii left their homes in Switzerland and, along with their neighbours, the Raurici, Tulingi, Latobrigi and Boii, began a migration west. The purpose of this mass movement of tribes, including women, children and livestock, was to move to western Gaul, to the lands of other Gallic tribes on which they intended to settle after defeating the inhabitants and forcing them to move on. These mass migrations of whole tribes were not unheard of, and a similar movement of German tribes in the late 2nd century BC had led to the clashes between them and Rome, leading to the catastrophic defeats of several Roman armies. The migration of the Helvetii did not come as a surprise to anyone, however, as extensive planning had been necessary. Preparations had begun three years previously. By the late 60s BC the Helvetii were feeling the pressure of space. Hemmed in by the mountains of Switzerland, they had little opportunity to expand their territory to cater for a growing population and to display their military prowess by occupying enemy land. The Helvetii were also concerned at the presence to the north of their land of German tribes which had been migrating westwards, particularly the aggressive Suebic king Ariovistus, who had settled in the territory of the Sequani after they and the Arverni had sought his support in local wars with the Aedui.

The Helvetii had begun their preparations in 61 BC, building up three years' supply of grain for the journey and for sowing the new lands they planned to take over in western Gaul. Other supplies were gathered, draught animals and wagons. Much of this was done under the leadership of a Helvetian noble, Orgetorix, who also secretly formed an alliance with two Gallic aristocrats, Casticus

of the Sequani and Dumnorix the Aeduan, the brother of Diviciacus who had close ties with Rome. The three seem to have planned to seize power in their tribes and lead a coalition, perhaps to conquer and partition Gaul between the three tribes or, more likely, either to drive the Germans under Ariovistus back east of the Rhine, or to oppose the increasing threat of Roman intervention or invasion, or perhaps both. Whatever the purpose of the plot, it was discovered and Orgetorix committed suicide before he could be put on trial for conspiring to make himself king. This did not deter the Helvetii from their migration plans, however; in the spring of 58 BC they burned their towns, villages and surplus grain to rule out the possibility of abandoning the migration, and with thousands of wagons started west, towards the Gallic lands west of the Rhône, and towards the Roman province.

Gauls and Romans were concerned by the prospect of the migration. The movement of several thousand people would cause huge damage to the lands they passed through, and could destabilise the whole of southern Gaul as tribes chose whether to join the Helvetii in a bid for land or to oppose them. At the end of their migration the Helvetii planned to seize land from other tribes, causing further disruption to the political balance of the area. Some tribes would have looked towards Rome for assistance, and in 60 BC the Senate had sent ambassadors to Gallic tribes in an attempt to discourage them from joining the Helvetii. The proposed migration threatened the security of Rome's allies including the Aedui and the Allobroges, as well as Provence with its desirable fertile lands. While it was unlikely that the Helvetii would have turned south to threaten Italy, memories of the disasters inflicted by the Germans may have made Rome somewhat

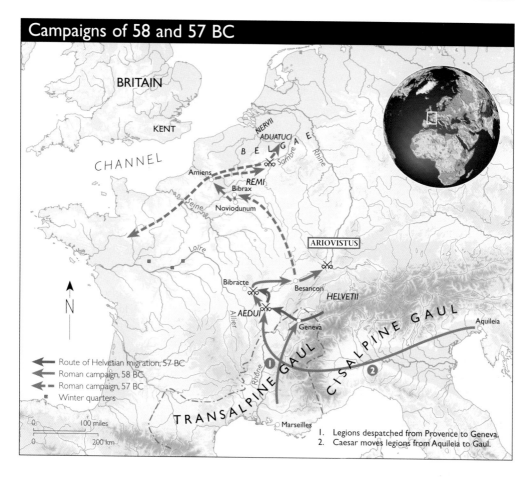

Campaigns of 58 and 57 BC

Route of Helvetian migration, 57 BC
Roman campaign, 58 BC
Roman campaign, 57 BC
■ Winter quarters

0   100 miles
0   200 km

1. Legions despatched from Provence to Geneva.
2. Caesar moves legions from Aquileia to Gaul.

concerned about migratory tribes, and there was a real worry over Germanic tribes moving into the vacated Helvetian lands. In Roman thought, Germans were less desirable neighbours than Gauls. Rome did not want upheavals on her northern borders and the preparations for the migrations led to thoughts of war in Rome. Ostensibly launched to protect Rome's interests, a war against the Helvetii would probably have led to the greater Roman intervention in Gaul that concerned Orgetorix and his allies.

A Roman war in Gaul was becoming inevitable by the late 60s. The consul of 60 BC, Metellus, seems to have been extremely keen to campaign against the Gauls and obtain a triumph. The leading Roman politician Marcus Cicero describes him as 'not over-happy at the reports of peace in Gaul', after Orgetorix's failed coup, and the consul of 59 BC, Julius Caesar, was

equally eager to make his mark militarily. The threat posed by the Helvetii to Provence and Gallic allies provided the *casus belli*, and the opportunity for Caesar to involve himself in Gaul, but had this not arisen, he may well have found some other excuse to campaign there. As it was, once the Helvetian threat had been neutralised, he swiftly found justifications to move deeper into Gaul and Gallic affairs to ensure sensational victories and conquests. These were easily found in the request by Rome's Aeduan allies for assistance against Ariovistus, and from there the Roman conquest of Gaul was Caesar's most likely aim. When Caesar, the new governor of Cisalpine and Transalpine Gaul, heard that the Helvetii were finally on the move, it was his duty to protect his province of Transalpine Gaul, which was directly in the path of the migrants. The Helvetii asked Caesar for permission to cross Roman

Trajan's Column in Rome illustrates campaigns of the early 2nd century AD, but many of the features shown, especially engineering skills and camp building, were just as important in the conquest of Gaul. In the top scroll, soldiers build a camp from turves to ensure the army is not attacked at night. (Ancient Art and Architecture)

territory and when he refused they turned north to continue their migration without trespassing on the Roman land. Although they were now no longer a direct threat to Rome, Caesar followed them and made an unprovoked attack on the Helvetii while they were crossing a river. The actions of the Helvetii were sufficient to warrant such a reaction, especially since the Romans considered them to be 'barbarians'. The conquest of Gaul was an aggressive war of expansion led by a general who was seeking to advance his career and standing amongst his peers, but who was acting within the expectations of Roman society and its value systems.

Invasion, siege and conquest

58 BC The first campaign

In the first year of his governorship, Caesar fought and won two major pitched battles and set himself up to conquer Gaul. The speed and decisiveness with which he operated must have impressed his political rivals in Rome, and terrified the Gauls. Caesar had freed them from the menace of the migrating Helvetii and the German king Ariovistus, but now he threatened their independence himself.

Caesar was still in Rome when news arrived in mid-March that the Helvetii were on the move, heading west towards Geneva and southern Gaul, dangerously close to the Roman province. He immediately headed for Provence, ordering the only legion stationed there to make for Geneva and to destroy the bridge over the Rhône. He levied auxiliary troops in Provence and raised two new legions in northern Italy. Playing for time, he agreed to consider a request that the Helvetii be allowed to pass, but then refused once his troops had built defences that forced the Helvetii away from Roman territory and into central France. He then dashed back to Italy to collect the two new legions and three veteran legions in garrison at Aquileia, marched them through the Alps in early summer and caught up with the Helvetii as they were crossing the Saône. Three-quarters had crossed, but Caesar attacked those remaining. Some escaped into the woods, but his legions slaughtered the rest. The casualty figures are not recorded.

Crossing the Saône in a single day on pontoons, Caesar caught up with the main body of Helvetii and trailed them at a discreet distance, refusing to be drawn into combat except on his terms. The Helvetii were keen to avoid battle and tried to negotiate, but Caesar's demands were too

severe, perhaps intentionally since he was probably eager to fight when the tactical situation became favourable. It did a few days later and a force under Labienus took the high ground above the Helvetian camp in preparation for an attack, but a veteran scout panicked and wrongly reported to Caesar that the flashes of arms he had seen on the hill were definitely Gallic, not Roman, so the attack had to be aborted.

Caesar continued to tail the Helvetii, but was finally forced towards Bibracte to collect supplies from his Aeduan allies, his own supply train being stuck on the Saône. Perhaps hoping to cut the Romans off from their supplies, the Helvetii decided to give battle and attacked the Roman rearguard. Caesar deployed on a slope under cover of a cavalry screen.

Battle against the Helvetii

The Roman forces consisted of six legions numbering c. 24,000–30,000 men, as well as unknown numbers of auxiliary infantry and cavalry. Two of the legions were newly recruited and many of the auxiliaries were Gauls. Their fighting capabilities must have been suspect.

There are no figures for the size of the Helvetian army; their allies, the Boii and Tulingi, numbered c. 15,000, and it is unlikely that the total Gallic army was more than c. 50,000 men.

Caesar deployed his two new legions and the auxiliary infantry on the high ground as a reserve and to guard the Roman encampment; the four veteran legions deployed as a *triplex acies* on ground sloping down towards the Helvetii. (Four cohorts were in the front line, with two further lines of three cohorts each as a reserve force.) The Helvetii formed up in very close order. They gathered their baggage, wagons and families

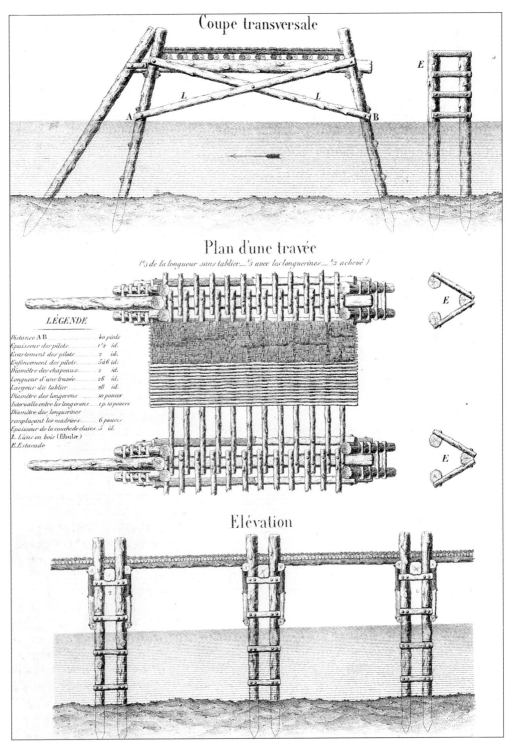

Coupe transversale

Plan d'une travée

(⅓ de la longueur sans tablier — ⅓ avec les longuerines — ⅓ achevé)

LÉGENDE

Distance A B	40 pieds
Épaisseur des pilots	1½ id.
Écartement des pilots	2 id.
Enfoncement des pilots	5 à 6 id.
Diamètre des chapeaux	2 id.
Longueur d'une travée	26 id.
Largeur du tablier	28 id.
Diamètre des longerons	10 pouces
Intervalle entre les longerons	1 p. 10 pouces
Diamètre des longuerines	
remplaçant les madriers	6 pouces
Épaisseur de la couche de claies	5 id.
L. Liens en bois (fibulæ)	
E. Estacade	

Elévation

The engineering skills of the Roman army are best illustrated by the bridge Caesar's soldiers built in 10 days across the Rhine. The bridge was built entirely of wood and required hundreds of timbers to be driven into the river bed from barges built specially for the purpose. Once they were in place, a timber roadway was constructed on top, allowing the Roman army to march across the river into Germany. (Glasgow University Library)

The battle against the Helvetii 58 BC

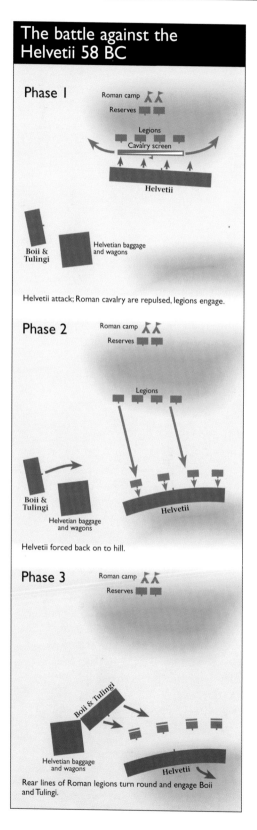

Phase 1

Roman camp

Reserves

Legions

Cavalry screen

Helvetii

Boii & Tulingi

Helvetian baggage and wagons

Helvetii attack; Roman cavalry are repulsed, legions engage.

Phase 2

Roman camp

Reserves

Legions

Boii & Tulingi

Helvetii

Helvetian baggage and wagons

Helvetii forced back on to hill.

Phase 3

Roman camp

Reserves

Boii & Tulingi

Helvetian baggage and wagons

Helvetii

Rear lines of Roman legions turn round and engage Boii and Tulingi.

beyond the left wing of their battle line, along with their allies, the Boii and Tulingi.

The first attack of the Helvetii was easily repulsed by the Romans, who had the advantage of the slope and superior weaponry in the form of their *pila*, which stuck into the enemy's shields, weighing them down and pinning them together. The Helvetii were forced back, but this attack may have been a feint. As the Roman cohorts followed the retreating Helvetii, the Boii and Tulingi outflanked the Roman right. At this point the Helvetii renewed the fight and the Romans were surrounded. Close-quarter infantry combat ensued. The brilliant tactical flexibility of the legion enabled Caesar to order the rear line of cohorts to turn round and the legions fought the battle on two fronts. The Roman reserves on the hill were not even engaged.

The Helvetii fled; the Boii and Tulingi were forced back against the wagons and slaughtered, along with the women and children.

In the aftermath of the battle, Caesar rested for three days to see to his wounded before continuing his pursuit of the Helvetii, who promptly surrendered. Concerned that Germanic tribes might move into the lands vacated by the Helvetii, Caesar ordered the survivors home. Caesar claims that of the 368,000 who set out on the migration, only 110,000 returned.

After dealing with the Helvetii, Caesar turned on the German tribes who occupied land on the left bank of the Rhine under their king Ariovistus. Caesar needed a good reason for attacking a king who was a 'Friend and Ally of the Roman People', and claimed that the Germans were raiding allied Aeduan territory and other Gallic tribes had asked for help. Both sides aimed to occupy the strategically important town of Besançon but Caesar got there first. Here panic spread through Caesar's inexperienced troops and even among some of his officers that Ariovistus and his army was going to be a much tougher prospect than the migratory tribes the Romans had so easily slaughtered. Caesar had to restore discipline by threatening to march off with only one of his legions. When he did march, with all his army, the two leaders met to parley but neither was prepared to damage his reputation by backing down and agreeing to the other's demands to vacate Gaul. Pitched battle was inevitable, although Caesar was more eager to force an engagement, perhaps because of his usual difficulties with his supplies. He was dependent for supplies on Gallic tribes whose reliability was sometimes suspect, and the speed with which he liked to operate on campaign only added to the uncertainties of his supply lines. Eventually, the Romans forced Ariovistus to deploy by marching in battle formation right at the German encampment.

The Germans parked their wagons behind their battle line, Caesar says to prevent the warriors escaping, but it may equally have been to prevent an outflanking manoeuvre by the Romans. The engagement began with the Germans charging so quickly that the Romans had no time to throw their *pila*, and an intense period of hand-to-hand combat ensued. The German left was routed by the Roman right under the personal command of Caesar, but the Roman left was coming under pressure. The officer in command of the cavalry, Publius Crassus, saw this and had the initiative to redeploy the third line of each legion to attack the German right. Again it was the flexibility of legionary tactics that turned the battle and the Germans fled, pursued the full 15 miles to the Rhine. The German losses are reported at 80,000 and the battle was clearly an outright victory for the Romans. In just one year Caesar was able to report to his rivals in Rome that he had defeated two of Rome's traditional and most feared enemies, Gauls and Germans. He wintered his legions near Vesontio and returned to northern Italy to attend to the civil aspects of his governorship.

57 BC Conquest of the east

By early 57 BC, if he had not already resolved to do so the previous year, Caesar had decided to conquer the whole of Gaul.

German cavalry tactics

Although the horses the German cavalrymen used were small and sometimes of poor quality, the cavalry itself was made particularly effective through the addition of a force of light infantry that worked in tandem with the cavalry. This provided the manoeuvrability of cavalry along with the staying power of infantry.

'With the six thousand cavalry was the same number of infantry, the swiftest and bravest men, each chosen from the whole army by a cavalryman for his own protection; they went into battle together. The cavalry would fall back on them; if the cavalry were in difficulties the infantry ran to help; if a cavalryman had been wounded and fallen from his horse, they surrounded him. They had become so swift through training that on a long advance or a quick retreat they could keep up by running, holding on to the horses' manes.'
Caesar, *Gallic War*

Some Gallic tribes were persuaded to form alliances with Rome because of the protection and influence such a relationship would bring within Gaul, and they may have felt, probably correctly, that as conquest was inevitable, it was better to be on the winning side. The Aedui in central Gaul were encouraged to remain Caesar's staunchest ally by his willingness to let them expand their influence over defeated Gallic tribes. The Remi in northern Gaul preferred to fight with Rome rather than against her, providing Caesar with intelligence during the campaign. However, the majority of Belgic tribes, feared Rome's growing power in the region and prepared to resist, soliciting help

A coin depicting the Celtic thunder god, Taranis, who is shown clutching a lightning bolt and standing next to a solar wheel, the symbols of his power. His rectangular shield closely resembles those of the Gallic warriors who fought against Caesar's legions (see also illustration on page 36). (Ancient Art and Architecture)

Caesar had under his command a number of officers who were also senators in Rome and whom he could appoint to senior positions. A quaestor was attached to the province of Gaul who had some financial responsibilities, and as a junior senator could also command troops, sometimes independently. Publius Crassus seems to have been a particularly able young man who, in 54 BC, went to join his father on the doomed campaign against the Parthians; he was killed at Carrhae the following year.

Caesar was also allowed to appoint a number of legates, usually more senior senators like Labienus who had held the Praetorship, a senior magistracy in Rome. These men could be placed in command of quite large forces of several legions plus cavalry, and trusted with independent commands. Labienus was left in charge of the entire province of Gaul during the expeditions to Britain. Appointing legates provided an opportunity to pay back political debts or to place others in your debt through patronage, although his debt to Caesar did not prevent Labienus from siding with Pompey in the Civil War.

from the Germans. Caesar claims they could muster an army of 200,000 warriors.

Caesar raised two more legions, bringing the total to eight (32,000–40,000 men, plus auxiliaries), and at the start of the campaigning season, headed for northern Gaul. His intention was to defeat the powerful Belgic tribes and cut them off from German support to the east. The Belgae caught up with him near Bibrax and tried to capture the *oppidum* from the occupying Remi who were being assisted by lightly armed missile troops Caesar had sent to help. Unable to capture the town, the Belgae instead ravaged the land and then turned towards Caesar's camp by the river Aisne. Neither side wished for battle at this point,

although Caesar had prepared by linking artillery redoubts to the camp by means of trenches to prevent a Belgic outflanking manoeuvre should battle ensue. Skirmishes followed, but still no battle. Eventually each side's supply requirements effected a result of sorts: Caesar attempted to precipitate a general engagement by sending his cavalry and light infantry against the Belgae because he was concerned about being cut off from his supplies. But the Belgae, too, were running short of supplies and because they had no logistical support, simply disbanded their army, to re-form if, or when, Caesar threatened them directly. They may also have recognised that Caesar's prepared battlefield made the terrain too unfavourable for a successful engagement.

The speed at which Roman armies could move proved an important factor in the success of this year's campaigns. Caesar pounced on the *oppidum* of the Suessiones at Noviodunum (on the river Aisne), hoping to capture it before the warriors returned after the Belgic army had disbanded. Though the warriors were able to sneak in at night, they quickly surrendered when they saw the siege preparations: clearly they had never experienced anything like Roman siege warfare before. The psychological effects of this surrender were widespread, with the Bellovaci and Ambiones surrendering to the Romans without resistance. The next tribe though, the Nervii, decided to resist, formed an alliance with the neighbouring Atrebates and Viromandui and planned to ambush Caesar's army as it was marching or at its most vulnerable when encamping. Making use of the terrain, the land patched with dense woodland and divided by high hedgerows, the Nervii set an ambush in woods on the far side of the river Sambre. The Romans began fortifying camp on the near side of the river, and their cavalry and light infantry crossed the water to scout and keep the Nervii away while the legionaries completed the encampment. They were easily repulsed by the Nervii, who then charged very fast at the entrenching Roman soldiers. Caesar had failed to deploy a screen of infantry to protect those entrenching, standard procedure when encamping in the presence of the enemy, and his legions were caught dispersed and unprepared. The two rookie legions forming the rearguard had not even arrived at the campsite.

Battle against the Nervii

Caesar employed eight legions, two of which were still marching, and an unknown number of auxiliary infantry and cavalry. The Nervii had at least 60,000 warriors of the Nervii, Atrebates and Viromandui.

Faced with a sudden attack, the Roman legionaries did exactly the right thing. Both they and their officers had a year's more experience than when they had panicked in the face of Ariovistus the previous year, and their training and discipline kicked in. They grabbed arms and automatically created a line of battle. The IX and X legions held the left wing, the VIII and XI the centre, and the VII and XII the right wing.

The Nervii created a very strong left wing; the Viromandui held the centre and the Atrebates the right wing.

The two cavalry forces were already engaged, with the Gallic cavalry mauling the Romans.

Despite the battle line being cut up by the hedgerows, the Romans held the line fast and withheld the Belgic onslaught. The Roman centre was successful and the left wing repulsed the Atrebates, pursuing them across the Sambre. This success left the half-built Roman camp and the right wing of the battle line exposed and the Gauls captured the camp.

Meanwhile, the Roman right wing was outflanked by the Nervii, several of the officers had been killed and the ranks had become too packed together to operate effectively: the situation was critical. Taking up position on foot with the front rank soldiers, Caesar ordered the ranks opened up and the two legions to form a square so they could defend themselves from attack on all sides. His own presence helped to stiffen resistance until help arrived in the form of the X Legion, which had been sent back to

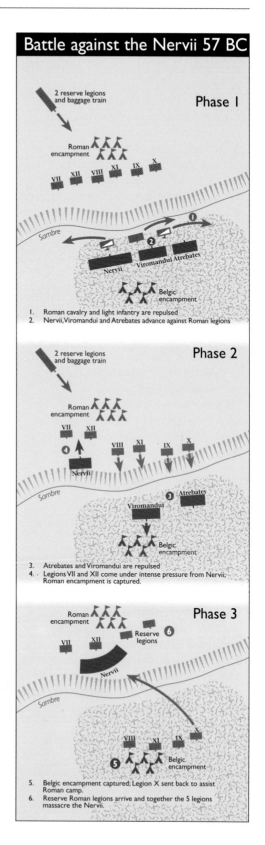

Battle against the Nervii 57 BC

Phase 1

2 reserve legions and baggage train

Roman encampment

VII XII VIII XI IX X

Sambre

Nervii Viromandui Atrebates

Belgic encampment

1. Roman cavalry and light infantry are repulsed
2. Nervii, Viromandui and Atrebates advance against Roman legions

Phase 2

2 reserve legions and baggage train

Roman encampment

VII XII

VIII XI IX X

Sambre

Nervii

Viromandui Atrebates

Belgic encampment

3. Atrebates and Viromandui are repulsed
4. Legions VII and XII come under intense pressure from Nervii; Roman encampment is captured.

Phase 3

Roman encampment

VII XII Reserve legions

Nervii

Sambre

VIII XI IX X

Belgic encampment

5. Belgic encampment captured; Legion X sent back to assist Roman camp.
6. Reserve Roman legions arrive and together the 5 legions massacre the Nervii.

assist after capturing the enemy encampment, and the two rookie legions of the rearguard which had finally arrived. The combined force of five legions turned the tide of battle and obliterated the Nervii who refused to surrender or withdraw.

Caesar's over-confidence had led to a dangerous situation, but his personal bravery and the experience of his army turned it into a significant victory. This successful engagement broke the power of the Belgae to such an extent that even German tribes beyond the Rhine sent envoys to Caesar offering submission. In operations towards the end of the year, one legion was sent to pacify the tribes on the Atlantic seaboard and with the remainder of his army, Caesar reduced the Aduatuci, who as allies of the Nervii were legitimate targets. Because they broke the terms of their surrender, all the Aduatuci were sold into slavery. The profit from selling 53,000 Aduatuci into slavery was, by rights, Caesar's alone.

Towards winter, Caesar sent one of his senior officers, Galba to open up the road over the Great St Bernard pass into Italy, allegedly for trade purposes. But he had been given an inadequate force of one under-strength legion and when Galba billeted his troops in the village of Octodurus he came under heavy attack from the local tribes who were concerned, probably rightly, that the Romans were more interested in conquest than trade routes. Galba's legion, the XII, was depleted after its mauling in battle with the Nervii and the poorly defended position they held was untenable. Galba was forced to abandon the campaign and break out, though according to reports they managed to kill some 10,000 Gauls on the way. Despite this setback, at the end of this second year, Caesar reported that Gaul was at peace and the Senate in Rome voted him an unprecedented 15-day public thanksgiving, which greatly increased his political and military reputation. He returned again to northern Italy to spend the winter; his legions were quartered in northern Gaul, the tribes there being forced to provide for the soldiers.

56 BC Naval warfare and the conquest of the west

Gallic resentment at the compulsion to feed the Roman legions over the winter showed itself when the Venetic tribes in north-western Gaul detained Roman officers sent out to procure grain and other supplies. Roman prestige demanded a heavy response.

The Aedui

Friendly relations between Rome and the Aedui had existed since 122 BC, and Aeduan warriors had served as auxiliaries in Roman armies, particularly as cavalry. Their support was vital for Caesar's campaigns in Gaul: they provided additional forces, food supplies, and a friendly place to fall back on should the Romans suffer a reverse. They were able to pressurise some tribes into allying themselves to Rome, such as the Bellovaci in 57 BC, but there was not unanimous support for Rome amongst the tribe. While Diviciacus, an influential aristocrat who had been chief magistrate of the Aedui, was a staunch supporter of Rome, his brother Dumnorix was just as passionately opposed to the alliance and though he was killed by Roman troops in 54 BC, some anti-Roman sentiment continued. Some Aeduan forces joined the revolt of 52 BC, but the tribe's involvement was by no means total. In return for Aeduan support, Caesar had allowed the tribe to extend its influence, letting them settle the Boii on their territory after their defeat with the Helvetii, for example, and picking them out as one of only two tribes spared punishment after the surrender of Alesia. Their favoured status and the willingness with which they embraced Roman culture resulted in the Aedui producing the first Gallic senator after the emperor Claudius admitted Gauls to that institution.

Since the Veneti were essentially a maritime force, ships were requisitioned from Gallic allies, warships were ordered constructed on the Loire, and oarsmen recruited in Provence with a view to beginning the naval campaign as early as the weather permitted. The Veneti knew that the capture of Roman officers would bring the invading army down on them and also prepared. They had the advantage of knowledge of both the land and the sea: warfare on the Atlantic with its storms and strong tides would be rather different from the kind of naval warfare Rome was used to in the Mediterranean. The Veneti fortified their hill forts, many of which were situated on isolated spits of land more accessible by sea than land, and gathered allies from Aremorica (modern Brittany), the Channel coast, and even the British tribes with whom they traded.

Caesar divided his forces and sent them to campaign in different parts of northern and western Gaul, proof that his claims that Gaul was at peace or had been conquered were something of an exaggeration. Throughout his governorship, Caesar was worried about incursions by German tribes and always kept a strong force in the Ardennes with cavalry to provide mobility against the Germans. This force also helped to hold down the Belgic tribes. Other forces were sent to Aquitania under Crassus, and Normandy under Sabinus. Caesar himself led a force of nearly four legions to meet with his newly gathered fleet, probably near the mouth of the Loire.

The Veneti
The Venetic campaign was a tough one. Sieges and assaults took care of the hill forts, but the wealth and resources of the Veneti were mobile and when one hill fort was about to be taken they loaded up their ships with people and possessions and simply sailed off to another. The newly built Roman fleet, designed for Mediterranean conditions and warfare, lacked the sturdiness needed to face Atlantic conditions and was stuck in harbour. The Romans, despite their professional army, sophisticated siege equipment and brand new fleet, were facing

an impasse and Caesar was forced to pause until his fleet could join him. Eventually the sea was calm enough to allow the Roman fleet to sail, and it encountered the Venetic navy off the coast of Brittany.

The size of the Roman fleet is not reported, but it consisted of Roman galleys, and ships provided by Rome's allies south of the Loire. The combined fleet of the Veneti and her allies numbered 220, although some may have been little more than fishing boats. The Venetic ships, designed for rough seas, were built of strong oak beams, too sturdy to be rammed by the galleys and too high in the water for the effective use of missiles.

Under the command of Decimus Brutus (who was later one of Caesar's assassins), the Roman fleet prepared grappling hooks to take on the Gallic sailing ships and then attacked. As with the famous *corvus*, the boarding bridge used against the mighty Carthaginian navy in the First Punic War, the Romans used the grappling hooks to overcome their disadvantage in naval warfare, cutting the rigging of the Gallic ships and rendering them helpless since they relied entirely on sail power. Unable to counter this new tactic, the Veneti decided to withdraw, at which point the wind dropped. Fortune favoured the Romans, who relied on oar power, and the galleys were able to go in and pick off the becalmed Venetic ships at their leisure. In an engagement lasting from late morning till sunset, most of the Venetic ships were destroyed.

Having lost their naval power, the Veneti could no longer retreat; they had nothing to protect them against the Romans or against other Gallic and British tribes and were forced to surrender. To serve as an example, Caesar executed the elders and sold the remainder of the population into slavery.

Normandy and Aquitania
Sabinus easily defeated a coalition of Venelli, Curiosolites and Lexovii when they charged the encampment he had located at the top of a long rise. They were so exhausted by the time they reached the camp that when the

Campaigns of 56 and 55 BC

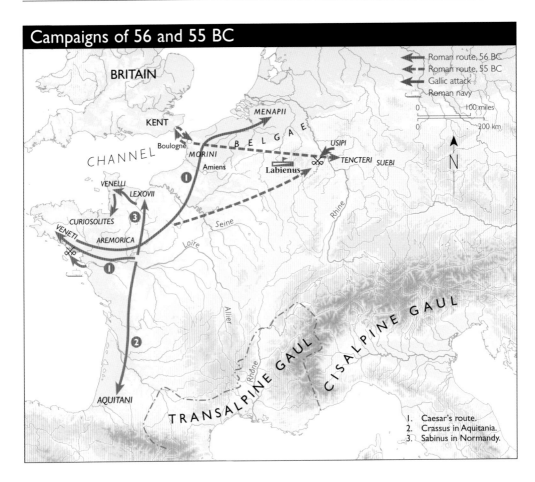

Romans sortied they routed them easily. All the tribes involved surrendered, placing the regions of modern Normandy under Roman control.

With just over one legion and a cavalry attachment, Publius Crassus had a tougher task against the tribes of Aquitania, so he raised additional infantry and cavalry from Provence and marched south of the Garonne and towards the Pyrenees, repulsing an attack by the Sontiates on the marching column. There was tougher opposition from the Vocates and Tarusates who had Spanish allies who had fought alongside the rebel Roman general Sertorius in the 70s BC. They aimed to cut Crassus off from his supply lines, a strategy that forced the Romans to seek pitched battle. But, having learned from the successful guerrilla tactics Sertorius had employed against Roman armies in Spain, the Gallic and Spanish tribes refused battle,

instead blocking roads and supplies, and attacking Crassus' marching column. If he wanted a result from the campaign, Crassus had to force an encounter, so his army attacked the enemy encampment. The camp was only properly fortified at the front, and once he learned of this, Crassus ordered reinforcements to circle round and attack the rear of the camp. The army of about 50,000 Gauls was taken by surprise and, completely surrounded, attempted to break out and flee, pursued by Crassus' cavalry force. Crassus reported to Caesar that only about 12,000 escaped the slaughter, and most of the tribes in the surrounding area surrendered. This was a significant victory and Crassus had succeeded in forcing the surrender of a huge area of south-western Gaul.

Towards the end of summer, Caesar turned on the Morini and Menapii on the Channel coast. They had supported the

Before Caesar's campaigns, Roman naval actions had been confined to the Mediterranean. The trireme illustrated on this civil war denarius was ill-suited to working in the tidal waters of the Atlantic seaboard and campaigns had to be halted until suitable conditions or vessels were available. (AISA)

Veneti and that was reason enough for an attack, but Caesar was probably already considering his campaigns for the following year, which would require a settled situation in northern Gaul. However, the poor weather and enemy tactics of withdrawing into forested and marshy land, meant that Caesar was only able to ravage farmland, rather than engage the enemy and he withdrew for the winter. The legions went into winter quarters in the land between the Loire and Saône that belonged to recently conquered tribes, their punishment for having resisted.

55 BC Publicity stunts

Caesar's two campaigns of 55 BC were dictated more by events in Rome than by military requirements in Gaul. His two closest political allies, the same men who were his greatest rivals, Pompey and Crassus, were consuls in Rome. The chief magistrates of the Roman state, their positions enabled them to seize all the publicity and buy the people's affections and votes with gifts, grain, and public banquets. Aware of the need to remain in the public eye, Caesar decided to enhance his reputation by being the first Roman to lead an army across the Rhine into Germany and over the 'ocean' to the mysterious island of Britain.

Two German tribes, the Usipi and Tencteri, had crossed the Rhine in search of

land after being ousted from their own by stronger Suebi, but following the policy he had established in his first year of office, Caesar refused to allow them to settle in Gaul. With a small force of 800 cavalry these

Roman soldiers building camp, their arms neatly stacked within reach. Caesar defied military theory by building camps near woods and consequently, his troops were attacked whilst entrenching. When the Nervii attacked his army in 57 BC, he was lucky that they were able to form a battle line and retaliate. (Trajan's Column, AKG)

A Celtic promentary fort in Spain, similar to those utilised by the Veneti in Brittany. Positioned on isolated spits of land, these forts were often accessible only by sea, which made attacks a difficult proposition for the invading Romans. (AISA)

German tribes then routed a Roman cavalry force (actually made up of Gauls) some 5,000 strong, killing 74. In retaliation, Caesar attacked their camp, caught them by surprise and massacred them, men, women and children, driving them into the nearby Rhine. Though there were probably nothing like the 430,000 casualties Caesar claims, it is likely that tens of thousands were killed, with no Roman losses. Roman warfare was often brutal, but this was excessively so, and Caesar's enemies in Rome threatened to prosecute him for war crimes once his governorship and its accompanying immunity from prosecution came to an end.

Caesar then decided to cross the Rhine to intimidate the Germans further, if they were not terrified enough by his massacre of the Usipi and Tencteri. Because this was a publicity stunt to gain prestige among both the Germans and his fellow Romans, Caesar decided to build a bridge and march across the Rhine rather than row across. In ten days, his troops had built a timber bridge on wooden piles driven into the riverbed and Caesar marched into Germany, burned some empty villages, marched back before the powerful Suebic army could muster, and destroyed the bridge. The first Roman invasion of Germany lasted 18 days.

The expedition to Britain was as brief as that to Germany. Caesar crossed the Channel late in the campaigning season, his justification for the campaign being the military assistance the British tribes kept giving the Gauls, but that was a mere excuse. The expedition to Britain was hardly an invasion; Caesar took only two legions with him, the VII and X, and the cavalry force never got across the Channel, seriously limiting Roman operations. It is not known where in Kent Caesar landed, but the land-fall was protected by cliffs and the Britons were waiting, so he moved seven miles up the coast to a flat, more open beach. The British had sent on their cavalry and chariots to oppose the landings and the deep-hulled Roman transports had to disembark the legionaries in deep water. Up to their waists in water and fully loaded with kit, the legionaries struggled ashore to be met by the terrifying barbarians, cavalry

and chariots. Despite artillery support, the legionaries were reluctant to leave the safety of their ships. They were inspired to do so by the example set by the famous eagle-bearer of the X Legion. Jumping into the sea, this unnamed soldier forced his fellow legionaries to follow him by taking the standard into battle. To lose a standard was the ultimate disgrace and the soldiers of the X Legion began disembarking. Once the scout ships began ferrying more legionaries to shore, the infantry was able to form up and force a landing. The Britons fled, but the failure of the cavalry to make the crossing meant the Romans were unable to finish the battle decisively.

In the following days the Roman expeditionary force suffered nothing but

Although this engraving depicts a romanticised view of Caesar's landing in Kent, it is possible that legionaries had to fight whilst still wading ashore, having disembarked in deep water. (Ancient Art and Architecture)

setbacks. Again, the cavalry failed to make the crossing, high tides caused serious damage to a number of the ships and transports, and the small Roman force was in no position to winter in Britain, as it was inadequately supplied. To cap all this, a detachment of the VII Legion was ambushed while harvesting grain and although a rescue party had driven the British off, this only inspired them to gather a large force to attack the seemingly vulnerable Romans. A short pitched battle ensued in front of the Roman encampment, but Caesar gives no details except that the Britons were easily repulsed and once again the lack of cavalry prevented any pursuit. Caesar demanded hostages from the defeated British tribes but could not wait for them to be handed over. With the rapidly approaching equinox and the likelihood of storms, Caesar withdrew, having never got beyond the coast of Kent. The expedition to Britain could have been a disaster. Caesar had risked everything by leading an under-strength and poorly supplied force to Britain. But the crossing of the Channel caught the imagination of the Roman public more sharply even than the bridging of the Rhine. Caesar became a hero and a public thanksgiving of 20 days was decreed in Rome, very satisfactorily trumping any popularity Pompey and Crassus had been able to achieve in the capital.

54 BC Back to Britain

Transports suitable for operations in the Channel were designed and built over the winter and a force of five legions and 2,000 cavalry made an unopposed landing in Kent in 54 BC. Caesar left three legions and a further 2,000 cavalry to hold down northern Gaul, and the fact that he took various untrustworthy Gallic chieftains to Britain with him indicates that Gaul was by no means pacified. Nonetheless, the Roman army disembarked and Caesar immediately took four of the legions and most of the cavalry to find the British who had gathered some 12 miles off. The Britons utilised hit-and-run tactics for most of the campaign and gained some success in hampering Caesar's advance. But the weather caused problems and again the ships were damaged by a storm. Caesar was compelled to return to the beachhead, fortify it securely and arrange for repairs to the ships before heading back out to find the British. The Britons used the delay to gather a larger army under the leadership of Cassivellaunus, king of the powerful Catuvellauni tribe.

The mobility of the British infantry, cavalry and especially the chariots, caused the Romans problems and forced them to remain in close formation on the march, lest they become isolated and picked off by the Britons. But when Cassivellaunus attacked a foraging party and was comprehensively repulsed, serious British resistance was crushed. The Romans crossed the Thames, aiming for the Catuvellaunian capital, a hill fort surrounded by trees, perhaps Wheathampstead in Hertfordshire. At this point, various tribes began surrendering to Caesar, offering hostages and grain. Caesar's willingness to accept these overtures encouraged others to capitulate, and once the hill fort was easily taken by storm, Cassivellaunus also requested terms. Eager to

withdraw from Britain before the equinoctial storms, Caesar agreed, demanding hostages and an annual tribute paid to Rome. The second expedition to Britain was far more successful than the first, and could truly be described as an invasion. Tribute had been exacted from the tribes and they could be considered subject to Rome. Caesar had no need to return to the island, and events in Gaul prohibited that anyway.

The winter of 54/53 BC was one of considerable disturbance in Gaul, showing how superficial much of the Roman conquest had been. Poor harvests throughout the province forced Caesar to divide his legions up when they went into winter quarters in north-eastern Gaul and probably increased discontent among the tribes, who were forced to supply scarce grain to the occupying legions. The scattering of the legions provided an opportunity, and within two weeks the winter camps were coming under co-ordinated attack.

Cotta and Sabinus

The furthest east of the winter camps, Cotta's was the most exposed Roman base and therefore the one most vulnerable to attack. One inexperienced legion and five cohorts were attacked by the Eburones under their dynamic leader Ambiorix, who claimed that all northern Gaul was in revolt and German mercenaries had crossed the Rhine to join in. He promised safe conduct to the Romans if they left their camp. Foolishly, Sabinus took him at his word and, despite the protestations of his fellow officers he led his force out of the safety of camp in a formation inappropriate to the tactical situation, straight into an ambush the Gauls had laid in a steep-sided valley. The inexperienced troops panicked, unable to maintain proper formation in terrain that denied them any opportunity to manoeuvre. The Romans were wiped out, Sabinus ignominiously being killed when trying to parley with Ambiorix, whom he still felt he could trust. A few escaped with their lives, others made it back to the encampment where they committed suicide during the night to avoid capture.

News of the second campaign in Britain 'We are waiting for the outcome of the war in Britain. It's known that the approaches to the island are surrounded by wall-like cliffs. It's also been established that there isn't a scrap of silver in the island and no hope of booty except for slaves – and I don't suppose you're expecting them to know much about literature or music!' Marcus Cicero, letter to Atticus, c. 1 July 54 BC.

'On 24 October I received letters from my brother Quintus and from Caesar, sent from the nearest point on the coast of Britain on 25 September. The campaign in Britain is over, hostages have been taken, there's no booty, but tribute has been paid and they are bringing back the army from Britain.' Marcus Cicero, letter to Atticus, late October 54 BC.

Quintus Cicero

Quintus Cicero, the brother of Rome's most famous orator, had one legion encamped in the territory of the Nervii. Encouraged by the massacre of Sabinus' force, the Aduatuci, Nervii and their dependent tribes attacked Cicero's camp, trying to sell him the same story about general revolt and a German invasion. Unlike Sabinus, Cicero refused point blank to discuss terms, strengthened the camp's defences and tried frantically to contact Caesar. Under guidance from Roman prisoners, the Nervii built a circumvallation of rampart and ditch and moved siege towers up to the Roman fortifications. There followed a desperate couple of weeks in which the legion successfully held off attacks that continued both day and night. Cicero's troops refused to leave the ramparts even when the barracks were fired and their possessions were burning, but injuries were taking their toll. By the time Caesar relieved the siege, the legion had suffered 90 per cent casualties.

When Cicero did finally get a message to Caesar, he acted immediately, redeploying his legions and hurrying by forced marches to Nervian territory, covering up to 20 miles a day. Though he had only two legions and a small cavalry force, Caesar destroyed a Nervian army 60,000 strong, which abandoned its siege of Cicero's camp to head off the relieving army. Cicero's dogged resistance and the outstanding bravery of his officers won high praise from Caesar.

53 BC

Following the disastrous winter of 54 BC, the season's campaigns concentrated on re-establishing Roman military superiority in north-eastern Gaul. Caesar recruited two more legions and borrowed one from Pompey, bringing the total to ten (40,000–50,000 legionaries). The size of the army allowed operations to be conducted, often simultaneously, against numerous tribes who had either been involved in the winter's uprisings or whom Caesar did not trust. At the end of the campaign most of the legions were quartered together on the Senones; the remaining four were quartered in pairs on the Treveri and Lingones, to prevent a repeat of the previous winter's attacks.

Before the campaigning season had properly begun, Caesar launched a surprise attack, concentrating on destroying property and capturing prisoners and cattle. The Nervii were swiftly forced to surrender and the legions returned to winter quarters.

In early spring Caesar marched suddenly on the Senones, taking them before they were able to withdraw into their fortified town or *oppidum*. With their people and supplies vulnerable, they had no alternative but to surrender.

Caesar marched into the Rhine delta with seven legions. Menapian tactics were to withdraw into the marshes, but the Romans built causeways to allow them access to the area, then destroyed all their property, capturing cattle and taking prisoners as they advanced. With their wealth destroyed, the Menapii were forced to surrender.

The Treveri were still unsettled after the winter and were awaiting promised German reinforcements before attacking Labienus, who was encamped with 25 cohorts of legionaries and a large cavalry force. Keen to defeat the Treveri before help arrived, Labienus tricked them into attacking on terrain that was very unfavourable to them. Labienus pretended to be withdrawing and the Treveri charged up a very steep riverbank to fall on the Romans. The Romans formed up their battle line and the Treveri, disordered and out of breath from their uphill charge, were routed within minutes of the battle commencing; Labienus' powerful cavalry force mopped up those fleeing. Help would never be forthcoming from the Germans now, so the whole tribe of Treveri surrendered.

For a second time Caesar bridged the Rhine and marched into Germany to punish the tribes for sending help to the Gauls and discourage them from doing so again. But supply problems limited the scope of operations and Caesar seems to have been unwilling to risk battle against the powerful Suebi so he withdrew.

In the Ardennes two columns of three legions each raided much of modern Belgium, destroying property and taking prisoners. The burning of crops threatened the Gauls with starvation and many tribes, including the Eburones, surrendered.

In the space of a year, northern Gaul was totally reduced through vicious punitive raids aimed at destroying the property and wealth of the tribes.

52 BC The great revolt

In the winter of 53/52 BC the general revolt which had been threatening erupted, perhaps

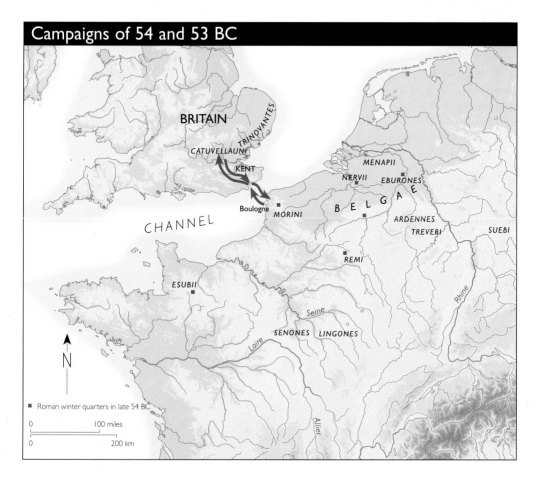

Campaigns of 54 and 53 BC

because the tribes realised that co-ordinated resistance could prove effective against the Romans, and possibly because a tribal council Caesar held the previous year indicated that Gaul was now being treated as a province of Rome. Taking advantage of Caesar's return to northern Gaul and the political turmoil and uncertainties in Rome caused by the death of the popular politician Publius Clodius, the Gauls began to plan their campaign. Amongst the tribes leading the call for revolt was the Carnutes, whose territory included consecrated land supposed to be the centre of Gaul, and where the druids met annually to settle disputes between Gauls. This sacred space was now being threatened by Roman advances and was of interest to all Gauls, encouraging them to put aside their previous differences. The massacre of Romans settled in the town of Cenabum (Orleans) signalled the beginning of the revolt and enabled a charismatic young Arvernian, Vercingetorix, to build a coalition of Gallic tribes around his own leadership. Caesar, who had been in Italy, reacted swiftly to try to prevent the whole of Gaul going up in revolt and rushed to Provence with a small force. Having arranged the defence of Roman territory, Caesar marched through the Massif Central and used Agedincum as his base to threaten Arvernian territory and force Vercingetorix to abandon an attack on Gorgobina, capital of the Boii who were still allied to Caesar.

The Roman route detoured in order to capture several *oppida* (the towns of Vellaunodunum, Cenabum, and Noviodunum), partly to spread terror, but perhaps more importantly, to capture supplies of grain and fodder. As it was still winter there was no forage available and the Roman army was finding it difficult to supply itself. The Gauls realised this and Vercingetorix's strategy was to avoid general engagements with the Romans, instead attacking foraging parties and supply trains. The Gauls cut off the Romans from all sources of food by withdrawing the population and supplies to the strongest *oppida* and adopting a scorched-earth policy,

abandoning all other *oppida*. Vercingetorix did not want to defend the *oppidum* of Avaricum (Bourges) despite its strong defences, but was persuaded to do so by the Bituriges. Caesar immediately invested it.

Avaricum

The *oppidum* was virtually surrounded by a river and marshes, but Caesar entrenched where there was a gap in the natural defences and constructed a siege terrace of earth and timber 330 feet wide and 80 feet high. Despite the cold, rain, sorties and attempts by the Gauls to undermine and fire the terrace, it was completed in only 25 days. Camped with a large force outside the *oppidum*, Vercingetorix had unsuccessfully tried to attack Roman foraging parties and wanted to abandon the defence of Avaricum before it was captured.

He was unable to persuade those whose home it was to do so, however: they were confident in the strength of their defences. Under cover of a heavy rainstorm when the Gallic sentries were less vigilant, Caesar ordered siege towers into position and his troops to assault the walls. The Gauls valiantly but vainly defended the breach and the Roman artillery took its toll, clearing an entrance for the legionaries who then took possession of the circuit of walls without risking street fighting by descending into the town proper. Once possession was secured the soldiers turned from disciplined attack to rape and pillage. No prisoners were taken and Caesar claims 40,000 died.

A coin of Vercingetorix who made himself king of the Arverni tribe and was able to unite the Gallic tribes under his sole leadership to create serious opposition to the Romans. Caesar called him a man 'of boundless energy', who 'terrorised waverers with the rigours of an iron discipline'. (Ancient Art and Architecture)

Vercingetorix

An ambitious young noble of the Arvernian tribe whose father had been executed for attempting to make himself king, Vercingetorix was ejected from the tribe by his uncle and other tribal leaders. They opposed his attempt to raise rebellion, but he was nonetheless able to raise a force and take control of the Arverni, then succeed where no other Gallic leader had, by forging an army under single leadership to resist Rome. His authority was so great that he was able to maintain Gallic morale even after a couple of reverses.

Campaigns of 52 and 51 BC

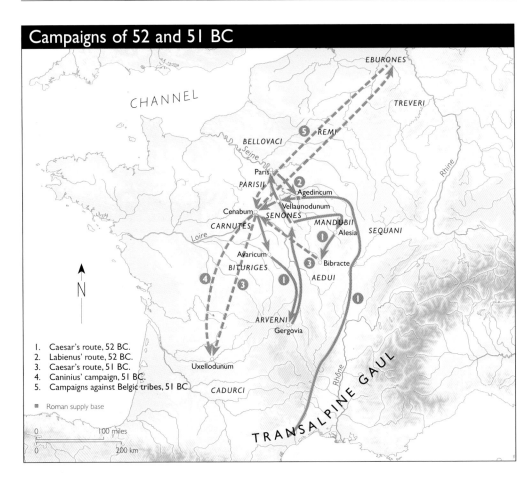

CHANNEL

EBURONES

TREVERI

REMI

BELLOVACI

Paris

PARISII

Agedincum

Cenabum   Vellaunodunum

SENONES

CARNUTES   MANDUBII

Alesia   SEQUANI

Avaricum

BITURIGES   Bibracte

AEDUI

ARVERNI

Gergovia

1. Caesar's route, 52 BC.
2. Labienus' route, 52 BC.
3. Caesar's route, 51 BC.
4. Caninius' campaign, 51 BC.   Uxellodunum
5. Campaigns against Belgic tribes, 51 BC.

CADURCI

TRANSALPINE GAUL

Roman supply base

N

0   100 miles
0   200 km

Artillery

Catapults were an important weapon in the armoury of the Roman army and were the ancient equivalent of canons and machine guns. Torsion artillery had been invented by the Greeks in the 4th century BC and developed during the subsequent Hellenistic period. By the late 1st century BC the machines available were both sophisticated and highly effective in warfare. There were two basic types of catapults, the *ballista*, which hurled stones, and the *scorpion*, which fired quarrels similar to the later crossbow. The catapults were powered by coils of rope or sinew, which could be tightened up using a ratchet, and when the stored energy was released, the missile could be projected with terrific speed and noise. Specialist architects and engineers were attached to Roman armies who would build and maintain these machines, but in

the field they would have been operated by the soldiers. In addition to the greater firepower such catapults provided to Roman armies, the presence of these engines of war on the battlefield or before a besieged town must have put considerable psychological pressure on the enemy. Gallic armies and communities were unused to such complex machinery; having to face a *scorpion* on the battlefield with its vicious sting cannot have been something they would have relished, and the very prospect of these machines may have put the Gauls at a disadvantage. Artillery mounted in boats was used, along with slingers and archers, to provide covering fire for the landings in Britain in 54 BC; Caesar says that the Britons were unnerved by the machines as they had never seen anything like them before, and this helped to drive them off the beaches.

Despite their technological superiority though, not all catapults were appropriate to Gallic warfare. Both types of catapults used by Roman armies were essentially anti-personnel devices. Although the largest stone-throwing *ballistae* might have been able to cause some damage to stone fortifications, they were not used primarily to knock down walls from afar: that was the job of battering rams and mines. They would have had little impact, in any case, against the earth ramparts of *oppida*, or the *murus Gallicus*, a combination of earth, timber and stone ramparts that fortified some *oppida*. But they were large and slow to move, and given the speed with which Caesar frequently operated, and the straightforward nature of most of the siege warfare he encountered, these larger catapults were probably not used. The *scorpions*, however, were much more mobile and could be used in both open warfare and sieges, adding to the missile barrage fired upon an enemy army in the opening phases of a pitched battle, for example. In preparation for a possible pitched battle against the Belgae, Caesar ordered the construction of trenches to protect his battle line and prevent outflanking manoeuvres by the enemy. At the end of each trench a redoubt was dug and artillery positioned in them. Had battle ensued, the *scorpions* in the redoubts would have provided considerable protection to the Roman army's flanks. Years later in the 'mopping-up' operations of 51 BC, Caesar positioned his battle line so that if pitched battle occurred against the Bellovaci, their battle line would be well within reach of the Roman artillery. While a volley of *pila* might be visible and Gallic warriors knew what to expect, *scorpion* bolts were swift, silent, and deadly. To be killed by one would not have been as glorious as being killed by an enemy warrior or soldier in open battle. In neither case, however, did the Gauls accept pitched battle: Caesar had so weighted the odds in his favour through use of topography and siting of artillery that the Gauls refused to engage. They were undoubtedly brave

warriors, but they were not so stupid as to throw their lives away.

Most Roman camps would have been defended by artillery and it is surprising that Caesar does not mention it having any role in defending Quintus Cicero's winter camp, which came under a sustained Gallic assault in the winter of 54 BC. It is unlikely that Cicero's winter quarters would not have been equipped with *scorpions* positioned in the gates and towers of the fortifications, something that was required by 2nd-century AD Roman textbooks on fortifying camps. Such artillery would have been especially useful, as the legionary strength defending the camp was depleted by the deaths and injuries that Caesar reports. It seems to have been the artillery that made the difference a few years later when an under-manned Roman camp at Gergovia came under attack by the Gauls: the machines could fire several bolts a minute and required far less physical effort to operate than hurling *pila* or lunging at the enemy with spears. When used by skilled operators, moreover, the *scorpions* could be deadly accurate.

The accuracy of *scorpions* is best illustrated through their role in Roman siege warfare. Carefully sited artillery could keep the defenders off the walls, while other soldiers operated battering rams, scaled with ladders or conducted undermining operations at the bottom of ramparts. At Avaricum they provided some protection for the legionaries constructing the huge siege terrace, at least until the besieged Gauls sortied *en masse*. But they were ineffective in preventing the Gauls from trying to set fire to the terrace. The Gaul who was throwing incendiary material onto the terrace was killed by a *scorpion*, but then another took his place. Caesar says they continued sacrificing themselves in attempting to fire the terrace and the *scorpion* kept on killing them until the fire went out and they gave up the effort. A *scorpion* must have been trained on one point and was able to fire accurate missiles

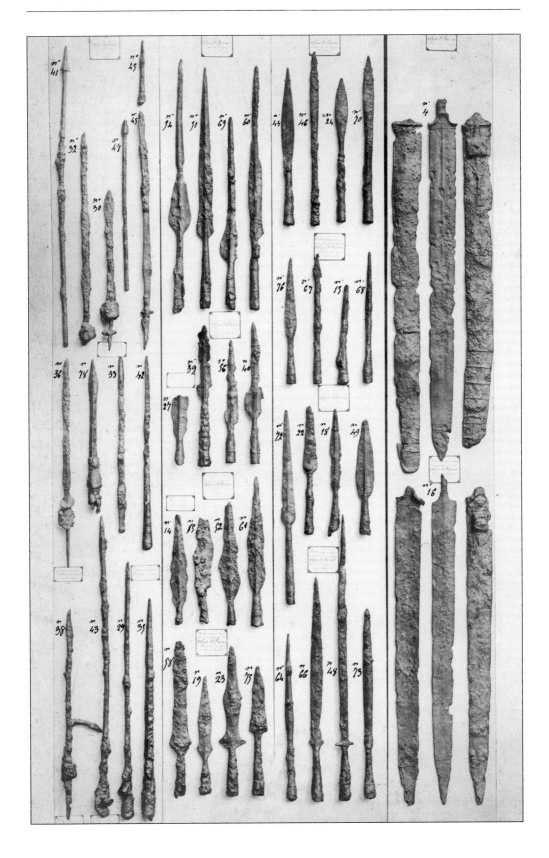

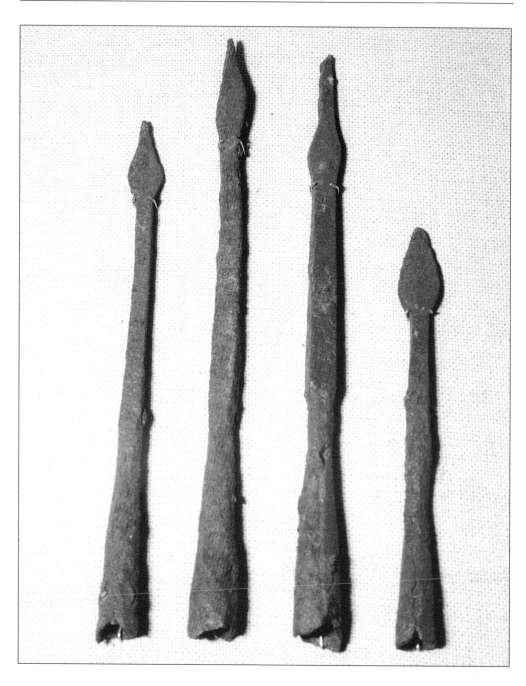

ABOVE These iron catapult bolts were excavated at Licenza, near Rome. Historians continue to debate the extent of Caesar's personal contribution to weapons development. (Ancient Art and Architecture)

OPPOSITE Finds of weapons from the Roman siege at Alesia. The site was explored by Napoleon III in the 19th century and many of these iron spearheads, *pilum* shafts and catapult bolts were found at Monte Rea where the fiercest fighting took place.

one after the other. Accurate artillery also helped to end the last siege of the conquest, at Uxellodunum in 51 BC. *Scorpions* positioned in towers prevented the Gauls from getting access to their only remaining water supply, though they did not actually surrender until the spring feeding the supply was diverted.

The Gallic coalition

Despite the setback at Avaricum, Vercingetorix had the authority to maintain the Gallic coalition and it was strengthened by the revolt of the Aedui. Some Aedui remained loyal and Caesar continued to command and use Aeduan cavalry, but it caused another blow to his already precarious supply lines, although the capture of supplies at Avaricum must have helped. Now the campaigning season had begun and fodder was becoming available in the open, Caesar ordered Labienus with four legions and cavalry to crush the Parisii and Senones, while he marched the remaining six legions down the Allier to Gergovia. Unlike Avaricum, which Vercingetorix had not wished to defend, this was one of the *oppida* he did intend to hold, probably because it was very strongly fortified, but perhaps also because it was the hill fort of his own tribe, the Arverni.

Gergovia

The hilly terrain dominated the Gergovia campaign. On arrival the Romans as usual entrenched camp, then captured a high hill opposite the *oppidum*, which dominated the principal water supply. Caesar had a smaller camp constructed there and linked his two camps with a wide ditch. This allowed him to move his forces around without interference from enemy sorties or cavalry. The next step was to capture another hill much closer to the hill fort and which actually adjoined the *oppidum*. The Gauls were not patrolling it properly and the legionaries were able to take it without much difficulty, crossing a six foot wall built to prevent such an action. In his *Commentaries* Julius Caesar claims he was only intending to take this hill and then halt the action. Either the soldiers failed to hear the recall he claimed to have sounded, and disobeyed orders, or he had actually intended to launch an attack against the *oppidum* itself if this first phase proved successful. Whatever the truth, the Romans did proceed to make a direct attack on Gergovia's defences, the enthusiasm of the

centurions for being the first onto the walls driving them on against the defenders who hugely outnumbered them. The Romans were driven back; 700 men were killed including 46 centurions. Caesar blamed his men for the defeat and may have been less than clear in reporting his intentions in his *Commentaries* to distance himself from blame for a serious setback.

Caesar's forced withdrawal from Gergovia must have greatly increased Vercingetorix's reputation and encouraged more tribes to join the revolt. He continued to attack the Roman supply lines while calling in reinforcements. The Romans, too, obtained reinforcements, from the Germans who proved effective in routing the Gallic cavalry attacks on the Roman marching columns. The next *oppidum* Vercingetorix decided to defend was Alesia in the territory of the Mandubii and after the victory at Gergovia he must have been confident of success.

Alesia

About 30 miles north-west of modern Dijon, Alesia was a large hill fort on a lozenge-shaped plateau protected by steep slopes and rivers on two sides. There was a plain at one end and at the other, the eastern end, the Gallic army was encamped. It was clear that an assault was out of the question, particularly after Gergovia, so the Romans would have to blockade. This was Vercingetorix's intention, for he allowed himself to be hemmed in at Alesia and ordered a relieving army to be gathered with all possible speed. The intention was to catch the Roman army in a pincer movement with simultaneous attacks by the besieged under Vercingetorix and a relieving army, which Caesar claims (perhaps dubiously) was nearly a quarter of a million strong.

The Roman siege works at Alesia were extraordinary in their size and complexity. After digging a deep ditch on the plain to prevent cavalry attacks on the working parties, the Romans built a rampart with palisade and towers at regular intervals, and

The siege of Alesia 52 BC

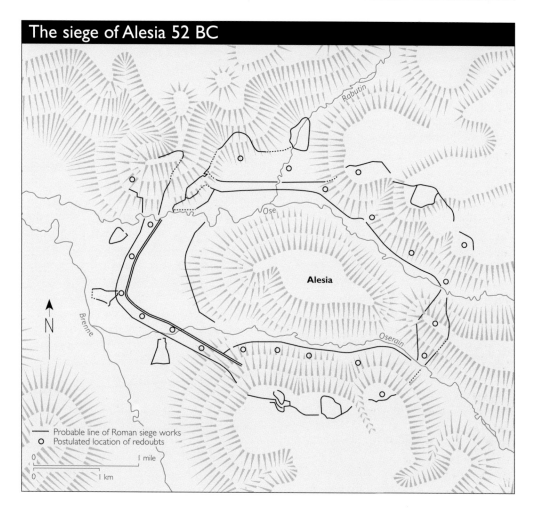

— Probable line of Roman siege works
O Postulated location of redoubts

a double ditch, one filled with water diverted from the rivers where possible; seven camps and 23 redoubts were added at strategic points. This line covered a circuit of 11 miles. Caesar was not happy even with this formidable system of defences, and lines of booby traps were extended for several yards in front of the trenches. These comprised rows of sharpened stakes, then covered pits with sharpened stakes planted in them, and finally rows of wooden stakes with barbed iron spikes stuck into them. Once this circuit was completed Caesar had another identical line built outside, 14 miles in circumference, to protect the besiegers from the relieving army. The whole system took about a month to construct. Archaeological investigations have indicated that the fortifications were

not as complete as Caesar suggests. There may have been gaps in the lines, particularly where the terrain provided natural protection, but the systems held up to concerted attacks by both Gallic armies even when they were prepared with bridging materials to cross the outer defences and ditches.

Ultimately, however, the Romans did not have to starve out the defenders at Alesia, and no attempts were made to take the *oppidum* by assault. Violent co-ordinated attacks by both Gallic forces on the Roman siege works had no effect and although the lines came under enormous pressure in one attack, reinforcements arrived in time and the Gauls were repulsed. It became clear that the extraordinary defences the Roman army had constructed were not going to break and the failure of the revolt and starvation for those shut in Alesia were inevitable. The relieving army disbanded and Vercingetorix surrendered. Caesar distributed most of the prisoners amongst his men in lieu of booty. Vercingetorix was kept, to be displayed six years later in Caesar's triumphal procession in Rome, after which he was ritually strangled.

> *The surrender of Vercingetorix*
> 'The leader Vercingetorix put on his finest armour and equipped his horse magnificently, then sallied out of the gate. After riding several times around Caesar who was sitting on a dais, he then dismounted, took off his armour and set himself at Caesar's feet where he remained in silence until Caesar ordered the guard to take him away and keep him for his triumph.'
> Plutarch, *Life of Julius Caesar*

51–50 BC Mopping up

The legions were distributed throughout Gaul over the winter to keep down the defeated tribes, and to protect the Remi who alone had been unswerving in their support for Rome. Caesar's last full year of campaigning in Gaul involved mid-winter terror raids against the Bituriges and Carnutes and, once spring had begun, Roman forces were sent which crushed all remaining thought of rebellion amongst the Belgic tribes, the Bellovaci, Eburones, Treveri and Carnutes. The only remaining serious resistance was in south-western Gaul. Here two men, Drappes, a Senonian who was nonetheless able to exert influence among other tribes, and Lucterius, a local Cadurcan, took over the *oppidum* of Uxellodunum which was extremely well fortified.

Uxellodunum

With only two legions, the general Caninius invested the *oppidum*, building three camps at strategic points and starting a circumvallation.

The reconstructed Roman siege-works of Alesia. Archaeological investigations at Alesia have shown that these defences were nowhere near as extensive or complete as Caesar claimed. Nonetheless, they were highly effective in repelling a joint attack by those besieged in Alesia and the Gallic relieving army. (Ancient Art and Architecture)

Drappes and Lucterius clearly knew what to expect because they sortied to collect supplies, but were intercepted by Caninius, and Drappes was captured. Roman reinforcements arrived during the siege, and Caesar personally attended to the final crushing of the revolt.

Despite the disaster that befell Drappes' foraging party, Uxellodunum was very well supplied and the forces bottled up there were nothing like as numerous as those at Alesia the previous year. Potentially, they could have held out for some time, but Caesar was

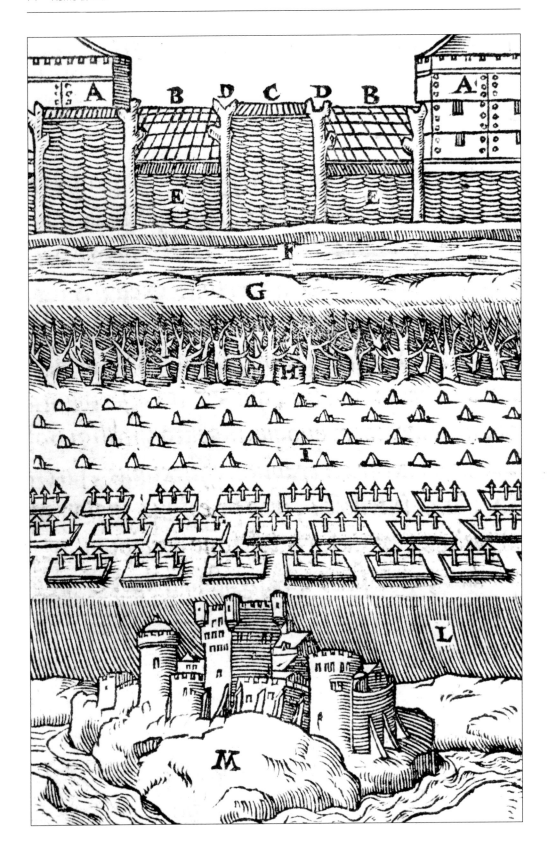

keen to take the town swiftly to serve as an example and so attacked the water supply. Like many Gallic *oppida*, Uxellodunum was dependent on an external water supply and artillery was set up to cut the defenders off from the rivers, leaving only a spring from which water could be obtained. The Romans then built a huge ramp and tower to dominate the spring and fire on those collecting water, and secretly dug tunnels towards it. Parts of the tunnels were discovered by archaeologists in the 19th century. The Gauls sortied in an attempt to destroy the siege ramp, rolling flaming casks down onto the woodwork, but their diversionary attack was repulsed and the Roman soldiers were able to extinguish the incendiary devices before serious damage was

LEFT A 16th-century woodcut of the Roman siege-works at Alesia showing the booby traps beyond the rampart and ditches, the sharpened stakes (*cippi*), half-buried wooden stakes (*lilia* or *lilies*), and iron spikes (*stimuli*), creating a formidable series of obstacles. (AKG Berlin)

Commius

One of the Gallic rebellion's leaders was Commius, chieftain of the Gallic Atrebates and an early ally of Caesar. He travelled to Britain in advance of the 55 BC expedition to gather intelligence for the Romans, and his reward was control over the neighbouring Morini and exemption from taxation for the Atrebates; but they still joined Vercingetorix. Commius was one of the commanders of the relieving army at Alesia and in 51 BC stirred up further rebellion amongst the Bellovaci. Labienus tried to have him assassinated at a parley but Commius escaped and later fled to Britain where he was able to establish himself as king of the British Atrebates.

BELOW Bronze of a dead Gaul, found at Alesia. Caesar does not provide the casualty figures from the Alesia campaign, but they were undoubtedly high. (Ancient Art and Architecture)

A scene from Trajan's Column showing an enemy leader being taken before the Roman commander. Traditionally, an enemy leader who was captured would be displayed in a triumphal procession in Rome and then executed – exactly the fate which befell Vercingetorix. (AISA)

done. Finally, the Roman tunnels reached the spring and the Gauls, ignorant of what had caused their ever-reliable spring to run dry, interpreted it as a divine signal and surrendered. Instead of massacring the defenders, Caesar cut off their hands and set them free, to serve as an example of the punishment meted out to those who resisted Rome.

So Gaul was conquered, or at least the tribes had all surrendered to Roman power. The legions were brigaded throughout Gaul over the winter and virtually no campaigning took place the following year because the province was largely at peace, and Caesar had already turned his attention back to Rome. Civil war was becoming inevitable and Caesar would be one of the key players.

The 'rules of war'

When the Gallic *oppidum* of the Aduatuci was being besieged by the Romans, the tribal leaders sent envoys requesting peace. Caesar replied that he would be merciful and spare the tribe, 'provided that they surrendered before the battering ram touched the wall of the *oppidum*'.

There were no rules laid down in antiquity about the treatment of the defeated in war. Ancient custom gave the victor total and absolute power over the defeated, whether they had surrendered voluntarily or been forced into submission. Defeated peoples, both combatants and non-combatants, could be executed, sold into slavery or even released, and their treatment was totally dependent on the decision of the victorious commander. Important captives, those of high social or political status, might be treated better than ordinary people, or they might be executed to set an example to others. Setting an example was one of the main factors in deciding the fate of the defeated, and linked with this were the overall aims of the conqueror. The difficulty of the campaign or battle might also have affected how the victor treated the conquered, along with whether the losing side had committed any atrocities during the course of the war. The slaughter of civilians at Avaricum was so brutal, Caesar tells us, because the siege had been a hard one and the Roman soldiers were avenging the massacre of Roman civilians at Cenabum.

We hear little of the Gallic treatment of Roman prisoners. Caesar gives a graphic description of the immolation of captured warriors by Gauls as a sacrifice to the Gallic war god Esus, but does not report this happening to any Roman captives.

Caesar's centurions

Centurions are often considered to be the backbone of the Roman legions, and rightly so. It may seem odd, but at the time of Caesar's campaigns the legion had no official commander; Caesar sometimes appointed a legate or quaestor to command one or more legions. It was not until the establishment of the Principate under Augustus that each legion had its own permanent commander, usually a senator, appointed by the emperor. The centurions (and the six military tribunes attached to the legion) had a vital role in providing the leadership, experience and stability that the legion needed to operate effectively. Centurions were the highest echelon of professional soldiers in the legion and their senior officers and commanders were politicians whose military experience and skill could vary considerably. The 60 or so centurions in each legion were appointed by the army commander – the provincial governor. While some may have been appointed because of their social status, the majority gained promotion through experience, leadership and conspicuous courage. This must have encouraged ambitious private soldiers to prove their worth on the battlefield to gain promotion to the rank of centurion. It also drove centurions to continue to prove themselves to their peers and to the soldiers under their command, so they led from the front, and often suffered disproportionately high casualty rates because of this. In the reverse at Gergovia, for example, 46 of the 700 killed were centurions.

These high casualty rates may have been exacerbated not just by centurions seeking to engage the enemy, but by the enemy deliberately targeting them. Centurions could have made themselves highly visible in battle, and probably did, through their armour, equipment, and particularly their helmets, which had distinctive transverse crests, as well as by wearing their decorations as a clear marker of their courage. A Gallic warrior who killed a Roman centurion would have greatly increased his reputation and therefore his influence within his tribe.

Sensible commanders recognised the value of their centurions not only in leading men into battle, but also in providing valuable advice based on their experience of war. Caesar regularly invited the senior centurions of his legions to the briefings and councils of war he held with his senior officers; he would have listened to their advice and used them to pass on information and orders to the rank and file. Their understanding of an intended battle plan was vital for success simply because they were the ones leading the men on the ground. The value Caesar placed on his centurions is also reflected in the good press he generally gives them in his account of the campaign in Gaul. When Caesar is prepared to give others credit for a Roman victory, the centurions are often praised; but they can also be blamed for a reverse like Gergovia. They were too eager, Caesar claims, to capture Gergovia, and led their men into difficulties through their desire to gain the plaudits and military decorations for a successful action. But they did die to save their men in the retreat.

P. Sextius Baculus

The XII Legion had been raised by Caesar in 58 BC in preparation for the campaign against the Helvetii, and although it consisted largely of new recruits, it had a core of experienced centurions who would have had to train their new soldiers on the job. The Chief Centurion (*Primus Pilus*) of

the XII was Publius Sextius Baculus, a man renowned for his bravery, but he would also have been an experienced and trustworthy leader for such an appointment. He was probably transferred from another legion, and would have been appointed by Caesar himself. During its second year in existence this legion suffered in the battle against the

The tombstone of M.Caelius, a centurion of Legion XVIII who was killed in the Varian disaster in AD 9. Promoted for their courage and leadership, centurions frequently suffered very high casualty rates in battle as they led their men from the front and strove to preserve their reputations for courage and valour. (Bonn Museum)

Nervii in 57 BC; most of the centurions were killed or injured, including all those from the legion's IV cohort. Baculus was seriously injured in the battle, but was able to remain with his legion or rejoin it later, after treatment in a camp hospital. Towards winter in the same year, Caesar sent the legion into the Alps with Galba. The legion was already under-strength and was probably still short of experienced officers following the battle with the Nervii, when it came under attack in the village of Octodurus and was pinned down by Alpine tribesmen. Baculus and a fellow officer, a military tribune, together advised Galba that the situation was too desperate to hold and they should break out. Galba listened to the advice of his juniors and in the ensuing break-out the XII Legion managed to turn the tables on the enemy and put them to flight with heavy casualties.

We hear nothing more of Baculus for the next three years, but he probably remained with his legion for the campaigns in northern and western Gaul. He reappears briefly in 53 BC during a German raid on a Roman camp garrisoned by the inexperienced XIV Legion, 200 cavalry and 300 legionaries from other legions who were on the sick list and recovering in camp. Baculus was presumably one of the sick, but we do not know if this was because he had been injured in battle again. A group of soldiers and camp servants out foraging was attacked by the German cavalry and some of them tried to make it back to camp. Baculus rose from his sick-bed and helped to hold the gates of the camp, allowing the rest of the garrison time to man the fortifications. Already weakened through illness, Baculus was seriously injured and fainted, but was dragged back to safety by his companions. He probably recovered

from this injury (Caesar would almost certainly have reported it had he died), but nothing further is known of him.

Centurions were promoted for their courage, but they were expected to continue to show bravery to justify their position, and to push for further advancement to the ranks of the senior centurions in the legion. Titus Pullo and Lucius Vorenus were two centurions in Cicero's legion who were in competition with each other for promotion to senior centurion. The attacks on Quintus Cicero's camp during the winter of 54 BC gave the two an opportunity to compete with each other to see who was the bravest. Both took part in a sortie, Pullo charging first with a spear but getting into trouble when his sword got stuck in its scabbard by a javelin which had pierced his shield and hit his sword belt. Vorenus came to his aid and forced the Gauls to retreat, but then tripped and became surrounded. Pullo rescued his rival and the two of them made it back within the fortifications after killing a few Gauls. Despite their rivalry they had saved each other's lives and had shown themselves to be equal in bravery. Caesar says nothing more about them so unfortunately we do not know if they were promoted.

At the end of their service, Caesar's centurions who had survived the wars in Gaul and the Civil War were probably wealthy men from the booty they had acquired and the bonuses they had been paid. Many of the soldiers of these wars were settled with land in military colonies in Provence or in northern Italy. The centurions were given larger allotments than the ordinary soldiers and often held public office in their local towns.

The impact of the conflict

War was central to the lives of both Romans and Gauls. In both societies one of the most effective ways for the aristocracy to maintain status was to be successful in war, and warfare touched upon the lives of everyone, rich and poor. For the Gauls, though, the Gallic War was different from the kinds of conflict they usually experienced in its range, intensity and destructiveness. Wars in Gaul tended to be on a fairly small scale, often little more than raiding parties against neighbours to grab easily portable property, livestock and slaves. These allowed the elite warriors to maintain their positions of authority in their tribes by demonstrating prowess in battle and the acquisition of wealth, which benefited the whole tribe. In particular the aristocratic leaders were able to display their position through the purchase of other 'status' goods from abroad, mostly from the Greek and Roman cities of southern Gaul. Younger warriors, too, could make their names through these raids and begin to acquire wealth. On a wider level, successful raiding increased a tribe's military reputation and could lead to the subjection of neighbouring tribes to dependent status, thereby lessening the likelihood of attack by other tribes. After the defeat of the Helvetii, for example, the Aedui allowed the beaten Boii to settle on their land because of their reputation for valour: the Boii would have become dependent on the Aedui, thus increasing the latter's military strength and influence in inter-tribal relations. So pressing was the need for increasing prestige in this way, that the Arverni and Sequani enlisted the help of German warriors in their campaign against the Aedui. Such raids caused some destruction and loss of property, including cattle, and Gallic peasants were often captured to be sold into slavery, but permanent conquests were rare.

The Roman approach to warfare was different. Whilst the Celtic style of warfare involved mainly those of warrior status, Roman society not only expected regular wars of conquest, but was prepared for it. A governor in Caesar's position would have been expected to campaign and possibly conquer new territory, and he had access to forces drawn from a mixture of conscripts and volunteers. The extra legions that were raised for the war in Gaul (six further legions during the governorship) were unlikely to have put considerable strain on the manpower of Italy. The majority of recruits came from northern Italy and would have welcomed the opportunity to serve in the legions (especially as many of them may well not have possessed full Roman citizenship and legionary service would have allowed them to assert their claims to it). Military service meant full integration into the Roman state, and the opportunity for enrichment from booty. So in terms of manpower and resources, the conquest of Gaul had little impact on the Roman state: it was, quite simply, what Rome expected. For the Gauls though, the intensity of Roman campaigning and particularly the speed with which their lands were reduced to provincial status must have been a terrible shock.

One of the main reasons for the extraordinary speed of the Roman conquest was the failure, or inability, of the Gauls to co-operate in their own defence. Caesar took advantage of the rivalry between Gallic tribes and when they were eventually combined under the leadership of Vercingetorix in 52 BC, it was too late to prevent the permanent establishment of Rome in Gaul and the creation of Roman provinces. We hear little from Caesar about the effects of the war on Gaul and its population (his audience would not have been particularly interested in these kinds of detail), but the effects must have been widespread, affecting the lives of wealthy and poor, influential and unimportant alike. Despite the turmoil caused by the campaigns of conquest though, the establishment of the Roman provinces ensured the continuation of the Gallic aristocracy in their dominance over the lower orders.

Loss of life

Ordinary Gauls were not always involved in the actual fighting, but they were all, men, women and children, legitimate targets in ancient warfare. Those tilling the soil or tending animals might be captured and carried off as slaves, or slaughtered by Romans in search of supplies or casual plunder. Such actions might be sanctioned by Roman officers and might even be organised on a large scale, particularly in the search for supplies, or carried out on the initiative of soldiers without their superiors' knowledge since there was unlikely to be serious punishment for such minor misdemeanours. The civilian population was particularly at risk because of the speed with which the Roman army moved: they could easily be caught out in the open, too far from the supposed shelter provided by *oppida*. During the campaigns of early 52 BC, Caesar's men regularly caught civilians in their fields and villages, as did the Gauls, who posed just as serious a risk to civilians from tribes who still supported Rome. Very high civilian casualties must have been caused during the destruction of the Helvetian army at the very beginning of the conquest, since the Helvetian warriors' families were at the battle site, watching from their wagons. They were almost certainly caught up in the slaughter following the capture by Roman soldiers of the Helvetian encampment. Worse was the massacre of the Usipi and Tencteri. The Roman troops fell on a poorly fortified encampment and met only minor resistance.

Caesar noted, 'Because they had brought all their possessions with them when they had abandoned their homes and crossed the Rhine, there were also many women and children, and they then began to flee in all directions. Caesar ordered the cavalry to hunt them down.' No mercy was shown, even to those who could offer no resistance. It was not surprising that Caesar's enemies in Rome pounced on the news of this slaughter and threatened to prosecute him for war crimes. But while some in Rome may have been genuinely appalled at this action, their concern was aimed more at destroying Caesar's reputation than exacting justice for the massacre.

Throughout the wars the majority of civilian casualties occurred during sieges. More often than not a tribe's civilians were caught up in the assault and capture of their hill forts or *oppida*, or in the blockades that occurred more rarely. Some of these *oppida* were well defended by Celtic standards (though not by Roman), and were basically fortified towns, some of which were flourishing with substantial buildings and populations by the mid-1st century BC. Civilians naturally sought refuge within their walls when an enemy army appeared on the scene, and when their armies were defeated in the field or chose not to face the Romans in pitched battle, they too retreated to the 'safety' of their *oppida*. These fortifications rarely posed much of a challenge to the Romans, however, and the lives of those inside, whether warrior or civilian, were in the hands of the Roman general. Under the accepted modes of behaviour in ancient warfare, if the place surrendered, then usually the defenders and civilians caught inside were treated with leniency, but if it resisted and was taken by force or starved into surrender after a blockade, then the treatment of all might be extremely brutal. Indiscriminate slaughter followed the capture of Avaricum by assault in 52 BC with nearly 40,000 Gallic casualties, according to Caesar. Many of them were women and children. The Aduatuci escaped this fate when they surrendered their *oppidum* to Caesar in 55 BC but because they then attacked the Roman guards, Caesar had the whole lot sold into slavery. Siege warfare brought a worse fate though for the civilian inhabitants of Alesia. The non-combatants of the Mandubii tribe whose town it was were thrown out of their *oppidum* by Vercingetorix, who was trying to conserve his food supplies. Caesar, following standard military procedure, refused to allow them through the Roman lines and sent them back in an attempt to hasten the Gauls' starvation and hence the end of the siege. Vercingetorix refused to allow them entry back into the town and they remained, gradually starving to death, in no-man's land within the siege works.

The Romans did not escape without losses, the most serious being the one and a half legions wiped out in the winter of 54 BC, anything from 5,000 to 7,000 men depending on how under-strength the legions were. Caesar is unusually frank about the seriousness of this defeat, mainly because he could place the blame firmly on his legate Sabinus, who had been commanding the detachment. He reports the losses at Gergovia as nearly 700, including 46 centurions, but elsewhere the general is fairly circumspect about the reverses and losses suffered by his own forces, not even providing the casualty figures from successful pitched battles which he must have known. Injuries, sickness and deaths must have reduced the strength of the legions, and by the end of the civil war with Pompey in 48 BC some of his legions were less than two-thirds of their proper strength. But because his *Commentaries* had a propaganda purpose, Caesar deliberately downplayed most of the reverses he suffered and the casualties his forces took. Few Roman civilians were caught up in the war: merchants and their families were massacred during the general uprising of 52 BC, and although there were enough of them to form an identifiable group within several towns, we can only guess at the numbers involved – probably not that many.

It is impossible to make any kind of accurate calculation of the total loss of life during the Gallic War. Gallic casualty figures are inflated for literary and political effect, whilst Roman ones are downplayed. An estimate of tens of thousands of Roman losses would probably be reasonable, while the casualty figures for the Gauls, Germans and Britons combined ran into the hundreds of thousands. Gallic warriors and men of military age are likely to have been particularly heavily hit with a resultant imbalance in the population, but the population of Gaul especially would also have been depleted by the numbers carried off into slavery.

Slavery

Slavery was a common feature of many societies in the ancient world. Rome was increasingly dependent on slavery in the late Republic with large numbers being employed in agriculture and the production of raw materials, especially in mines and quarries. Gauls also kept slaves, procuring them during raids on other tribes, and there was a thriving trade in slaves from Gaul to Rome, with luxuries and particularly wine being exchanged for them. Slaves were one of the most common acquisitions from Rome's extensive wars of conquest since prisoners of war were generally sold into slavery. An influx of Gallic slaves was probably expected when Caesar began his campaigns in 58 BC. Traditionally, the slaves taken in a campaign were the property of the commanding general, and they represented one of the most lucrative immediate sources of income for him. This must have been particularly important for Caesar, who had bankrupted himself during his election campaigns for various magistracies in Rome, and especially in buying the position of *Pontifex Maximus* (Chief Priest) in 63 BC. Despite his right to possession of the slaves, Caesar was generous to his soldiers and gave them the slaves captured in some of the campaigns. This made him extremely popular with his men and increased their loyalty, an important factor in the succeeding civil war.

Caesar reports that his army captured huge numbers of prisoners during his wars of conquest and many of these were sold into slavery. He claims that 53,000 men, women and children of the Aduatuci tribe were captured when he took their *oppidum* in 57 BC, and this may have been the majority of the entire tribe. Because of their perfidy (they had surrendered but then during the night had rallied and attacked the Romans), Caesar had all of them sold into slavery. This was done by auction, one of the reasons merchants would have been keen to accompany an army on campaign, and Caesar pocketed all the proceeds which must have been a vast sum. The following year he

treated the Veneti in a similar manner. Many tribes that resisted Caesar escaped fairly lightly and did not have their populations taken as slaves, but the Veneti were treated differently because, like the Aduatuci, they had shown themselves to be untrustworthy in Roman eyes, detaining Caesar's envoys (admittedly to requisition grain supplies during the winter, which they may have felt legitimately aggrieved about given that they were not at the time subject to Rome). The Venetic elders were executed and the entire population, men, women and children (or at least those who were rounded up), were sold into slavery.

While the slaves captured during the campaigns were a useful source of much-needed wealth for Caesar, their worth lay principally in their numbers. As individual slaves they were less valuable, relatively, than slaves from other parts of the Mediterranean world, for they were unskilled. In a letter to his friend Atticus, Marcus Tullius Cicero makes a snide remark about the perceived barbarous culture of the Celts, indicating that the slaves were illiterate and 'uncivilised'. Rome had not yet reached the point when thousands of prisoners of war were sacrificed in the arena by emperors for the amusement of their subjects; many of the slaves from the Gallic wars would have been sold for their muscle, to work in the fields, in quarries and mines, often in appalling conditions with a very short life expectancy. Some, including women and children, may have ended up in Rome, but the majority were probably put to work in northern Italy, Provence and Spain.

It is just as impossible a task to estimate the numbers of Gauls enslaved as it is the casualty figures; whatever the actual numbers though, Caesar's Gallic War must have dealt a major blow to the size and balance of Gaul's population. Those not

Column base from Mainz, Germany, mid-1st century AD. Two captured barbarians are chained together to be sold into slavery. Slaves formed one of the main sources of income from foreign conquests, and although Caesar could have claimed all the profits from the sale of Gauls, he shared them with his men. (Landesmuseum, Mainz)

killed or captured and auctioned off as slaves by the Romans did not avoid the suffering themselves: the war brought widespread destruction and hunger.

Destruction

Ancient warfare, by its very nature, was nothing like as destructive as more modern forms of war; the demolition of property and possessions would usually have been quite well targeted, at least when sanctioned or specifically ordered by Roman officers. What we do not hear about, but must assume happened, was casual raiding, destruction and looting by Roman soldiers. They are not reported in the ancient accounts of the campaigns because of the political nature of the narrative that Caesar was producing: ill-disciplined soldiers did not reflect well on him and he wanted to tell his audience about successful operations, battles and conquest, not the minor details of soldiers looting. But we hear about such activities from narratives of other wars and campaigns from the Roman period, and there is no reason to assume that the behaviour of the Roman soldiers in Gaul was any different. As with casualties, it is impossible to quantify the amount of destruction; that carried out on orders was probably precisely directed and tribes friendly to Rome such as the Aedui and the Remi probably escaped more or less unscathed. Siege warfare obviously resulted in the destruction of a great deal of property as towns were captured and sacked, but the countryside was also devastated. The enormous siege terrace at Avaricum and extensive fortifications at Alesia must have required huge quantities of timber for their construction, and the countryside surrounding these *oppida* must have remained scarred for a generation after the conquest.

The campaigns against the Menapii and Morini were primarily destructive. Because the population withdrew into inaccessible marshes, the Romans simply destroyed all the livestock, farms and villages they could find in the hope or expectation that this would force the Gauls into surrender. It did, for with their wealth and livelihoods gone they had no option. Despite being able to cause widespread destruction and casualties, however, Rome rarely resorted to uncontrolled ravaging of the countryside or mass slaughter as a means of defeating her enemies. In a highly emotive passage, the Roman historian Tacitus, writing in the early 2nd century AD about Roman provincial policy, claims that the Romans 'made a desert and called it peace'. But in creating her empire this was not Rome's approach, as there was no point in making a province if the land was unworkable and unable to sustain a population who could pay taxes to Rome.

The Gauls, too, resorted to destruction of property: in 52 BC, the entire strategy of the revolt was based on a scorched-earth policy and the expectation that the Roman army would face such severe supply problems especially early on in the campaigning season that it would be forced to retreat. Given the annual problems that Caesar did face in supplying his army, this was a perfectly sound strategy, and so excess supplies of food, fields, livestock and towns with all their contents were destroyed. After the complete failure of the revolt, the following winter must have been a desperate one for the Gauls and it is likely that there was widespread famine and starvation throughout central Gaul. Many of the Gallic tribes probably suffered food shortages during the winter because of the very presence of the invading army, when military requisitioning affected both subjected and allied tribes.

Food supply

The Gallic economy was based mainly on agriculture and we have already seen how the war disrupted the lives of the population in some areas of the country through the deliberate destruction of crops and livestock. Shortages were also caused by requisitions imposed by Caesar on many of the tribes in Gaul. Although it used one of the most advanced logistical systems of any ancient army, the relatively slow speed of contemporary transport meant that Roman armies had to arrange the provision of additional supplies from the theatre of war or from other nearby areas. In Gaul this burden was placed partly on newly conquered tribes, but also on allies such as the Aedui, part of the price they paid for Roman support. The obligation to provide for a large standing army, unlike the Gallic armies that dispersed to their homes over the winter, put a considerable strain on the tribes. Caesar relied on the Aedui for supplies, particularly during the early campaigns before he had established clear supply routes. When trailing the migrating Helvetii in 58 BC, he was intending to divert to the Aeduan capital of Bibracte to obtain supplies from his allies, and he regularly demanded grain from defeated tribes and even allies, particularly at the start of the campaigning season when little fodder would have been available in the fields.

The heaviest demands for grain and other supplies from the Gauls came over the winter months during the closed campaigning season. The legions were put into winter quarters, usually a well-fortified encampment rather than being billeted in Gallic towns, but their stationing was carefully chosen. For the most part, legions spent the winter on the lands of newly conquered tribes to keep an eye on them, perhaps to impress on them the idea that Rome was there for good with a military presence that did not disband over the winter, and to punish the tribes for opposing Rome by forcing them to feed the occupying force over the winter. These demands could place considerable strain on a tribe's grain supply and threaten their survival. But there were no 'neutrals' in this campaign and even tribes in areas far away from the campaigning who had not even opposed the Romans might have demands made upon them. The Veneti were still an independent tribe in western Gaul who had not fought against Caesar when, during the winter of 57/56 BC he sent officers to requisition grain. Not surprisingly they were unhappy at the demands made of them and detained the officers.

Religious and social change

Gallic tribes were already undergoing social and political change before the Roman conquest. It was caused by the interaction between the Greek and Roman culture in the south of France and the Gallic tribes of central France. The incorporation of Gaul within the Roman empire led to the emergence of a Gallo-Roman culture, a fusion of the two civilisations, but this was a gradual process of assimilation that had barely begun by the end of Caesar's campaigns. The conquest of Gaul did not lead to a fundamental shift in the balance of power in the provinces, at least at the level of the Gauls. The hierarchical structure of Gallic society suited the way Rome liked to administer her provinces, relying on existing oligarchies to rule the subject population. This allowed provinces to be run by a Roman governor with a very small administrative staff. Pro-Roman chieftains may well have been able to maintain their positions of power and status within their tribes.

Rome did not seek to impose a particular set of religious beliefs on the peoples she conquered, and local gods were often incorporated into the Roman pantheon, usually in association with a Roman god. It was extremely rare for Rome to persecute or attempt to crush a religion it encountered in the provinces, but druidism proved to be the exception and Julius Caesar began the attempt to eradicate it. Druids had considerable influence in Gallic society that was not just confined to religion: they also had a political role and could be highly influential within their tribes. The fiercely anti-Roman Aeduan aristocrat and druid Dumnorix was able to wield considerable power, and Caesar was clearly concerned that he might attempt to seize control. The principal reason for Rome's condemnation and persecution of druidism, though, was its associations with human sacrifice.

All the Gauls are very superstitious; so people with serious illnesses and those about to enter the dangers of battle make or promise to burn human beings as sacrifices, and the druids

officiate at these sacrifices ... When they have decided to fight a battle, they promise to dedicate the spoils that they capture in battle to Mars. If they are victorious they burn the captured animals and pile up all the other spoils at one point. (Caesar, Gallic War)

A shrine at Ribemont-sur-Ancre in Picardy appears to illustrate this sacrifice of warriors defeated in battle quite clearly. The dismembered remains of over 200 people, mostly young men, were arranged around a central area, along with captured weapons just as Caesar describes. The site was in use from the 3rd century BC but may have continued in use until the Roman conquest. The site seems to have been destroyed at that point, probably by the Romans. The poet Lucan describes how Caesar ordered the destruction of a shrine at Marseilles which displayed the skulls of sacrificial victims. Such shrines have been excavated at Roquepertuse, Glanum and Entremont in southern France. To Roman sensibilities, human sacrifice was 'barbarous' and it was inappropriate to bury the dead within the precincts of shrines, so druidism was outlawed, human sacrifice was banned and the shrines destroyed.

Rome

As already indicated, the conquest of Gaul would have had minimal impact on the lives of most Romans whatever their status. We know that Caesar's peers, particularly his political rivals, followed his exploits, and they tried to make life difficult for him, threatening him with prosecution for war crimes and at one point attempting to have his governorship terminated. But there was also considerable excitement amongst the Roman public to hear the latest news of the campaigns, particularly the crossing to Britain: 'I look forward to receiving Britannic

RIGHT Roman soldiers foraging, Trajan's Column, 2nd century AD. Caesar relied heavily on his Gallic allies for grain and fodder, but during the campaigning season foraging parties supplemented the normal supply routes. With their attention elsewhere, soldiers foraging could, and did, get into difficulties. (Ancient Art and Architecture)

Porch from a Gallic shrine at Roquepertuse, Provence. The niches allowed the display
of human skulls, the kind of practice that fuelled Roman prejudice of the 'barbarian'
Gauls and the alleged brutality of Gallic cults. (Ancient Art and Architecture)

letters from you', Marcus Cicero wrote to a young friend, Trebatius, who was expecting to go with the expedition of 54 BC.

Caesar's rivals were right to be worried about him, though. During the campaigns he received unprecedented plaudits for his successes, granted to him by the senate and people in Rome; his popularity with the ordinary people, already solid, increased. He acquired a massive fortune, having been almost bankrupt only a few years previously, and most importantly he acquired a fanatically loyal army of veteran legionaries and auxiliaries drawn from the Gauls and Germans he had been fighting. With this military strength he felt confident to risk gambling his political future and his very life, and was ready to resort to civil war to obtain the domination he felt was due to him.

Roman merchants

The first Romans to settle in Gaul were almost certainly merchants and traders. Merchants from Rome and Italy could be found in towns and cities all over the Mediterranean, from Egypt to Spain, well before these areas were taken over into direct Roman control. They settled especially in centres of production or communication which acted as trade centres, and could become extremely wealthy from the commerce between Rome and her neighbours. By the time Caesar began his campaigns in the mid-1st century BC, Romans had moved well beyond the boundaries of the Roman possession of Provence and there were identifiable communities of Romans living in several Gallic towns, including Cenabum (Orleans), Gergovia, Cabillonum (Châlons-sur-Saône) and Novoidunum (Nevers). The Roman presence in these towns helped in the spread of Roman culture and language, and the Roman and Italian merchants must have picked up something of Gallic culture and language themselves. There is no evidence to suggest that Romans and Gauls did not co-exist peacefully in these towns, at least until the arrival of Caesar with his armies. The creation of a new province might have offered the prospect of greater opportunities for the Roman merchants already based there, but the campaigns caused disruption and danger to the lives of civilians, both Roman and Gallic. The Roman merchants were probably a group easily identified with the invaders, and during the widespread uprising of 52 BC, they became a clear target for the Gauls.

Traders and other 'hangers-on' also accompanied Roman armies on their campaigns. They do not seem to have been considered a part of the army as they camped outside the fortifications, and did not have an official role in supplying the army. They followed the army at their own expense, even hiring their own ships to accompany Caesar across the Channel on his invasions of Britain, in the hope of obtaining booty and perhaps opening up new trading opportunities. However, they provided a number of useful services for armies on campaign and so were tolerated by most generals. These traders were particularly useful during the winter and soldiers could supplement their probably fairly monotonous rations with more interesting fare, including pastries and other culinary luxuries from home. They might also have purchased booty from the soldiers, enabling them to exchange their spoils of war for more portable wealth in the form of coinage. Other 'hangers-on' included soothsayers and prostitutes; some of the more disciplinarian generals considered the presence of these non-combatants to be a drain on the army's morale and ejected them from the encampment. Caesar appears to have been more tolerant, and their presence probably had a positive effect on the soldiers' morale. By following the army, however, these traders, both Gauls and Romans, exposed themselves to the same dangers as the army. When the German cavalry attacked Quintus Cicero's camp in 53 BC the merchants who were encamped just outside the Roman ramparts had no chance to escape and were cut down, the Germans not bothering to discriminate between soldiers and non-combatants.

Traders were a useful source of information and military intelligence both for the tribes living in Gaul and for the invading Romans. It seems to have been normal for Gallic tribes to interrogate passing traders to acquire the latest news, and Caesar obtained information particularly from

Roman traders based in Gaul. At Besançon before setting out against Ariovistus, the Romans questioned both Gauls and traders about the Germans. The informants seem to have exaggerated the physique and military prowess of the Germans, causing widespread fear among the Roman army; intelligence gained from merchants might not have been very accurate, especially on military capabilities. Before crossing to Britain for the first time, Caesar had tried to extract information about the geography of the island, the size and customs of the inhabitants, including their fighting habits, and especially about harbours. He does not seem to have got much information of particular value for his expedition and was forced to dispatch one of his officers, Volusenus, to scout for harbours. He, too, was unable to enlighten Caesar on this subject. The merchants must have been Gauls in this instance, because they immediately reported the Roman plans to the Britons. Clearly merchants were able to move with comparative ease throughout the tribes of

northern Europe, and it is not surprising that some Roman traders spoke Gallic, and could thus act as interpreters for Caesar.

Merchants could be influential men of equestrian status, the rank below men of the senatorial class like Caesar, and they could be very wealthy. Gaius Fufius Cita was a merchant of equestrian rank who was a member of the Roman community of Cenabum massacred in the uprising of 52 BC. Caesar had placed him in charge of the grain supply for his army, probably because of his business, and possibly language skills, and in return Cita would probably have expected the governor to favour him in the granting of business contracts such as mining, quarrying, and supplying the army once Gaul was reduced to provincial status. It is debated how much influence the wealthy

A Roman sculpture from Germany of a merchant ship transporting casks of beer or wine indicates the importance of trade between Rome and northern Europe both before and after the conquest of Gaul. Gallic chieftains had been importing Roman wine for decades before Caesar's invasion. (Trier Museum)

merchants could have had on Roman foreign policy. Caesar claims that the opening up of a route through the Alps in the winter of 57 BC was to provide merchants with a safer route free of duties levied by the Gallic tribes, but it was just as likely to have been for military reasons. Military success and personal advancement were the principal reasons for campaigning and conquest by Roman generals, but opening up commercial opportunities (from which the general could expect to benefit considerably financially), and thus profiting merchants of equestrian status are very likely to have added further encouragement. The equestrian vote could be hugely influential in elections for public office in Rome. It is very likely that the hostility of the Venetic tribes to Rome was caused by worry about Roman encroachment on her lucrative trading routes with Britain and along the whole Atlantic coast of Gaul. The Roman advance into Gaul, then, provided plenty of opportunities for merchants to benefit financially and they were the first to spread Roman culture among many of the Gallic tribes.

Roman triumphs

There is no single incident or date at which the Gallic War can be said to have ended. Caesar was waging war against numerous tribes who came together in 52 BC in a concerted but failed attempt to eject the Romans from their lands. Throughout the years of campaigning, the tribes had to be defeated individually or in small coalitions. Even the surrender of Vercingetorix at Alesia did not signify the end of the war, though it was the end of serious resistance to Rome, at least for the time being. Caesar portrayed Vercingetorix's surrender as the climax of his whole governorship. He had not only conquered all of Gaul, he claimed, but had completely crushed the revolt led by the charismatic Gallic chieftain, a hero worthy of his prominent position in Caesar's narrative. Caesar stopped compiling his commentaries on the war after the crushing of the revolt of 52 BC, because he had been granted a further 20 days' public thanksgiving and no longer needed to boast to those in Rome of his military successes. But the campaigns continued; Aulus Hirtius, one of Caesar's officers, continued the commentaries, taking the story down to 50 BC and the eve of civil war. Small-scale campaigns rumbled on into 50 BC and only stopped because of the needs of the civil war: Caesar took most of the garrison out of Gaul to fight against Pompey. Gaul was not fully reduced to provincial status until the reign of the first emperor Augustus, and even after that there are indications of the need for further campaigns. But there was no doubt who was the victor; the campaigns had been largely one-sided, and the capitulation of the tribes by the late 50s was all but total. Surrender had been unconditional.

Seven legions marched against the Bellovaci in 51 BC, which may have been an over-reaction, but Caesar wished to make an example of those who continued to resist. He forced the surrender of Uxellodunum, an *oppidum* in south-western Gaul that was being held by the remnants of the revolt of the previous year, and punitive campaigns took place against several tribes in the north. The last military action in Gaul reported by Aulus Hirtius occurred at the end of 51 BC, after the legions had been sent to winter quarters. Commius, a chief of the Atrebates tribe who had once been an ally of Caesar but had then joined Vercingetorix, began causing problems. In the account, Aulus Hirtius claims that the Atrebates as a tribe were peaceful and submissive to Rome, and that Commius was little more than a bandit, riding around with a group of warriors disturbing the peace. The fact that Commius was actually attacking military targets, successfully ambushing supply convoys, suggests that in reality he was attempting to continue resistance, albeit on a fairly small scale. The Roman legate Volusenus was detailed to wipe out Commius and a series of encounters took place, coming to a head in a small skirmish in which Volusenus received a lance through the thigh courtesy of Commius. Commius and his followers were promptly put to flight and agreed to Roman demands that he live where told and surrender hostages to guarantee his compliance. But Aulus Hirtius does not give us the full story. A brief account by the 1st-century AD writer Frontinus claims that Commius tried to escape from the Romans in a boat but it was stranded by the low tide. The cunning Atrebatan hoisted the sails despite being grounded and the pursuing Romans, believing him to be getting away, abandoned the pursuit. Commius made it to Britain where he managed to establish himself as king of the British Atrebates.

The Romanisation of Gaul was a slow and gradual process. Celtic style buildings, such as these reconstructed examples, would have continued to exist and be built for some decades after the Roman conquest; eventually a 'Gallo-Roman' culture evolved. (Ancient Art and Architecture)

By the late 50s it had become apparent to many Gallic tribes that there was little point in further resistance to the Roman conquest, even if they had had the manpower and resources to do so. Much of the land in central Gaul had been devastated, particularly in the revolt of 52 BC when the Gauls devastated their livestock and grain supplies in order to deny the Romans; many of the tribes that had been heavily involved in the fighting must have been short of warriors. With Roman armies wintering in Gaul and never disbanding, it was clear that, unlike most of the enemies they had faced previously, the Romans were not simply going to go away. At the time, submission must have seemed to many to be the only option short of annihilation. Viewed from two millennia away, this outcome was virtually inevitable. Caesar may have ridden

his luck many times and taken some appalling risks, but the Roman army was too well trained and equipped to be defeated in such a war, too organised, with a strong command structure, logistical system (which worked well at least some of the time), and the ability to maintain an army in the field year in year out. If Caesar had not conquered Gaul, some other Roman general would have done.

The remainder of Caesar's tenure as governor was spent in conciliating the Gauls he had so recently conquered, the next stage in creating a Roman province. Civil war blocked the normal procedure: the sending out of a senatorial commission to establish the provinces, and it was not until much later that these were established by Augustus. Caesar aimed at establishing a working relationship with the tribes he had recently

Vercingetorix, the Arvernian who united the Gallic tribes against Gaul, became a symbol of French unity during the 19th-century resistance to Prussian aggression. This huge sculpture by the French artist J. F. Millet of an idealised Vercingetorix was erected on the site of Alesia by Emperor Napoleon III. (Ancient Art and Architecture)

Caesar, shown here on a coin minted during his dictatorship, was as aware of the importance of 'image' as any modern politician, and ensured that his exploits in Gaul were regularly reported to the Senate and people in Rome by writing up the campaigns on an annual basis. (Ancient Art and Architecture)

been fighting against, especially with the tribal elites. He bolstered the positions of those he trusted through concessions and gifts, thus ensuring their loyalty to Rome, and also to himself, something that he would benefit from in the ensuing civil war. The tribal system was allowed to remain, based initially round the *oppida*, and these or later more Roman-style settlements nearby formed the foundations of the *civitates*, the towns of Roman Gaul on which the

government and administration of the provinces were centred. A tribute was set for the subject tribes throughout Gaul that was not light, but nor was it oppressively heavy.

Public thanksgivings were offered by the Senate and People of Rome for the last time in 52 BC. Caesar had been awarded an unprecedented number of tributes for his various exploits, so his successes were being celebrated in Rome in his absence. The formal celebrations for victory in the war had to wait for years, until 46 BC, when the civil wars had run their course and Caesar had made himself dictator of Rome. Then he held a triumph; this was the procession through Rome of the successful general in a chariot, followed by tableaux illustrating the

campaigns, and his troops who traditionally sang dirty songs about their commander:

'Home we bring our bald whoremonger;
Romans, lock your wives away!
All the bags of gold you lent him, went his
Gallic tarts to pay.'
(Suetonius, *Life of Caesar,* translated by Robert Graves)

The Gallic triumph was one of four; the others celebrated campaigns in Turkey, Africa and Egypt. Money was given to the people of Rome who watched the procession and to the soldiers, a particularly generous donation in this instance because of their loyal support throughout the civil wars. While

Silver coin of 48 BC showing a Gallic captive in front of a Gallic shield, struck by L Hostilius Saserna to celebrate Caesar's victories in Gaul.
(Ashmolean Museum, Oxford)

Caesar was the star of all four triumphs, 'second billing' in the Gallic triumph was given to Vercingetorix. The Gallic chieftain had been imprisoned in an Italian town for six years, waiting the day of the triumph when he would be processed round the streets of Rome in chains, and then taken to the Tullianum prison in the Roman Forum to be strangled. Caesar undertook huge building projects in Rome financed partly through his spoils from the war. He built the Temple of Venus Genetrix not only to honour the legendary divine founder of his family (and his lover Cleopatra), but also to display the spoils from his campaigns, probably weapons and particularly wealthy booty, including from Britain, to remind his fellow Romans that he had been the first to cross the Ocean and invade the mystical island.

Caesar's lightning campaigns and conquest of a huge area meant that some parts were not thoroughly conquered and further campaigns would be necessary. But he got out of his governorship what he had intended and what he needed to secure his political future. He had set out to make himself a fortune and a military reputation and to do that he had precipitated an encounter with the Helvetii and engineered a campaign against the Germans, giving him the excuse to conquer the whole of Gaul. He had the means by 50 BC to wage successful civil war and make himself dictator.

Pax Romana

Facts and figures were an important part of any narrative of an ancient war and Caesar's account is no exception. He regularly enumerates the size and type of enemy forces he was facing and often gives a figure for their casualties. The accuracy of these figures is rather suspect and as already indicated there were good political reasons for exaggerating both the size of the enemy force and the number of casualties inflicted. Casualty figures were a kind of currency of military success, not least because a general needed to have inflicted at least 5,000 enemy casualties in battle in order to claim a triumph back in Rome. So figures are likely to have been inflated to stress the military skill and prowess of the commander and his troops. And the rule on minimum figures for triumphs may have encouraged the slaughter in the aftermath of battle to go on longer than strictly necessary, just to make sure enough were killed. The figures given in the *Gallic War* for sizes of enemy forces and casualties must be regarded as very rough estimates that are severely exaggerated. Sometimes they become almost unbelievable. It is highly unlikely that the Gallic relieving army at Alesia was anything like the 240,000 Caesar claims, even though to give his figures a suggestion of authenticity he lists each individual tribe and the number of warriors they contributed. Along with the alleged 80,000 Gauls trapped in the *oppidum* with Vercingetorix this represents an unlikely concentration of troops. Caesar was probably never as seriously outnumbered as he likes to suggest. Despite the problems with numbers, however, the total casualties in the nine years of fighting must have been appalling. Some tribes were all but wiped out, or else their influence declined so much because of crushing defeats with high casualties that little is heard of them again. The Helvetii

thought of themselves as one of the bravest and most influential of the Gauls, but after they were forced back to their homelands little is heard of them again.

Caesar was unlikely to be criticised for killing Gauls and Germans though, especially since he managed to do it without suffering any really serious defeats himself. The one major defeat with the loss of one and a half legions in the winter of 54 BC was blamed squarely on his subordinate officer Sabinus, who is portrayed as an inept coward. As far as Caesar's fellow Romans were concerned, killing Gauls and Germans in large numbers was perfectly acceptable and usually to be praised. Both peoples had inflicted serious defeats on the Romans in the past (in the very distant past in the former case), and so the destruction of Gallic and Germanic armies by Caesar was seen simply as revenge for previous losses and a defence against anything like it ever happening again. Caesar goes to a great deal of trouble in his accounts to link the enemies of his first campaigns to tribes who had actually been involved in earlier defeats of Roman armies. So the Tigurini, the Helvetians massacred at the Saône in 58 BC, had defeated a Roman army in 107 BC; Ariovistus was a German king; the Aduatuci descended from the Cimbri and Teutones who had destroyed several Roman armies in the late 2nd century BC. To the Romans, these people were also barbarians, and it would not be going too far to suggest that in the Roman mentality the only good barbarian was a dead one.

Despite this outlook, there were moves by some politicians in Rome to have Caesar removed from his governorship and charged with what would today be termed 'war crimes'. Charges would probably have included waging war outside his own province (which was, of course, limited to Cisalpine and Transalpine Gaul), and attacking peoples without justification, a necessary factor for a just war in antiquity. The outcry at the massacre of the Usipi in 55 BC may represent genuine repugnance at the slaughter of so many women and children on so flimsy a pretext. But it is important to remember that the men working to bring these charges against Caesar were bitter political rivals who saw him as a threat to the stability of Rome. Most of their actions to try to get Caesar removed and put on trial were motivated more by a desire to destroy him than genuine concern for the treatment of the enemy. In his *Life of Caesar*, Suetonius noted, 'He did not ignore any opportunity to wage war regardless of how unjustified it was or how dangerous. He attacked enemies and barbarians without provocation, and even allies, so eventually the Senate sent legates to report on the condition of Gaul. Several suggested that Caesar should be handed over to the enemy (for punishment for his actions)'.

No major advances were made by either side in military terms. The Roman style of fighting, and indeed their equipment, was entirely suitable for facing taller Celts and Germans with their long slashing blades, and the flexibility offered by the cohortal organisation of the legions was ideal for dealing with an enemy that did not maintain disciplined rank formations. Many modern historians have suggested that Caesar made alterations to the *pilum* (javelin). He is credited with fitting the *pilum* with an iron shank that was partly untempered. This ensured that it was likely to be a far less effective weapon for the enemy to throw back if the shaft had bent, and if it pierced an enemy shield and subsequently bent, it would be very difficult to extract in a hurry and might force the enemy to throw away his shield and fight unprotected. This is the effect that Caesar notes during the battle with the Helvetii and it is this observation that led modern historians to claim that he made the alterations himself. Examples of such *pila*

with bent shanks have been excavated at Alesia, so clearly his reporting of the effect of the *pilum* is not only plausible but also reliable. However, there is no evidence at all to associate Caesar with any experimentation with the *pilum* or change in its design. Marius had done so previously, replacing two of the iron rivets fastening the shank to the wooden shaft with wooden pegs in order to create the same effect in a *pilum* with a fully tempered shank, but it would be wrong to credit Caesar with this further development.

The Gauls learned during the conquest of their lands that pitched battle was not the way to defeat the Romans: they were too well trained and disciplined to be beaten in open warfare. Hit-and-run tactics were far more effective, as were ambushes, and as the Gauls gained more experience of Roman techniques, they made more use of these methods. Crassus had encountered them first in Aquitania where the Gallic tribes were assisted by Spaniards from across the Pyrenees who had learned the effectiveness of guerrilla warfare against Roman armies when fighting for the Roman renegade Sertorius against Pompey in the 70s BC. The Gallic strategy of 52 BC was based on a scorched-earth policy, hit-and-run tactics to cut the Romans off from their supplies, and an avoidance of pitched battle. It failed because of the Romans' skill in siege warfare. Guerrilla warfare remained the most effective form of military opposition to Roman armies in western Europe, as illustrated by the spectacular success of Arminius' ambush of three Roman legions in AD 9, ending Roman hopes of the conquest of Germany.

The transition from conquered lands to provinces was a slow one. Any major advances in this direction were put on hold by the impending civil war between Caesar and Pompey, but even during his last year as governor Caesar had turned his attention back towards Rome. His actions in setting tribute were a stop-gap and although only a skeleton garrison remained in Gaul during the civil wars there is little sign of any serious attempt at an uprising: the tribes were probably still licking their wounds and recovering from the crushing defeats inflicted by the Romans. Others, like the Aedui and Remi, must have been counting their luck that they had chosen to side with Rome. As far as possible, the existing hierarchies within tribes were maintained. Caesar did not attempt to impose a different method of rule on the Gauls but, in keeping with usual Roman policy towards provinces, preferred to work with the systems of rule that the people were used to. The Gallic tribes and their internal structures fitted in well with Rome's preference for rule by wealthy oligarchies, whether that was tribal chieftains in Gaul or elite magistrates in cities in the eastern Mediterranean. The existing tribal territories were for the most part maintained, becoming the lands administered by the towns that grew up or were established, often close to Gallic *oppida*, but generally without fortifications. 'Civilisation' had arrived.

This 'civilisation', literally meaning 'living in a town', was not imposed on the Gauls by the Romans, but during his dictatorship Caesar established a number of citizen colonies in Gaul, mostly in Provence. They served a dual purpose: providing land and retirement rewards for the soldiers who had served Caesar during the civil war, and forming a core of experienced veterans who could be called on in times of emergency, but who could also illustrate to the locals the advantages of being Roman. It was some time, however, before all the tribes in Gaul accepted this. Though Gaul seems to have remained remarkably quiet during the civil wars, it was not entirely trouble free. In 39 BC the Roman governor Agrippa (who later won the battle of Actium for Julius Caesar's great-nephew Octavian, effectively making him emperor of Rome), campaigned in the same areas of north-eastern and south-western Gaul that had never been fully settled by Caesar. He also established a road network that provided Gaul with a strong infrastructure that helped in both the continuing pacification of the area and with economic development and the spread of Roman culture. Octavian, who became the

emperor Augustus, visited Gaul several times, probably increasing his prestige among the Gauls by stressing his relationship to the man who had conquered their lands. Roman camps in north-eastern Gaul may date to these campaigns, but very little is known about them. In 27 BC Augustus established three provinces probably based on the three parts of Gaul that Caesar had defined at the very beginning of his *Gallic War*. The provinces were Aquitania, Gallia Belgica and Gallia Lugdunensis, the latter having as its provincial capital the city of Lugdunum or Lyons, founded as a Roman veteran colony in 44 BC. Many of the towns that were founded as the 'capitals' of the individual Gallic tribes flourished and remain important towns in modern France, including Soissons, Bayeux, Tours and Autun (with its Roman name Augustodunum, 'town of Augustus'), which was the new capital of the Aedui.

Further campaigns took place in the Alps between the 20s and 15 BC before Roman attention turned towards Germany. Military disaster there in AD 9 brought the frontier between Gaul in the Roman empire and Germany to more or less the line of the Rhine, and a very strong legionary force was stationed along the river. Like the new towns in Gaul, these legionary bases also left their mark on the later history of the region as most of the fortresses spawned civilian settlements that outlived the Roman empire: Strasbourg, Bonn and Mainz all began in this way. Despite the strong military presence, however, there are indications that Gaul was still not completely settled and the occasional outburst of resistance materialised. A revolt broke out in AD 21 led by two noblemen, Julius Florus, a Treveran, and an Aeduan, Julius Sacrovir, who had both commanded Roman auxiliaries and been granted Roman citizenship. The cause was very probably related to the collection of taxes, but it failed to gather widespread support and was put down with the help of other Gauls. The recent discovery of a legionary fortress near Dijon dating to about the AD 70s suggests that things were still not completely quiet even a century after Augustus' formal establishment of the provinces, but there is no evidence of widespread destruction. Gaul was on its way to becoming a 'Romanised' province, clearly indicated by the decision of the emperor Claudius to allow Gallic noblemen to enter the senate.

Julius Caesar claimed to have conquered Gaul. He did defeat the tribes and force them to surrender, but he left Gaul still unsettled in order to pursue his personal ambitions. His fame as the conqueror of Gaul comes from his own hand, as the author of his *Commentaries*; he did not on his own turn Gaul into Roman provinces – that was for his political successors to do. The conquests brought Gaul into the Roman empire and began a process that had a profound political and cultural impact on western Europe; and it provided Caesar with the springboard to establish himself as dictator of the Roman world.

Part II
Caesar's Civil War
49–44 BC

The First Triumvirate

Following his triumph over Marius, Sulla ruled as dictator with absolute power for nearly two years and only laid this down when he went into voluntary retirement. Before he did so, Sulla attempted to restore the Senate's position within the Republic, confirming its traditional powers and filling it with his supporters. He passed a law that was intended to prevent army commanders from following his own example and using their legions outside their own provinces without permission. The career pattern (*cursus honorum*) followed by Roman senators was also to be regulated more closely. The Republic was not to be dominated by a few individuals, but guided by the collective wisdom of the 600 senators.

Sulla's reforms were reactionary, impractical and weakened by the example of his own rise to power, so that many Romans did not consider them to be legitimate. Most importantly Sulla had failed to do anything to cater for the demands of the army on a permanent basis, so that discharged soldiers continued to have no source of livelihood and were therefore still inclined to follow any commander who promised them land. The chaos of the civil war and the rapid collapse of the Sullan constitution fostered a continuation of political disorder and eventually the renewal of open war in 49. This period also had a profound influence on the careers and attitudes of the main protagonists in 49–45. Caesar himself first rose to prominence during Sulla's dictatorship, narrowly avoiding execution by the dictator when he publicly celebrated his relation by marriage to Marius at a family funeral.

However, a far more dramatic role was played by Cnaeus Pompey, who in 83 came to the support of Sulla at the head of three legions raised from his family's estates and veterans who had served under his late father, Pompeius Strabo ('squinty'). At the time Pompey was only 23 and, having never held public office, had no legal authority on which to base his power. Fighting with distinction in Italy, Sicily and north Africa, Pompey was granted the title Magnus ('The Great') by Sulla, though this may have been more than a little ironic. After Sulla's retirement, the Senate continued to employ the services of this private citizen and his personal army to suppress an attempted coup in Italy in 78 and then to fight the last of Marius' adherents in Spain. Employing Pompey, rather than a legally appointed magistrate under their control, set an exceptionally bad precedent. Probably the Senate felt that, since Pompey and his legions existed, it was better to use him than risk his turning against them.

In 71 Pompey returned victorious from Spain, and decided to stand for the consulship for the following year. He was too young, and had held none of the normally required junior magistracies, but he kept his legions outside the city as a scarcely veiled threat. Marcus Licinius Crassus, who had just returned from suppressing Spartacus's slave rebellion, took the opportunity to retain his own army and in turn declared himself a candidate for the consulship. Crassus was exceptionally wealthy, his fortune based originally on property confiscated from Sulla's executed opponents. The Senate was forced to permit their candidature and the Roman people, who were on the whole well disposed to both men after their successes, duly elected Pompey and Crassus as consuls for 70. Thus Pompey at the age of 36 entered the Senate directly as a consul, an utterly unprecedented action. His military record was already spectacular, but, given his age, he clearly expected to be given further important tasks.

Since Sulla's reforms, a magistrate remained in Rome itself during his year of office. He was then appointed as a promagistrate to govern a province. Former consuls, or proconsuls, were sent to the most important provinces while former praetors, or propraetors, went to the less significant areas. The appointment as governor was normally made for a year, but could, if the Senate chose, be renewed for additional 12-month periods at the end of this time. As governor, the promagistrate possessed supreme military and civil power within his province, dispensing legal decisions or leading an army as the situation required. He could not be recalled or prosecuted until his term of office expired. A governor's powers (or *imperium*), lapsed as soon as he re-entered Rome and he became a private citizen again, simply one senator among many.

The Senate had traditionally chosen the provinces for each new political year, although individual magistrates were then

Bust of Cnaeus Pompeius Magnus (Pompey). Joined with Crassus and Caesar to form the First Triumvirate but after the death of Crassus, relations with Caesar broke down and led to Civil War. (Ancient Art and Architecture Collection)

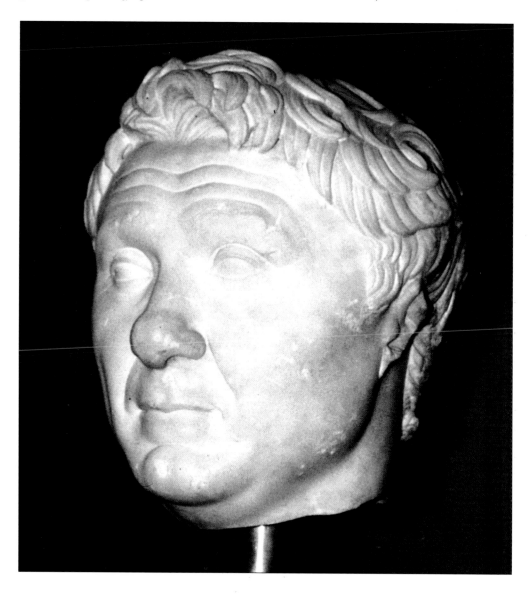

normally allocated a task by lot. In 88 Marius had arranged for a popular vote giving him the command in the Asian War, a move which prompted Sulla's march on Rome. In 67 Pompey employed the same method of a vote in the People's Assembly (*concilium plebis*) to give him a wide-ranging command against the pirates plaguing the Mediterranean. A combination of careful organisation, massive resources, and a willingness to accept the surrender of pirate communities and resettle them elsewhere, allowed Pompey to achieve victory in under two months. In 66 another law was passed by the people sending Pompey to Asia to fight against Mithridates of Pontus. This meant that the existing commander in this war, Lucullus, who had achieved great success, was replaced in spite of the Senate's desire to leave him in charge. Since the war was virtually over before he arrived, it took little time for Pompey to complete the defeat of Mithridates, who committed suicide when his own son turned against him. Pompey then proceeded to campaign throughout the near east, for instance, intervening in a domestic squabble between the kings of Judaea. After a three-month siege, Pompey took Jerusalem. He and his officers went into the Holy of Holies in the Great Temple, although they declined to take any of its treasures. This was a great propaganda success, the Roman aristocracy always striving to be the first to do any spectacular deed. As well as his military operations, Pompey carried out extensive administrative reform of the east. Provincial boundaries were altered, cities founded or refounded with new constitutions and relations with client kingdoms regulated. Many aspects of his settlement would endure for over 500 years.

Pompey had acquired so much glory and plunder on his campaigns that he had no serious rival within the Senate, and there was growing fear of what he would do when he returned to Italy. Many wondered whether he might copy Sulla and seize absolute power by force. In fact, Pompey behaved in a manner that was scrupulously correct,

disbanding his army almost as soon as it had landed in Brundisium, and returning to Rome to celebrate an especially lavish triumph. He seems to have simply wanted to take his place as one of the Senate's most important members, but he also had two immediate political objectives. The first was to gain formal approval for all of his reforms in the eastern provinces. The second was to secure grants of land for the soldiers who had served him so well. In spite of his tremendous prestige, and in part because he had spent so much time on campaign and so little at Rome, Pompey was a poor politician. His speech in the Senate fell flat, and he did not seem to know how to use his great reputation and wealth to achieve his ends. He was opposed, most notably by Crassus, who was jealous of Pompey's prestige; Lucullus, who resented having been superseded in the command against Mithridates; and Cato the Younger, who disliked the revolutionary nature of Pompey's career and was reluctant to see him prosper. Time and again this opposition thwarted any attempt to ratify Pompey's settlement or grant land to his veterans. The impasse dragged on for nearly two years and was finally resolved in a manner that astounded most senators.

In 60 Julius Caesar returned from Further Spain, where he had served as a propraetorian governor and campaigned with success against local tribes. Six years younger than Pompey, Caesar's career had been fairly conventional up to this point, although his lavish spending on games and public feasting, combined with his rakish lifestyle, had won him numerous political enemies. Having won the right to celebrate a triumph, Caesar hoped this honour would permit him to win the consulship for 59. However, candidates had to present themselves for election in the city itself, and a general, still in command of the troops who would march in procession behind his chariot during the triumph, was not permitted to enter Rome until the day of the ceremony. Unable to gain an exemption, Caesar gave up his right to a triumph, dismissed his troops, and entered the city as a civilian. Thwarted, his opponents arranged for one of the consular provinces for the next year to be the supervision of the forests and country paths of Italy, a command without any troops or opportunities for profit and glory.

Around this time Caesar made approaches to both Crassus and Pompey and managed to reconcile them. Together the three men formed a secret political alliance, which is known by historians as the First Triumvirate. To cement the alliance, Pompey married Caesar's daughter Julia, a union which, for all its political inspiration, proved to be a remarkably happy one. In return for supporting his candidature, Caesar undertook to gain land for Pompey's veterans and to secure the ratification of his Eastern Settlement. Crassus paid off the massive debts Caesar had incurred in the promotion of his career, and gained a secure place as one of the most powerful men in the state. Caesar won the election and during his year of office was able to override his consular colleague, Lucius Calpurnius Bibulus. On several occasions large numbers of Pompey's veterans packed into the forum and voting assemblies, using threats or actual force to control the voting. One common joke at the time was that this year Rome had two consuls – Julius and Caesar. Together the three members of the triumvirate possessed massive patronage. Many senators owed them money, especially Crassus, who was highly skilled in using his fortune to win influence, and all had to go to the triumvirs if they wished to secure an appointment to any of the more senior positions in the army or government. Both Crassus and Pompey were highly satisfied and, in return, Caesar was granted a far more important province by popular vote. A special command consisting of three normal provinces, Illyricum, Cisalpine Gaul and Transalpine Gaul (modern-day Provence in southern France) was allocated to him for five years.

Caesar departed for his province in 58, never to return to Italy until the beginning of the Civil War. Crassus had covered his immediate debts, but Caesar was in great need of money to further his career. Very much the junior partner in the triumvirate, he also needed military glory to rival Crassus and, especially, Pompey. At first he appears to have contemplated a Balkan war against the Dacian King Burebista, but the news of the migration of a Gallic tribe towards Transalpine Gaul shifted his focus away from Illyricum. Over the next years Caesar campaigned throughout Gaul, twice bridged the Rhine and marched into Germany, and led two expeditions across the sea to Britain. That island remained mysterious to the Romans, and the euphoria over Caesar's expeditions could be compared to the excitement that greeted the moon landing in 1969. Caesar won massive glory during his Gallic campaigns, and produced his *Commentaries*, probably published in annual instalments, to celebrate his achievements. As well as gaining glory, Caesar became one of the wealthiest men in the world from plunder and sale of slaves, hundreds of thousands of whom were captured during the conflict.

Though unable to leave his province without also laying down his command, Caesar took care to keep a close eye on affairs in Rome, and spent every winter as close as possible, overseeing the administration of Cisalpine Gaul. He supported a radical politician, Publius Clodius, a demagogue who employed a gang of political thugs to force his legislation through. Rome had no police force, nor was it permitted for troops to be stationed within the city, so the state had no force with which to combat this violence. Clodius passed laws that complemented the legislation of Caesar's consulship, but which also attacked prominent figures within the Senate. In 58 Cicero was forced into exile, a success Clodius celebrated by leading a riot which burned down his house. Next Clodius turned his attention to Pompey, a move that presumably was not sanctioned by Caesar. Pompey responded by backing another gang of thugs led by Titus Annius Milo. Running battles were fought in and around Rome as the city descended into chaos. In 57 Pompey

The Roman World in 50 BC

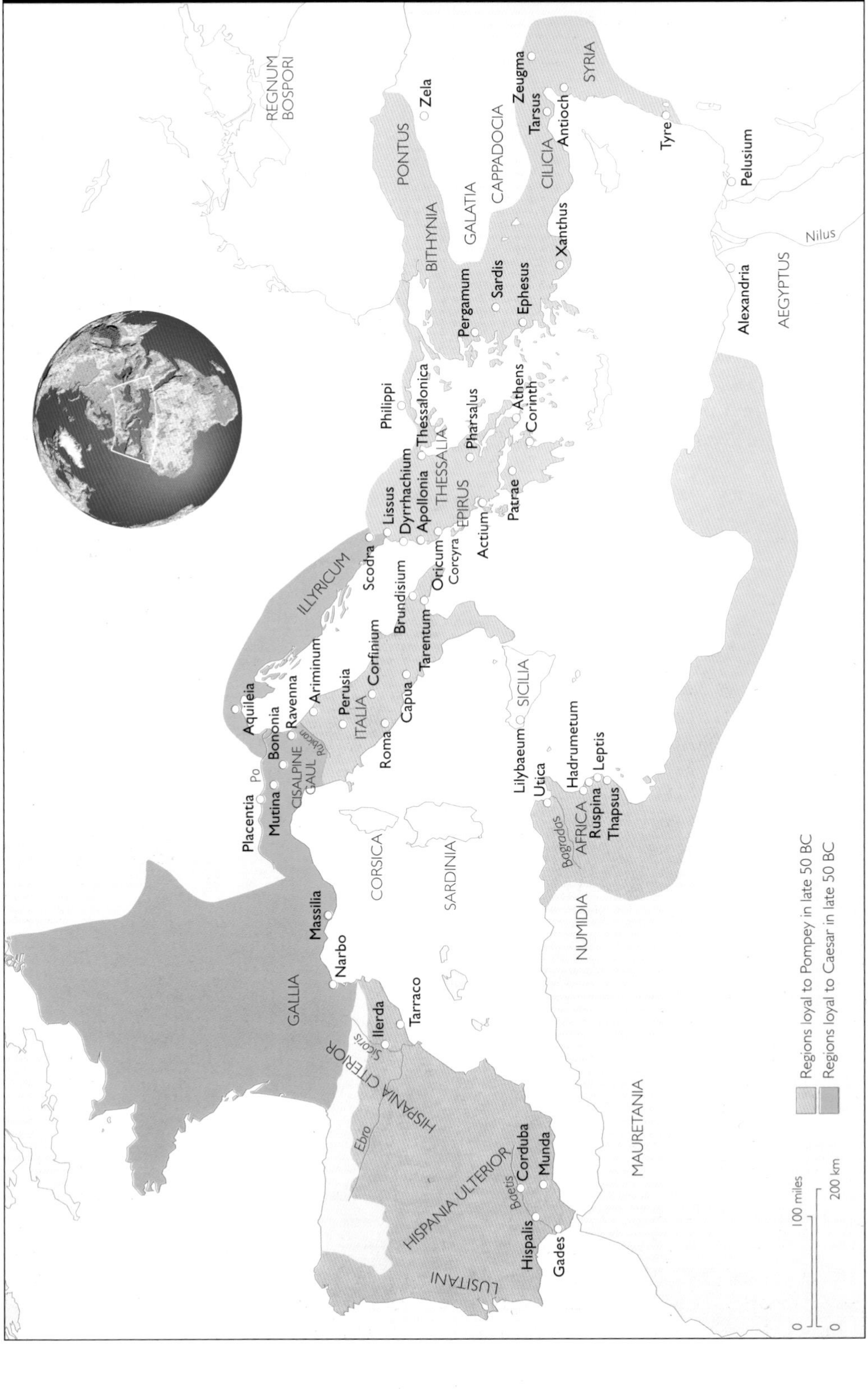

REGNUM BOSPORI

SYRIA

Zela

Zeugma

PONTUS

CAPPADOCIA

Tarsus

GALATIA

Antioch

BITHYNIA

CILICIA

Tyre

Pelusium

Xanthus

Sardis

Pergamum

Ephesus

Nilus

Alexandria

AEGYPTUS

Philippi

Thessalonica

Athens

THESSALIA

Pharsalus

Corinth

Dyrrhachium

Apollonia

EPIRUS

Lissus

Patrae

Scodra

Oricum

Corcyra

Actium

ILLYRICUM

Brundisium

Tarentum

Aquileia

Ariminum

Bononia

Ravenna

Corfinium

Perusia

ITALIA

Roma

Capua

SICILIA

Placentia   Po

Lilybaeum

Hadrumetum

Mutina

CISALPINE GAUL

Utica

Ruspina   Leptis

Bagradas

Thapsus

AFRICA

CORSICA

SARDINIA

NUMIDIA

Massilia

Narbo

GALLIA

Ilerda

Tarraco

Sicoris

HISPANIA CITERIOR

MAURETANIA

Ebro

HISPANIA ULTERIOR

Baetis   Corduba

Munda

Hispalis

Gades

LUSITANI

Regions loyal to Pompey in late 50 BC

Regions loyal to Caesar in late 50 BC

100 miles

200 km

0

0

sponsored a law recalling Cicero. Three days after Cicero's return, that is on 7 September, Pompey was given the major responsibility of overseeing the City's corn supply and once again displayed his considerable talents for organisation in rapidly remedying the situation. His return to the public eye provoked a renewal of rivalry with Crassus and it was clear that the triumvirate was coming under strain.

Crassus went to consult Caesar in his province and, after some cajoling, Pompey travelled to join them in April 56. In the town of Luca the triumvirs, along with a hundred or so senators who had accompanied them to show their goodwill, held a conference in which the alliance was patched up. Pompey and Crassus would both stand for the consulship in 55 and, since both their fame and the presence of a considerable body of Caesar's soldiers on leave ensured success, they were able to arrange matters to the benefit of all three. Caesar's command was extended for five years, although there is some doubt as to precisely when in late 50 or early 49 it was to expire. Pompey received both the Spanish provinces, but in an unprecedented move was allowed to remain in Rome and command through subordinates. Crassus was given Syria, from which he planned to lead an invasion of Parthia, for it seems that he felt the need to rival the conquests of his colleagues. Aged almost 60, he was considered rather old for active command by Roman standards and there were doubts about the legitimacy of a war with Parthia, but the triumvirs were too strong for any opposition to stand much chance.

In 54 Julia died in childbirth, and Crassus left to join the army in Syria. The following year he was defeated by the Parthians at Carrhae, and then killed when his army was forced to retreat. In spite of these blows, Pompey appeared still to consider himself bound to Caesar and in 53 sent one of his Spanish legions to reinforce Caesar's army in Gaul. Rome continued to be plagued by political violence, as Clodius' and Milo's followers clashed with renewed frenzy. In

52 Clodius was killed and his supporters carried his body into the Senate House, where they cremated it, burning the building to the ground in the process. In the face of anarchy, the Senate appointed Pompey sole consul and charged him with restoring order, for the first time permitting troops to guard Rome itself. Milo was put on trial and forced into exile as order was restored.

Caesar knew that he had many opponents in the Senate, chief among them Cato the Younger. In spite of his new wealth and the freedom with which he had tried to buy support, Caesar knew that a good number of influential men loathed him, and would not forgive him for his actions in 59. As a serving magistrate he was not subject to prosecution, but as soon as his office expired and he returned to civilian life this protection was withdrawn. He did not believe that he would receive a fair trial. During the Gallic campaigns Cato had even once suggested that he ought to be handed over to the Germans for war crimes. Defeat would mean exile and the end of his political career. To avoid this, Caesar wanted to go straight into a second consulship, after which he would be given another military command, perhaps against the Parthians. In this way he could continue to serve the Republic in a distinguished capacity.

In 52 Pompey passed a law which stipulated a five-year interval between a magistracy and a provincial command, although he specifically exempted Caesar in a clause apparently written in his own handwriting. However, around the same time he married the daughter of Publius Metellus Scipio, a known opponent of Caesar. Pressure on Caesar mounted, as incoming consuls lobbied to have him replaced in his province, since the war in Gaul appeared to be over. Pompey's attitude appeared increasingly ambivalent and the extension of his Spanish command gave him military might to match against Caesar. The latter was being forced into a corner. He had either to give up his command and trust to Pompey to protect him from the inevitable prosecution or to fight.

Legion against legion

Rome's civil wars split the state into factions, and the army with it. Since there were no ethnic, ideological or social differences between the rival sides, it was inevitable – even more than in any other civil war – that the organisation, tactical doctrine and equipment of their armies was virtually identical. The main strength of the Roman army lay in the legions, units with a paper strength of about 5,000. In theory the legions were recruited only from Roman citizens, but during the civil wars many non-citizens were enlisted to bolster numbers. In his *Commentaries*, Caesar frequently emphasised the heterogeneous nature of the enemy armies, but he had himself formed an entire legion, Legio V Alaudae, from Gauls, only later giving them the franchise as a reward for distinguished service. Given the dominance of the Roman military system, some allied kings had remodelled their armies after the Roman style. King Juba of Numidia included four legions in his large army, while Deiotarus of Galatia formed two which would later be amalgamated and formed into Legio XXII Deiotariana as a fully fledged part of the Roman army.

In this period a legion consisted entirely of heavy infantry. It had no permanent commander, but the practice had evolved of appointing an officer, usually one of the general's representatives, or legates, to fulfil this role. Much of the unit's administration was overseen by the six military tribunes, probably assisted by a small staff. These were largely equestrians (the class immediately below the Senate and possessing similar property) and at that time many were career soldiers of considerable experience. The basic tactical unit of the legion was the cohort of some 480 men. There were ten of these in each legion, and the cohort in turn was

This scene from the 1st-century monument to Domitius Ahenobarbus shows legionaries wearing a uniform which would not have been out of place during the Civil War. They wear mail armour, Montefortino-type helmets and carry long oval shields. (AKG Berlin)

subdivided into six centuries of 80. The century was led by a centurion, supported by an *optio* (second-in-command), *signifer* (standard-bearer), and *tesserarius* (guard commander). Centurion represented a grade of officer rather than a specific rank and these men differed greatly in seniority. On several occasions Caesar mentions rewarding brave centurions by promoting them to a higher grade, often in a newly formed legion that would benefit from having experienced officers. One of the six centurions probably acted as commander of the cohort, either the man with longest service or the centurion of the senior century, the *pilus prior*.

All legionaries were equipped with the same basic defensive gear, consisting of a bronze helmet (most often of Montefortino or Coolus patterns), cuirass (usually mail but sometimes of scale), and a large semi-cylindrical bodyshield constructed from three layers of plywood to give it both flexibility and strength. The latter seem most often to have been oval in shape, but it is possible that the transition to a more rectangular shape was already underway. Such shields were heavy – reconstructed examples weighing in at 22lbs – but offered good protection. They could also be used offensively, the soldier punching forward with all his body weight behind the shield's bronze boss. We are told that one of Caesar's soldiers, in spite of having his right hand chopped off almost as soon as he had boarded a warship, was able to clear the deck

of enemies by knocking them down with his shield during the fighting off Massila. A soldier's other offensive equipment consisted of a short sword, the famed *gladius*, sometimes a dagger, and a heavy throwing javelin known as the *pilum*. The *pilum* consisted of a wooden haft about 4 feet long, topped by a narrow iron shank 2 feet in length and ending in a pyramid-shaped point. When thrown, all of its great weight was concentrated behind this small tip, giving it formidable penetrative power. It was designed so that once it punched through an enemy's shield, the slim iron shank would slide easily through the hole made by the point and had the reach to wound the man behind. Soldiers may have

The Coolus-type helmet (the name is modern) was one of the commonest patterns worn by legionaries in the Late Republic. Made from copper alloy and following Gallic design, it offered protection to the top of the head whilst cheekpieces protected the face. Many examples from this period are of poor quality, the bowl spun rather than beaten into shape, probably because of the need to equip mass armies. (British Museum)

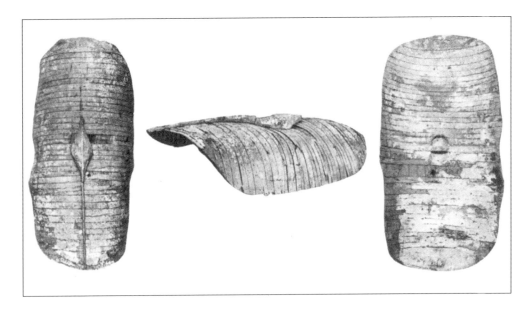

The Kasr el-Harit shield. This shield found in Egypt just before the Second World War was originally identified as Gallic but is most probably Roman. Made of three layers of plywood, it is remarkably similar to the Roman shield described by the Greek historian Polybius in the late 2nd century BC. (Nick Sekunda)

carried two *pila* on campaign, but only one on the day of battle itself. The doctrine of the period was to deliver a massed volley at very short range – some 15 yards or so – and follow this up with a charge, sword in hand.

Roman legionaries were not simply soldiers, for many were trained as engineers or artillerymen. Such men remained with their cohorts until required, and were then formed in temporary units to complete a task. The Civil War would be marked by many remarkable feats of engineering.

In battle a legion most often formed in three lines, four cohorts in the first line and three each in the second and third. Intervals were maintained between each unit and the cohorts from the next line stationed to cover these gaps, creating something resembling a checkerboard formation. However, since all cohorts were armed uniformly, the legion was perfectly capable of fighting effectively in other formations, and we also hear of armies in four or two lines, although a single line was considered too brittle to be

employed save in dire need. The legion was a very flexible force. Its structure and size made it an important subunit within the battle line, but one or several cohorts could as easily be detached for smaller operations. As with all armies throughout history, theoretical unit sizes were rarely reflected in the field. At Pharsalus the cohorts of Pompey's legions averaged around 400 men apiece, while Caesar's force was little more than half that size. Campaign attrition reduced one of Caesar's legions to less than 1,000 men during the Egyptian campaign.

The legions were the mainstay of any army, especially decisive in pitched battles, but both sides supplemented their numbers with allied soldiers or auxiliaries, fighting in their own traditional style. Such troops were especially useful in providing cavalry and light infantry. In most cases they were locally recruited and led by their own native chieftains. At first Caesar's auxiliaries came primarily from the Gallic and German tribes, and Pompey's from his provinces in Spain and his many clients in the east, but as the war progressed, troops were recruited wherever possible and the pattern became more complex.

By the end of the Gallic campaigns, Caesar commanded ten legions (numbered V to XIV). Two more, XV and I, the latter on loan from Pompey's Spanish armies, had been withdrawn earlier in 50 to be sent against the Parthians. The majority of these troops were seasoned veterans, utterly devoted to Caesar and confident in their own and their commander's ability. In support were bands of excellent Gallic and German cavalry. To match against this Pompey had seven legions garrisoning his Spanish provinces, although these had little actual combat experience. There were also the I and the XV which had not yet left for the east and were still in Italy, but as both had recently served under Caesar their loyalty

By the time of the Civil War the Roman army had stopped employing citizen cavalrymen like the figure depicted here on the altar of Domitius Ahenobarbus. However, many young aristocrats, including the orator Cicero's son, volunteered to serve as junior officers with the Pompeian army. (AKG Berlin)

appeared questionable. However, he boasted that he had only to stamp his foot in Italy for more legions to appear, and was also sure of the loyalty of the eastern provinces which he had reorganised just over a decade before. In the long term, Pompey could probably claim greater resources than Caesar, but it would take time to mobilise these into field armies.

In 49 Pompey was almost 58, but remained an extremely fit and active man, and others marvelled at the energy he showed in joining the training exercises of his soldiers. His military record was extremely good, even if he had made something of a habit of arriving in the last stages of a conflict to claim the credit largely won by someone else. He was certainly a brilliant organiser, as the campaign against the pirates, as well as, more recently, his supervision of Rome's

corn supply, had shown. In his youth he had been a bold commander, on several occasions leading charges in person, but his aggression, in a properly Roman way, had always been based on sound preparation. However, although he was only six years older than Caesar, Pompey had spent the last decade in Rome and had not served on campaign since 62. His performance during the Civil War would suggest that he was past his best as a general. He was not helped by the presence of so many distinguished senators in his camp. Unlike Caesar, whose followers were undistinguished and whose authority was unchallenged, Pompey was always under pressure to alter his plans. Most of the senators who flocked to his cause had more prestige than ability, and on more than a few occasions proved a positive hindrance. The ablest of his subordinates, Titus Atius Labienus, had served with Caesar throughout the Gallic campaigns. It is probable that he had a prior connection with Pompey, for he defected from Caesar's camp at the beginning of the war. On hearing of this, the latter ordered his baggage to be sent on after him.

Caesar failed to attract any distinguished supporters from the senior members of the Senate. Now in his early 50s, he was still very much at the peak of his ability, and was fresh from a decade of successful fighting in Gaul. His strategy during the Civil War, as in Gaul, was based on rapid offensives, sometimes in the face of great odds. Though often criticised for recklessness by modern commentators, it is important to emphasise that such boldness was characteristically Roman, and should not

conceal that much preparation underlay these enterprises. Although subject to occasional epileptic fits, he was in other respects an extremely healthy and active man, capable of massive effort and rapid long-distance travel. Caesar promoted and lavishly rewarded any soldiers who distinguished themselves, but even more than this it was his remarkable charisma that ensured that his soldiers were devoted to him. Throughout the war, desertions from the Pompeian forces were common, but all of our sources claim that there were no defections in the other direction. Fighting a war to protect his own honour and status, Caesar's objective was clear and obvious, giving the Caesarian war effort a unity of purpose not displayed by the other side. Yet it also meant that it was much easier for him to lose. If Caesar were killed, or his army defeated so heavily that he was discredited, then the war would effectively have been over. Only the Pompeians could suffer defeat after defeat and still prolong the struggle.

It is hard now to say whether Pompey or Caesar was the better general. The vast bulk of our evidence comes, directly or indirectly, from Caesar's version of events. His *Commentaries* obviously present his own actions in a favourable light, while dismissing those of the enemy. However, they also provide evidence that allows the wisdom of some of Caesar's decisions to be questioned. Yet, for the Romans the answer was obvious, for the most important attribute of a great general was that he won his wars. Caesar defeated Pompey, and in the end there was no more to be said.

Prominent figures in the late Republic

Afranius, Lucius: one of Pompey's officers who fought for him in Spain, Macedonia and Africa.

Ahenobarbus, Lucius Domitius: consul in 54 BC and a leading opponent of Caesar in the build-up to the Civil War. Defeated at Corfinum and Massilia, and finally killed in the aftermath of Pharsalus.

Antony, Mark (c. 81–30 BC): one of Caesar's subordinate officers, he was given both administrative and military posts. Emerged as one of the main leaders of Caesar's supporters after his assassination.

Brutus, Marcus Junius (c. 85–42 BC): influential younger member of the Senate who fought against Caesar in 49–48 BC. Captured and pardoned, he was one of the leaders who led the conspiracy against him.

Caelius Rufus, Marcus: friend of Cicero, but sided with Caesar during the Civil War. The unstable Caelius Rufus then rebelled against him and was killed.

Caesar, Caius Julius (100–44 BC): maverick politician and brilliant commander, Caesar rose through Civil War to establish himself as dictator. Murdered by a conspiracy of senators, Caesar's fame has nevertheless endured to the present day.

Cassius Longinus, Caius (c. 85–42 BC): having won a name for himself by defending Syria after the death of Crassus, Cassius sided with Pompey during the Civil War. Captured and pardoned, he and Brutus led the conspiracy against the dictator.

Cicero, Marcus Tullius (106–43 BC): the greatest orator of his day, Cicero was more a politician than soldier. He survived the Civil War only to be executed on Mark Antony's orders. Cicero's correspondence and writings are a valuable source for this period.

Cleopatra (c. 69–30 BC): queen of Egypt and subsequently mistress of first Caesar and then Antony.

Crassus, Marcus Licinius (85–53 BC): the man who suppressed Spartacus' rebellion and later one of the triumvirate with Pompey and Caesar. Crassus mounted an invasion of Parthia in 54 BC and was killed the next year after the defeat at Carrhae.

Curio, Caius Scribonius: reckless young senator who was bribed to join Caesar and defended his interests as tribune of the plebs in 50. Killed in Africa the following year.

Domitius Calvinus, Cnaeus: one of Caesar's subordinate officers, elected to the consulship in 53 and 42 BC.

Juba, King: ruler of Numidia and Gaetulia, he sided with Pompey, but took his own life after the defeat in 46 BC.

Marius, Caius (c. 157–87 BC): a man of humble background, but great military talent, Marius reformed the Roman army and had a spectacular career, but also provoked Rome's first civil war in 88 BC.

Octavia: sister of Octavian, she was married to Antony to cement their political alliance. However, he subsequently discarded her for Cleopatra.

Octavian/Augustus (Caius Julius Caesar Octavianus, 63 BC–AD 14): Caesar's nephew and adopted son. His rise to power and eventual defeat of all rivals led to the creation of a form of monarchy known as the Principate.

Petreius, Marcus: one of Pompey's senior subordinates, he commanded large forces in Spain, Macedonia and Africa, but committed suicide after the defeat at Thapsus.

Pompey the Great (Cnaeus Pompeius Magnus, 106–48 BC): Pompey rose to fame at a young age during the Sullan Civil War, forging a career which was as spectacular as it was unconstitutional. Joined with Crassus and Caesar to form the First Triumvirate, but, after the death of Crassus, relations with Caesar broke down and led to Civil War.

Pompeius, Cnaeus: elder son of Pompey, who fought against Caesar in Spain and was defeated and killed at Munda in 45.

Pompeius, Sextus: younger son of Pompey and a gifted naval commander, he fought with success against Octavian until his final defeat in 36.

Scipio, Quintus Metellus Pius Nasica: one of Caesar's main opponents in the Senate, he proved an inept commander and was defeated at Thapsus in 46.

Sulla, Lucius Cornelius the dictator (138–78 BC): the first man to lead a Roman army against Rome and the victor in its first Civil War, he became dictator and attempted to reform the Roman state.

Sulla, Publius Cornelius: nephew of the dictator, he served as one of Caesar's officers, but died in 45 BC.

Crossing the Rubicon

'They wanted it. Were it not for the support of my army they would have passed judgement upon me in spite of my achievements.' (Caesar looking at the bodies of dead senators after Pharsalus)

By 50 the mood in Rome was increasingly tense. The fear was similar to that in anticipation of Pompey's return in 62, but probably even worse, for Caesar was perceived now as a more open revolutionary, and his province, with its large, veteran army, lay on Italy's own border. Many Romans feared that this force would be turned against the state in a bid for dictatorship. A much smaller group of senators, led by Cato and including many of the House's most influential members, was determined that Caesar should not be allowed to return to normal politics, since his new-found wealth and prestige would make it difficult to oppose him. Were he allowed a second consulship, it was feared that his behaviour this time would be even worse than in 59. Everyone realised that Pompey's attitude would be decisive, but his intentions remained unclear. Stopping Caesar from arranging to stand *in absentia* (and so retaining his army) for the consulship required at the very least Pompey's inaction, while if it came to a war, he was the only one capable of matching Caesar's military might. Yet if Caesar was defeated and killed or exiled, this would remove Pompey's last serious rival, leaving him with massively greater power, influence and wealth than anyone else within the Republic. This in itself threatened monarchy, but Cato and his supporters clearly believed this to be the lesser of two evils. At worst Pompey was a less skilful politician than Caesar and so would have greater difficulty in exploiting his position, but it seems likely that they hoped in some way to negate him.

Perhaps the only real chance for the Republic would have been to accept Caesar's return and continue to have two leading senators or *principes* far outstripping their fellows and so balancing each other's power. Even if this had occurred, there was always the risk that the two would fall out at a later date and that a war would result. In the event, intransigence on both sides prevented any compromise.

In 51 Caesar had tried to have his command extended until the very end of 49, presumably so that he could then move directly into the consulship for 48, but the measure was successfully opposed in the Senate, in part because Pompey failed to support it. This was followed by several attempts to have Caesar recalled immediately, using the argument that the war in Gaul had already been completed. Pompey opposed these moves, and in March 50 made it clear that Caesar ought to be permitted the original extent of his governorship, no more and no less. The failure to support his old ally more fully encouraged the belief that there was a split between the two.

In the meantime Caesar had been employing the profits of his campaigns to buy influence and friends at Rome. One of the consuls of 50, Lucius Aemilius Paullus, allegedly received 36,000,000 sesterces (as a guide an ordinary soldier was paid 1,000 sesterces a year), enough to cover the great debts he had incurred in restoring the Basilica Aemilia (originally built by an ancestor) in the forum. Paullus did not support his colleague Marcellus in his attacks on Caesar. More active support was purchased from the tribune of the plebs Caius Scribonius Curio, at the cost of 10,000,000, which also went mainly to his many creditors. Curio was highly talented,

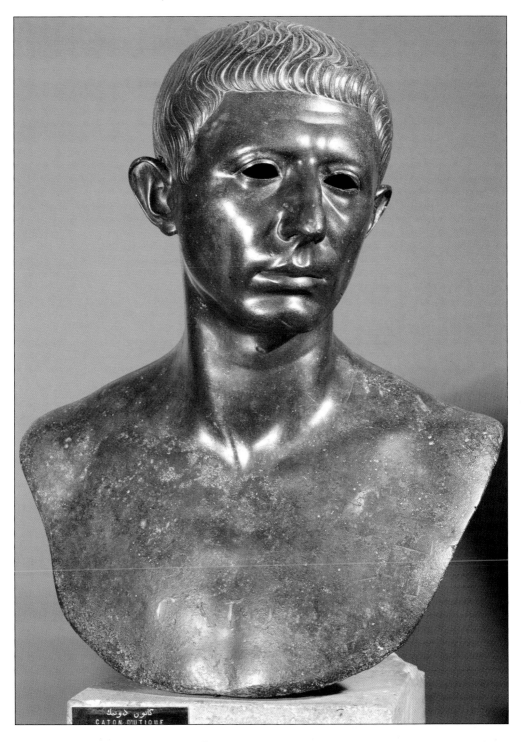

Marcus Porcius Cato commanded tremendous respect, if only moderate practical support, in the Senate due to his outspoken and sternly moral views which recalled those of his famous ancestor, Cato the Elder. His intransigence was a major factor in making the Civil War inevitable. (AKG Berlin/Erich Lessing)

but unreliable, having been involved with many of the scandals of the last decade, and had previously been vocal in his condemnation of Caesar. Now he proved vigorous in his support of Caesar's objectives throughout his year as tribune. In the Senate he argued that Pompey's Spanish command should end at the same time as Caesar's post, although it in fact had several years still to run. More than a few senators responded favourably to this idea, hoping that in this way open war between the two men could be averted. When the Senate finally voted on this proposal on 1 December 50, it was carried by 370 votes to 22. However, in the same session Marcellus arranged for them also to vote separately on whether Caesar and Pompey should be removed from their commands. A large majority was in favour of Caesar laying down his governorship, and as big a majority against forcing Pompey to do so. Rejecting the Senate's decision that both should give up their armies, Marcellus and a group of supporters went to call on Pompey. Giving him a sword, they requested that he take action to preserve the Republic. Pompey neither accepted nor declined this task, and the city's uncertainty deepened. Then, a few days later he seemed to have declared himself openly, and took command of two legions, I and XV. Veterans from his old armies were summoned to Rome.

Curio's term as tribune expired later in the month, but another of Caesar's supporters, Mark Antony, had been elected to the office and continued his work. In the meantime Caesar had written to the Senate, recounting his many victories won on Rome's behalf and his other services to the state, reminding them that he had already been granted the right to stand for consulship *in absentia*, and offering to lay down his command, provided that Pompey did the same thing. If he did not, then Caesar felt that he was obliged to retain his legions as protection against the faction opposed to him. The letter included the scarcely veiled threat that he was also willing to free Rome from the tyranny of this faction. On the same day that this was read in the Senate, Scipio, Pompey's father-in-law,

proposed issuing a decree that Caesar must hand over his legions by a set date – probably some time in the summer – but the measure was vetoed by the tribunes. Another group of senators, this time headed by Caesar's father-in-law, Calpurnius Piso, asked leave of absence to visit Caesar in his province and negotiate with him, but this was refused. Curio acted as Caesar's representative and proposed various compromises, at first that Caesar would give up the main military province, Transalpine Gaul, later extended to Cisalpine Gaul. He would remain governor of Illyricum with command of just one legion, but must be allowed to stand *in absentia* for the consulship. If the offer was serious, and we have no reason to doubt that it was, this would have made it virtually impossible for Caesar to fight a civil war and seize power by force. Pompey seems to have been tempted, but Cato and his associates so detested Caesar that they simply would not accept his standing for election without first becoming a private citizen, and therefore subject to prosecution. Another suggestion, supported by Cicero, was that at the same time Pompey should leave Italy and actually go to govern his Spanish provinces. One of the consuls for 49, Lucius Lentulus Cornelius Crus was violently opposed to any compromise, and continually insulted both Antony and Curio.

On 7 January 49 the Senate met and passed its ultimate decree, the *senatus consultum ultimum*, which called on the magistrates to use any means to defend the state. Caesar's supporters among the tribunes felt threatened with physical assault if they remained in the city. Disguised as slaves, they were hidden in carts and fled north to join Caesar, as did Curio. In the coming months Caesar's propaganda would exploit the threats made to the tribunes of the plebs, for this office was held in particular respect and affection by the population as a whole. In the days to come Pompey and the Senate began to prepare the war effort against Caesar. Scipio was given command of Syria and Lucius Domitius Ahenobarbus, consul in 54 and a long-time opponent of Caesar, received the Gallic provinces.

The news reached Caesar at Ravenna on 10 January. He spent the day watching gladiators training and held a previously arranged dinner in the evening, but secretly issued orders for several parties of soldiers to travel in civilian clothes carrying concealed weapons to Ariminum (modern Rimini), the nearest town in Italy. With him he had only a single legion, XIII, and apparently some 300 cavalrymen. Late in the evening he excused himself to his guests, and then departed for Ariminum in a carriage drawn by two mules. One tradition claims that in the night they lost their way, and it was only after they had found a local guide that they returned to the right road and reached the river Rubicon, which marked the boundary of his province. Commanders were barred by law from leading troops outside their province without the Senate's express permission, so crossing the river would turn Caesar into a rebel. In some versions Caesar paused uncertainly for some time, discussing with his officers what he should do. One of these was Asinius Pollio, who later wrote a history of the war (now sadly lost), so it is possible that he was truly indecisive and that these accounts are not simply inventions intended to heighten dramatic tension. Less likely is the story that they were confronted by the vision of a god playing pipes. However long it took, Caesar crossed the Rubicon, uttering the famous line 'the die is cast' – *alea iacta est* in Latin, although some versions claim that he spoke in Greek.

Caesar and his men occupied Ariminum without a fight and were soon joined by the tribunes. There was widespread fear of what he would do next. Cicero's correspondence from the early weeks of 49 is filled with gloomy forecasts of the bloodshed which everyone was sure would accompany the advance of the Caesarian army. In Gaul, Caesar and his legions had fought very aggressively and often with extreme brutality, some sources claiming that over a million people had been killed in less than a decade. Perhaps, as some modern commentators claim, many expected the legions to behave in no less harsh a manner now that they had

burst into Italy, and Cicero on one occasion even wondered whether Caesar would not prove more like Hannibal than a Roman general. Yet we should remember that nearly all Romans, including Cicero and many opponents, had revelled in Caesar's victories over foreign enemies. Cato had wanted to have Caesar prosecuted for breach of faith when he attacked during a truce, and was not primarily concerned with the massacre of barbarian tribesmen. Far more worrying to contemporaries was the precedent of every civil war and rebellion fought in the previous 40 years. Marius had massacred any opponents he could catch when he seized Rome in 87. Sulla had made the process more formal, with the proscriptions, long lists of names posted in the forum. Any citizen proscribed lost all his legal rights; this made it legitimate for anyone to kill them and in doing so they would gain a share of the victim's property that would otherwise go to the state. Rome's civil wars were not fought between rival political ideologies but rival individuals, and normally ended in the death of all those on the losing side. There was no reason to suspect that Caesar would be any different, and the political violence he had employed during his consulship only seemed to make this more likely.

In fact the war did not begin as anyone had expected. Caesar moved quickly, seizing towns with the limited forces at his disposal rather than waiting to gather his legions. He was largely unopposed, but the advance of his army was not accompanied by massacre or atrocity and his soldiers were under strict orders not to loot. There was a strange, phoney war quality to the first few weeks. Caesar in particular, was trying to show that he was still willing to compromise. Messages went back and forth as he suggested various compromises. Pompey and his allies replied by saying that they could not negotiate while Caesar commanded troops on Italian soil, and that he must return to Cisalpine Gaul before anything could be discussed. Yet Pompey did offer to leave for Spain once Caesar had laid down his command. Caesar refused the offer, perhaps not trusting the

Mark Antony acquired at an early age a reputation for wild living and radical politics. Though abler than most, he was fairly typical of the disreputable supporters on which Caesar had to rely. After Caesar's death he emerged as one of the most important leaders of the Caesarean faction. (Kingston Lacy, National Trust Photographic Library)

Senate or maybe feeling that he had gone too far to withdraw at this stage. Even so, both sides continued to claim publicly that they still hoped for a negotiated settlement, and were only thwarted by the enemy's intransigence.

Civil War

'Blitzkrieg' – the Italian campaign – January–March 49

The suddenness of Caesar's advance surprised and unnerved his opponents, just as he had intended. Pompey left Rome in the second half of January, declaring that it could not be defended. He was followed by most of the magistrates, including the consuls, who left in such haste that it suggested panic. Many Romans were still uncertain about just how firmly committed each side was to fighting,

and this open admission of military weakness made many wonder whether Pompey could really be relied on to defend the Republic.

The first clash came at Corfinum, where Domitius Ahenobarbus had mustered some 30 cohorts of new recruits and planned to hold the city. This was in spite of Pompey's repeated pleas for Domitius to bring his men south to join his two legions (I and XV) at Capua. It was the first sign of the great divisions between the commanders opposing Caesar. Caesar's army now mustered two

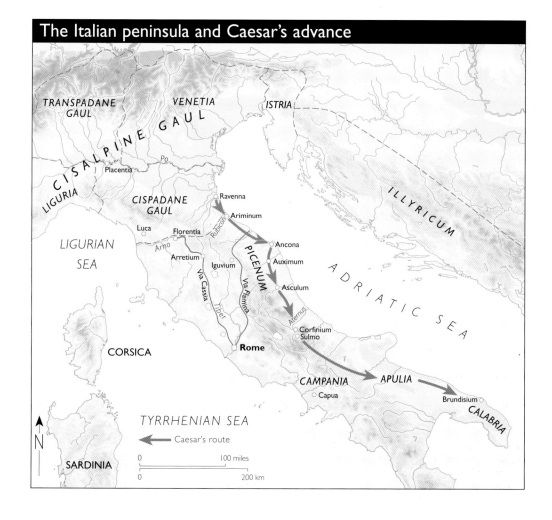

The Italian peninsula and Caesar's advance

TRANSPADANE GAUL

VENETIA

ISTRIA

CISALPINE GAUL

Po

Placentia

CISALPINE

LIGURIA

CISPADANE GAUL

Ravenna

Ariminum

ILLYRICUM

Luca

Florentia

Rubicon

LIGURIAN SEA

Arno

Arretium

Iguvium

PICENUM

Ancona

Auximum

ADRIATIC SEA

Via Cassia

Via Flamina

Asculum

Tiber

Aternus

Corfinum

Sulmo

CORSICA

Rome

CAMPANIA

APULIA

Capua

Brundisium

CALABRIA

TYRRHENIAN SEA

← Caesar's route

N

SARDINIA

0   100 miles

0   200 km

legions, for he had been joined by the XII, plus some Gallic cavalry, although some detachments from these units were probably still scattered as garrisons in the towns already occupied. In February Corfinum was surrounded and Ahenobarbus learned that Pompey had no intention of coming to his aid. Caesar tells us that Ahenobarbus then panicked and planned to slip out of the city and escape, abandoning his soldiers to their fate. Hearing of this, the garrison mutinied and surrendered themselves and the town. Ahenobarbus and the other senators were brought before Caesar, who made a great display of formally telling them of the grievances that had prompted him to march into Italy, and then allowing all who wished to, to go free. This was the first important display of Caesar's clemency (*clementia*), a policy to which he would adhere throughout the conflict, in marked contrast to his opponents, who employed the more brutal methods normal in past civil wars. The ordinary soldiers and most of their officers took an oath of allegiance to Caesar and were taken into his own army.

Pompey had probably already decided to abandon Italy altogether and cross the Adriatic to Greece. In the eastern provinces he had many clients and allies who could provide him with soldiers. The only properly trained troops in Italy had until recently been serving under Caesar, and Pompey was reluctant to test their loyalty so soon by advancing on the enemy. With Domitius's army gone, he was in any case outnumbered. He would go east, recruit and train a vast army and fleet and deal with Caesar in due course, returning to invade Italy by sea. Often he is supposed to have declared that 'Sulla did it, why shouldn't I?', referring to the dictator's successful return from the east in 83. Militarily this plan made perfect sense, but politically it was very damaging. Many Romans felt abandoned, and one senator sarcastically reminded Pompey that if he was short of soldiers to fight Caesar then perhaps he ought to start stamping his feet.

Pompey retreated south to Brundisium. Caesar followed in pursuit as quickly as he could, but a large number of recruits and senators had already been shipped across the Adriatic before he arrived outside the city. Pompey remained with about two legions, waiting for the ships to return and complete the evacuation. Caesar's engineers began to supervise the construction of a huge mole, intended to block access to the harbour. At first a solid breakwater was built out from the shore, but in deeper water this was continually swept away, so instead they began adding large rafts to the structure. Pompey used merchant vessels mounting hastily constructed three-storey towers and equipped with light artillery to attack and hinder construction. Pompey's fleet returned before the mole was complete and were able to enter the harbour and embark the garrison. The city's gates were blocked and a small force left as rearguard to allow a smooth evacuation, but the citizens of Brundisium, either through hostility towards Pompey or fear of Caesar's men, helped the attackers in and the retreat became more hasty than planned.

In less than two months Caesar had seized control in Italy. Pompey had escaped, with the best of his soldiers, and many leading senators. At present Caesar lacked a fleet and was in no position to follow him. On 18 March he was back in Rome, trying to persuade as many senators as possible to convene. His clemency had surprised and relieved many who were neutral or wavering, though some were still convinced that this was simply a ploy and that, in time, Caesar's own cruel nature or that of his disreputable followers would prevail. When he led his soldiers to seize the state Treasury held in the

RIGHT This early 2nd century AD relief shows a Roman soldier leading a chained Germanic captive. During the Gallic campaigns Caesar enslaved an enormous number of prisoners. The profits from these sales not only paid off his debts but made him an extremely wealthy man. (Author's collection)

FOLLOWING PAGES There was some naval fighting during the Civil War but the most decisive encounters occurred on land. However, sea battles would figure prominently in the fighting after Caesar's death. (AKG Berlin)

Temple of Saturn, and Caesar threatened to execute the tribune Metellus who stood in his way, such fears seemed confirmed.

Curio was sent with two legions to secure Sardinia and then Africa. Caesar himself decided to set out for Spain overland and defeat Pompey's legions there. These were the best of the enemy troops then in existence, but their strategic role was unclear now that Pompey had shifted his main focus to the eastern Mediterranean. Caesar is supposed to have claimed that he went first to fight an army without a leader, before going to fight a leader without an army.

'An army without a leader' – the Spanish campaign – April–August 49

The main Pompeian army in Spain was at Ilerda (modern Lérida) commanded by Lucius Afranius and Marcus Petreius. Between them they had five legions, 80 cohorts of Spanish auxiliaries – a mixture of both close- and open-order infantry – and 5,000 cavalry. The other two legions, again supported by auxiliaries, remained far to the west in Further Spain under the command of Marcus Terentius Varro. To face the force at Ilerda, Caesar was able to muster six legions, along with 3,000 cavalry of various nationalities which had served with his army throughout the Gallic campaigns, and the same number of recently recruited Gauls. Also mentioned is a force of 900 horsemen kept as his personal bodyguard, but it is not entirely clear whether these were included in the above total. Most of this force was sent on in advance under the command of Caius Fabius. As Caesar marched to join them, his tribunes and centurions offered to loan him money with which to pay the soldiers. Gratefully accepting this gesture, their commander felt that this commitment helped bond both officers and legionaries to his cause.

Ilerda lies on a ridge to the west of the river Sicoris (modern Segre). A small force covered the bridge outside the town, but the main Pompeian camp was situated further south on the same high ground, where they had gathered considerable store of provisions from the surrounding area. On arrival Fabius built two bridges across the river and crossed to camp on the west bank. Finding it difficult to gather food and fodder, he sent a foraging expedition of two legions back across to the eastern side, but this was threatened when one of the bridges unexpectedly collapsed and only rescued when a force was sent to its aid.

Caesar arrived in June, and immediately advanced and offered battle at the foot of the ridge. When Afranius refused to be drawn, Caesar had the third of his three lines dig a deep trench – a rampart would have been more visible and would therefore have invited attack – and then camped behind it. It took several days to complete the defences of this camp to Caesar's satisfaction, and after that he attempted to seize the hill between Ilerda and the enemy camp. Three legions formed for battle, and then the front line of one advanced to capture the height. The Pompeians responded quickly, and, moving swiftly and operating in a looser order learned in fighting the tribes of Lusitania (roughly the area of modern-day Portugal), occupied and defended the hilltop. Both sides fed in reinforcements throughout the day, although the narrow slope only allowed three cohorts in the fighting line at any one time. In the end, Legio IX charged uphill and drove the enemy back for sufficient time to permit Caesar's army to withdraw. They had lost 70 dead, including the senior centurion (*primus pilus*) of Legio XIV, and over 600 wounded, while the enemy had suffered 200 fatalities including five centurions.

Two days later heavy rainfall raised the level and power of the river and swept away the bridges used by Caesar's army, largely cutting them off from supplies. Coming under increasing pressure, Caesar's soldiers built boats of the type they had seen in Britain. Ferrying a legion across the Sicoris at night, they secured a bridgehead and permitted the construction of a new bridge, allowing the army once again to operate effectively on the eastern bank as well as the west, winning several small engagements. This success

The early 1st century AD Arch of Orange commemorated the Roman defeat of the last of the Gallic rebellions. This relief depicts Gallic military equipment piled and captured by Roman victors. Caesar's successful campaigns in Gaul provided him with a loyal and extremely effective army willing to fight for him against other Romans. (Topham Picturepoint)

encouraged many local communities to join Caesar, providing new sources of food. His engineers then dug canals off from the main river, lowering its level and creating a serviceable ford for men on horseback much nearer to the army's camp than the bridge. More Gallic cavalry had arrived, giving Caesar's horsemen a considerable numerical advantage over the Pompeians which soon made it increasingly difficult for their foraging parties to operate.

The Ilerda campaign

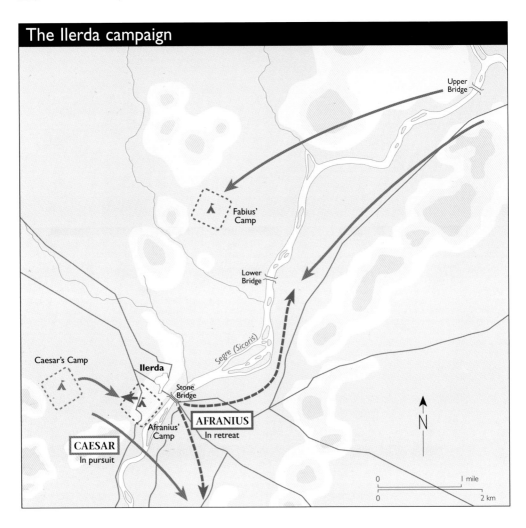

Afranius and Petreius decided that they could no longer maintain their position and so, using barges gathered from along the river as pontoons, they threw another bridge across the Sicoris and under cover of darkness crossed to the east bank, before turning south. Caesar's scouts reported this activity and in response he sent his cavalry to harass the enemy retreat, the rest of the army following at dawn. His men waded through the rudimentary ford, the infantry moving between two lines of pack animals to slow the flow of water. In the next days, Caesar's patrols discovered a more direct path than the enemy and by hard marching he was able to get in front of them. The enemy were now at a severe disadvantage, but Caesar refused the pleas of his officers and men to fight a battle,

saying that he hoped to win with as little loss of Roman life as possible. Camped close together, the legionaries on both sides began to fraternise. Nervous of their men's loyalty, Afranius and Petreius massacred all of Caesar's men they could catch, though their opponent released all the Pompeian soldiers in his camp unharmed. They then made their officers and men swear an oath not to abandon the cause. In spite of this, within a short time, the generals, their troops cut off from all supplies, capitulated. The commanders were pardoned

RIGHT This scene from Trajan's column showing legionaries constructing a fortified camp dates to the early 2nd century AD. Segmented armour of the type shown here, does not appear to have been introduced until several decades after the Civil War. (Author's collection)

and allowed to go free, some of the army incorporated into Caesar's own and the rest disbanded. Varro and the two legions in Further Spain surrendered immediately on the approach of Caesar's forces. In a matter of months, and through a mixture of boldness and skilful manoeuvre, Caesar had overrun Spain at minimal loss to himself. Appointing Quintus Cassius Longinus as governor – an extraordinary appointment for a man serving as tribune of the plebs – he returned to Italy.

Massilia – spring–summer 49

En route to Spain, Caesar had been refused admission to the great trading city of Massilia (modern Marseilles) by the authorities there, who claimed that they wished to remain neutral. The claim was immediately discredited when Domitius Ahenobarbus sailed into the harbour and took command

This wall mural from Pompeii shows two war galleys manoeuvring in battle. Naval fighting was not as important as land battles during the fighting between Caesar and Pompey. However, the failure of the vast Pompeian fleet, commanded by the former consul Bibulus, to oppose Caesar's army as it sailed from Brundisium to Greece with almost no protection had a considerable impact on the following campaign. (AKG London)

of the city. Leaving Caius Trebonius with three legions and Decimus Brutus with a fleet to prosecute the siege, he had then moved on to Spain. The defenders proved very active, displaying especial skill in the small but fierce naval actions fought outside the harbour. Yet the attackers persisted in spite of heavy damage inflicted on their siege works by enemy sorties, and in the end the Massiliotes decided to surrender. Ahenobarbus learned of this, and fled by sea. Caesar, returning from Spain in late September, was present to accept the surrender, installing a garrison of two legions, but generally being lenient to the city.

Curio in Africa – spring–summer 49

Curio occupied Sicily without fighting, and then crossed with three legions to Africa, where the governor, Publius Attius Varus had declared against Caesar. The latter was supported by the Numidian King Juba, who commanded a large, if sometimes unreliable army. Curio had little military experience – none at all of high command – and was considered brilliant but unreliable by most contemporaries. His army consisted of troops originally raised by the Pompeians who had

This carved stone relief from Osuna in Spain shows an Iberian cavalryman. Spanish horsemen served on both sides during the Civil War. It is hard to know whether they still employed traditional equipment or had adopted more Roman styles. (AISA)

taken the oath to Caesar after their surrender at Corfinum. Curio landed successfully near Utica, surprising the enemy, and soon came into contact with Varus' army. The two sides formed for battle on either side of a steep valley. Varus' brother, Sextus, had been at Corfinum and appealed to Curio's legions to desert and return to their original loyalty. However, the soldiers refused and, after a success in a cavalry skirmish, Curio led them in a bold, uphill attack which swiftly routed Varus' army. Encouraged by this success,

Curio acted on what proved to be faulty intelligence, and attacked what he believed was a detachment of Juba's army. In fact, the bulk of the king's forces was there and, after an initial success, the Romans were ambushed and virtually annihilated. Curio was surrounded with the remnants of his troops on a hilltop and died fighting. Only a small fraction of the army, including the historian Asinius Pollio, escaped to Sicily.

'A leader without an army' – Greece – January–August 48

The report of Curio's defeat was not the only bad news reaching Caesar in late 49, for Mark Antony had suffered a lesser defeat in

Illyricum. Even more serious was a mutiny involving four of his legions, and in particular Legio IX, at Placentia (modern Piacenza) on the river Po. The troops complained that many who had served throughout the Gallic campaigns were now long overdue for discharge, and that no one had yet received the donative of 500 denarii per man (double their annual salary) promised by Caesar at Brundisium some months before. Caesar's response was harsh, berating them for their impatience and declaring that he would decimate Legio IX, which meant executing one man in ten. In the end he relented, and only had the 12 ringleaders killed.

Dyrrachium

Caesar spent a short time at Rome, having been appointed dictator before he arrived and held the post for 11 days, using his powers to hold elections in which he was voted to the consulship. He was eager to move against Pompey, and near the end of the year went to join the army of some 12 legions along with 1,000 cavalry which had been assembled at Brundisium. Attrition meant that it was unlikely any of the legions mustered more than 3,000 men, and some units were closer to the 2,000 mark. Nevertheless, this was still a formidable total to ship across the Adriatic and to supply once there. Caesar exhorted his soldiers by saying that this next campaign would be the culmination of their labours, and then told them to carry only the absolutely essential baggage and to leave nearly all servants, slaves and families behind. On 4 January 48, there were sufficient ships to embark seven legions and 500 cavalrymen. The crossing was a great gamble, for Caesar had no significant naval force with which to oppose the vast Pompeian fleet, currently commanded by his old enemy and consular colleague in 59, Bibulus. Yet the enemy did not expect him to move in winter when the weather was poor, and Caesar landed without opposition at Paeleste in Epirus. Bibulus was alerted by the time the transport ships headed back to Brundisium and intercepted some of them. For the moment it proved impossible for Mark Antony to run the blockade and bring the remainder of the army across to join Caesar.

Caesar was isolated and severely outnumbered by the enemy. Pompey had had more than nine months to muster his forces, and by this time they amounted to nine legions, supported by over 5,000 light infantry and 7,000 cavalry. A further two legions under Scipio were on their way from Syria. Pompey, always a great organiser, had taken care to gather plenty of food and fodder to supply his troops even in the winter months. Caesar's men had to make do with the little they had brought with them and whatever could be gathered from local communities. The situation was increasingly desperate, but Caesar was not really strong enough to open a full-scale offensive. Some manoeuvring took place, along with further attempts at negotiation, but there was no serious fighting. At one point he put to sea in a small ship during appalling weather, hoping to reach Brundisium and hurry his reinforcements over, but the weather proved so bad that he was forced to return to the shore. In was not until 10 April that Mark Antony managed to bring the remaining legions across the Adriatic. Pompey responded too slowly and failed to prevent the union of the two forces.

Caesar had all 11 legions, but was still outnumbered and continued to have supply problems. Nevertheless he immediately resolved to make a bold attack on one of the enemy's major supply dumps at the port city of Dyrrachium. Outmarching the enemy, he managed to get between Pompey and the city, although he was not able to seize the latter. Pompey camped on the coast on a hill called Petra, overlooking a natural harbour which continued to allow him to receive supply shipments. Caesar's main camp was on a hill further north, but he continued to have supply problems as the harvest was not yet ripe and the region had been thoroughly plundered by the enemy. A line of hills ran around Pompey's camp and Caesar began construction of a line of forts connected by a ditch and wall, which were intended

This scene from Trajan's column shows the Emperor Trajan and a group of his senior officers planning for their campaign. The general's council (*consilium*) was an important opportunity for him to explain his intentions and issue orders. These were held frequently during a campaign and always preceded a battle. (Author's collection)

eventually to surround the enemy completely. This provided some protection for his patrols and foraging parties from the more numerous enemy cavalry, although in part the rugged ground made the operations of the enemy cavalry less effective. More importantly the willingness of Pompey, with a numerically superior army, to be hemmed in by the enemy would be a public humiliation, perhaps weakening the loyalty of his allies. Pompey replied by beginning his own line of fortifications parallel to Caesar's. There was considerable skirmishing between the two sides as they fought for possession of key positions or simply to hinder each other's progress. Pompey's more numerous army had the advantage of being on the inside and so having to build a shorter line, which eventually measured only some 15 miles to the more than 17 miles of the Caesarean works. In effect two armies were conducting a siege instead of the more normal forms of open warfare which, for Caesar's forces, were reminiscent of some of their conflict in Gaul.

Both armies, and especially the Caesareans, were on very short rations, but Pompey's army had a very large number of animals, both cavalry mounts and baggage animals, which began to suffer. Priority went to the cavalry and soon pack and draught animals were dying in great numbers. Caesar managed to dam the streams that carried water into the enemy positions. For a while Pompey's men survived by digging wells, but these did not really provide sufficient quantities and after a while the bulk of his cavalry and their mounts were shipped out. In the meantime, Caesar's legionaries dreamed of ripening crops and survived by eating barley rather than wheat, consuming far more meat than usual, and using a local root called charax to make a kind of bread.

On seeing an example of this bread, Pompey is said to have declared that they were fighting beasts and not men.

The work went on as each side extended its fortifications further and further south. Pompey's army mounted a heavy attack which was easily repulsed by the troops led by Publius Sulla. The enemy retreat was so

precipitate that some of Caesar's officers felt that an immediate all-out attack might have won the war there and then. However, Caesar was not present and praised Sulla for not going beyond his orders, feeling that such an important change of plan was the responsibility of the commander, not that of a subordinate or legate. On the same day a series of diversionary assaults were also made in some force. All failed at the cost of some 2,000 casualties, but especially heavy fighting occurred around a small fort held by three of Caesar's cohorts under Volcatius Tullus. Heavily outnumbered, the defenders suffered many wounds from the vast number of missiles shot into the camp by

The battle of Dyrrachium

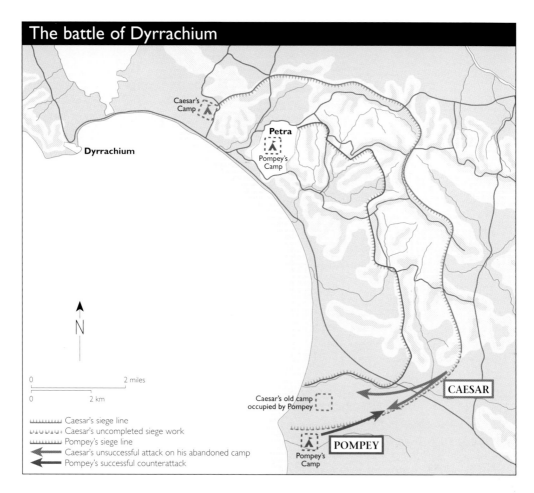

Caesar's Camp

Petra

Dyrrachium

Pompey's Camp

N

| 0 | 2 miles |
| 0 | 2 km |

Caesar's old camp occupied by Pompey

CAESAR

POMPEY

Pompey's Camp

ᴜᴜᴜᴜᴜᴜᴜ Caesar's siege line
ᴜᴜᴜᴜᴜᴜ Caesar's uncompleted siege work
ᴜᴜᴜᴜᴜ Pompey's siege line
⟵ Caesar's unsuccessful attack on his abandoned camp
⟵ Pompey's successful counterattack

the hordes of slingers and archers supporting the attacking legion. Nearly all the defenders were wounded, four out of six centurions in one cohort losing their eyes, but somehow they held on. Caesar rewarded his officers and men lavishly, and they were granted extra rations, which at the time may have seemed even more satisfying than promotions and medals.

Soon after this success, two Gallic chieftains, Roucillus and Egus, defected to Pompey, along with their closest followers. Caesar claims that they had been caught claiming pay for non-existent cavalrymen

LEFT This early 2nd-century AD relief from Adamklissi in Romania shows a legionary in the uniform of the period fighting a half-naked barbarian. The Roman has punched his opponent with the boss of the shield to unbalance him and then stabbed him in the stomach. (Author's collection)

and feared punishment. The desertion raised enemy morale and provided Pompey with considerable intelligence about Caesar's dispositions. Using this information, he planned a powerful attack on an incomplete section at the southern end of Caesar's fortifications, the main body striking from his own lines, while detachments of light troops were taken by sea and landed behind the enemy. The attack achieved some initial success, but as Antony and then Caesar himself led up reserves the tide was turned and the enemy driven back. To regain the initiative, Caesar replied with a heavy counter-attack against a camp originally built by Legio IX, subsequently abandoned and now occupied by the enemy. His troops moved through dead ground and woodland and achieved initial surprise, breaking into the camp, but then things began to go wrong. One of the attacking columns got lost, mistaking another wall for the rampart of the camp and following it towards the sea. Pompey shifted reserves to the area. The leading attackers began to flee and the panic spread rapidly as most of the 33 cohorts involved dissolved into rout. Caesar tried to stop standard bearers as they fled past him – a common gesture used by Roman commanders to rally their men – but all rushed on, some leaving the standard in his hands, and one even trying to stab him with its butt-spike, prompting a bodyguard to slice off the man's arm. Losses amounted to over 960 men and 32 tribunes and centurions killed and more taken prisoner. Fortunately, Pompey failed to follow up his advantage so soon after the failure of his own attack, prompting Caesar to declare that he would have lost if only the enemy commander had known how to win. Labienus was allowed to take charge of the prisoners and had them all executed. Parading his army, Caesar publicly punished several of the standard-bearers and tried to inspire the rest. Judging that their morale was at a low ebb, he decided that they needed to be encouraged before he risked a major action. Evacuating his sick and wounded, Caesar decided to withdraw, sending his baggage train out of camp at night to conceal his intention from the enemy. The main column was then able to withdraw with little hindrance. Only a few Pompeian cavalry managed to catch up with the retreating army and these were defeated by Caesar's cavalry, closely supported by a picked unit of 400 infantry.

Pharsalus

Caesar headed into Thessaly, hoping to join up with a detachment under Domitius Calvinus which he had sent to intercept Scipio and his two legions. His army began to recover its strength as they passed through unplundered land and were able to harvest the now ripening grain. However, the reverse at Dyrrachium made some communities doubt Caesar's prospects of victory and the city of Gomphi refused to

admit him or provide food. Caesar stormed the place and, for one of the very few times during the Civil War, allowed his men to sack the town. Some sources claim that the next day's march was more like a drunken revel, but also that the overindulgence appeared to cure much of the sickness from which many soldiers were suffering.

Pompey now had several options. One would have been to use his fleet to cross to Italy, now largely unprotected, but this would still mean that Caesar had to be defeated at some future date, and might be seen as running from his opponent. His personal belief was that they ought to shadow Caesar's army, but avoid open confrontation, hoping to wear him down by depriving him of supplies. This was a well-recognised Roman strategy, often known by the nickname of 'kicking the enemy in the belly'. However, there was massive pressure from the senators with the army to bring matters to a swift conclusion by bringing the enemy to battle. In early August the two armies camped near each other on the plains of Pharsalus. Several days were spent in the manoeuvring and formal challenges to battle that so often preceded the battles of this period. The pressure on Pompey to fight grew stronger and stronger. Many of the senators were so confident that arguments broke out over who should receive Caesar's post of Pontifex Maximus, one of the senior priesthoods in Rome, as well as what punishment was appropriate for those who had supported him or tried to remain neutral.

On the morning of 9 August Caesar was preparing to move his camp to another position where the army could more easily find food, when he noticed that the Pompeian army had advanced much further from the rampart of their camp than was usual, and had come fully onto the level ground by the river Enipeus. Quickly, the order was passed for Caesar's men to take off their packs and then re-form in columns, wearing only the equipment necessary for battle. Then the army marched out and formed up facing the enemy. Altogether

This relief shows a Spanish warrior carrying a long oval shield and wielding a curved sword or falcata. He appears to wear some sort of crested sinew cap. As with the cavalryman shown on p.134. it is uncertain to what extent the Spanish infantry in the Civil War were dressed in this traditional fashion or had adopted Roman equipments. (Museo Arqueologico Nacional, Madrid/AISA)

The battle of Pharsalus, phase one

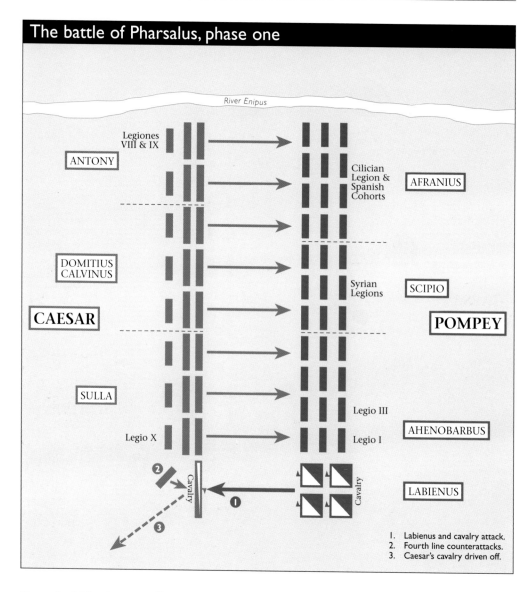

River Enipus

Legiones VIII & IX

ANTONY

Cilician Legion & Spanish Cohorts

AFRANIUS

DOMITIUS CALVINUS

Syrian Legions

SCIPIO

CAESAR

POMPEY

SULLA

Legio III

AHENOBARBUS

Legio X

Legio I

Cavalry

Cavalry

LABIENUS

1. Labienus and cavalry attack.
2. Fourth line counterattacks.
3. Caesar's cavalry driven off.

Caesar had 80 cohorts totalling 22,000 men and 1,000 cavalry. He formed the legions into the usual three lines, with the most experienced units on the flanks. Legio IX had suffered heavily at Dyrrachium, so it was combined with the almost equally depleted but veteran Legio VIII into a single command and placed on the left, next to the river. On the right flank was Caesar's favourite unit, Legio X. The entire army was split into three commands, Mark Antony on the left, Cnaeus Domitiius Calvinus in the centre and Sulla on the right. Caesar was free to move to wherever a crisis developed, but in fact was to spend nearly all the battle with Legio X. The cavalry were all massed on the right.

Pompey's army was significantly larger, with the 110 cohorts in its three lines totalling 45,000 men and an enormous force of 7,000 cavalry on the left flank, supported by significant numbers of archers and slingers. Next to the cavalry were the two legions that had once served with Caesar, I and XV (now renumbered III). In the centre were the legions from Syria and on the right nearest the river the legions from Cilicia, plus some troops from Spain. The army was

The battle of Pharsalus, phase two

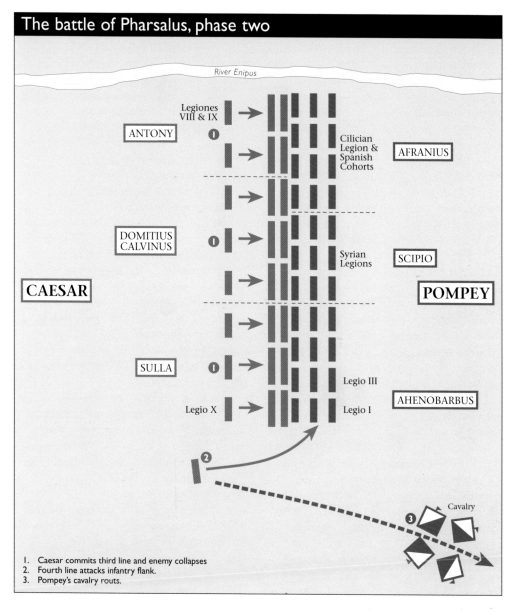

River Enipus

Legiones VIII & IX

ANTONY

Cilician Legion & Spanish Cohorts

AFRANIUS

DOMITIUS CALVINUS

Syrian Legions   SCIPIO

CAESAR

POMPEY

SULLA

Legio III

AHENOBARBUS

Legio X   Legio I

Cavalry

1. Caesar commits third line and enemy collapses
2. Fourth line attacks infantry flank.
3. Pompey's cavalry routs.

also divided into three commands, with Ahenobarbus on the left, Scipio in the centre and Afranius on the right. The main line was formed very deep by Roman standards, with each cohort deploying in ten ranks. Caesar's men must have been in four or five ranks, much closer to the Roman norm. Pompey had also given his infantry an unusual order, telling them not to advance to meet the enemy, but to remain stationary and throw their *pila* as soon as the enemy came within range. Both of these decisions suggest that

Pompey doubted the effectiveness of his own legionaries compared with Caesar's more experienced soldiers. Instead of relying on them, he planned to win the battle with his cavalry. Concentrated on the left flank, they outnumbered Caesar's horsemen by around seven to one. They would advance to open the battle, smashing their opponents and then wheeling round to take Caesar's infantry from the flank and rear. Labienus was in charge of this attack, and may even have devised the plan.

The enemy's deployment made the massive superiority of their cavalry obvious. To counter this, Caesar took a single cohort from the third line of each of his legions and stationed this force behind his own cavalry, probably echeloned back from the infantry line. This fourth line was concealed behind the horsemen and Legio X and not observed by the enemy. Both armies were now ready for battle, though some delay may well have elapsed as the commanders encouraged their men. For the battle Caesar's army were given the password 'Venus, Bringer of Victory' and Pompey's men 'Hercules, Unconquered'.

The battle began with an advance all along Caesar's line. Most of the Pompeians remained in position, but their cavalry surged forward against Caesar's horse, which gave way. During the charge and subsequent combat the Pompeians seem to have fallen into some disorder, the individual squadrons losing formation and merging into one great mass. Many of these horsemen were relatively recent recruits and neither officers nor men had much experience of operating in such large numbers, but there was always a tendency for this to happen if cavalry became too crowded. Suddenly, Caesar gave the signal for his fourth line to attack. The legionaries charged forward, yelling their battle cry and sounding their trumpets, and then using the *pila* as spears. The result was almost immediate panic, which spread throughout the mass of enemy cavalry until there was a great stampede to the rear. The supporting light infantry were abandoned and massacred or dispersed by the legionaries. Pompey's main attack had failed.

In the meantime the main infantry lines had come into contact. Caesar's men had begun their charge at the usual distance, turning their steady forward march into a run preparatory to throwing their *pila*, but had then noticed that the enemy was not moving. To prevent the cohorts from running too far, losing their formation and maybe wasting their missiles, the centurions halted the line. The nonchalance with which Caesar's men paused and redressed their ranks such a short distance from the Pompeians was another indication of their superb discipline. Re-

formed, the attack went in, the legionaries waiting until they were within 50 feet or so of the enemy before throwing a volley of missiles and charging sword in hand into contact. The Pompeians replied with their own *pila* – though it is doubtful if the men in the rear ranks of each cohort can have thrown their weapons effectively. A hard struggle developed, the second line of each army, which always acted as close supports to the first line, soon being drawn in. However, the fourth line followed up its success by attacking the exposed left flank of the Pompeian infantry, throwing that section of the line into disorder. Caesar gave the signal for his third line to advance and renew forward momentum in the fighting line. The pressure on the enemy was too much. At first the Pompeians went back slowly, but more and more units began to dissolve into rout. Caesar sent officers out to ensure that enemy legionaries were permitted to surrender, although his men were allowed to massacre the foreign auxiliaries.

Pompey had left the battlefield almost as soon as his cavalry had been swept away. He had ridden back to his camp, instructing the guards there to maintain a careful watch, and then gone to his tent. Later, as the rout of his army became obvious, he laid aside his general's cloak and left for the coast. If these accounts of his behaviour are accurate – and there must be some doubt, as they all come from hostile sources – his command at Pharsalus was remarkably spiritless, and his behaviour, being the first rather than the last to despair, utterly inappropriate for a Roman general. Caesar also claims that his men were astounded by the luxuries that they discovered in the Pompeian camp, items more suitable for effete Orientals than true Romans, although again this could well be propaganda.

Pompeian prisoners numbered 24,000, with supposedly another 15,000 killed. Nine eagles (the standard of an entire legion) and 180 signa (the standard of a century) were among the trophies. Once again most Pompeians were pardoned by Caesar, and he is supposed to have been especially pleased when his men brought in Marcus Brutus, son

This iron helmet, known to modern scholars as the Agen type, was one of several Gallic designs adopted and developed by the Roman army. Such helmets were certainly in use with many of the Gallic auxiliaries in the Civil War and may also have been worn by some legionaries, especially in Caesar's legions, which had been serving in Gaul for some years. (Schweisz Landesmuseum, Zurich)

of one of his former mistresses and later leader of the conspirators who would murder him. Many other Pompeians escaped, but Ahenobarbus died in the pursuit. Some fugitives went to north Africa, but Pompey travelled to Egypt. Caesar's own loss was comparatively light at 200 men, along with 30 centurions. Such a disproportionately high loss among these officers was not uncommon, the result of their aggressive and inevitably dangerous style of leadership.

Egypt – September 48–August 47

Caesar rested only for a very short time after the victory. Mark Antony was sent back to Italy, while Domitius Calvinus went with three legions, mainly consisting of former Pompeians, to Syria. Caesar himself took Legio VI, now reduced to a mere 1,000 men, another legion mustering some 1,400 men, and 800 cavalry and rushed in pursuit of Pompey; until he had been taken or killed there could be no end to the war. News arrived that Pompey had gone to Rhodes and then taken ship for Egypt, hoping to receive aid in rebuilding an army.

Egypt was wracked by its own civil war at this time, for the old King Ptolemy XI Auletes (or flute-player) had left the throne jointly to his son Ptolemy XII – a boy of about 14 – and his eldest daughter Cleopatra. The boy king was dominated by his advisers, Pothinus the eunuch and Achillas the commander of his army, a force that effectively included two Roman legions which had been in the province since 55 and had largely 'gone native'. Pompey's ship arrived on the coast near Ptolemy's camp and he appealed to the young king for aid. Since the king was unwilling to support a loser and eager to win favour with the victor, Pompey was lured ashore and murdered, the first blow being struck by a centurion who had served under him during his Asian campaigns.

Caesar landed at Alexandria on 2 October 48, and was met by a deputation

This coin is believed to be a portrait of Cleopatra VII, queen of Egypt and in turn the mistress of Caesar and Mark Antony. Our sources describe her as not classically beautiful but with a fascinating personality. She was certainly intelligent and highly educated in the Hellenistic tradition. (British Museum/AKG Berlin)

from Ptolemy that presented him with Pompey's head and signet ring. Caesar is supposed to have wept, distraught at the loss of his former friend and missing the opportunity of pardoning him. This emotion may have been genuine, as indeed may his alleged desire to spare Pompey, but it is equally possible that he simply wished to distance himself from the cruelty of an act from which he derived political benefit. Nevertheless he gave honourable burial to Pompey's remains, the tomb surviving to be desecrated by Jewish rebels in the second century AD. Preceded by his lictors – the attendants carrying the fasces, the bundle of rods and an axe that symbolised the power of Roman magistrates – Caesar marched in great pomp to the palace. This display enraged the volatile Alexandrians and provoked some rioting. Caesar's soldiers responded with force and, since the late king had recommended his children to Rome, declared that both sides in the Civil War should disarm and submit to his arbitration. Some time in the next few days Cleopatra visited Caesar. The most famous story is that she was wrapped up in a carpet or blanket and carried secretly into the palace by a faithful Greek attendant, before being unrolled in front of a mesmerised Caesar. Cleopatra was 21 – more than 30 years younger than Caesar – exceptionally attractive if not quite flawlessly beautiful, highly educated, intelligent, and with a fascinating personality. Thus began one of the most famous romances in history.

It was not long before Ptolemy's advisers felt that their cause could not compete with his sister's for Caesar's favour. Leading their army to support the mob of Alexandria, they besieged the palace, blockading Caesar's men for six months. His soldiers were close to panic when the water supply was cut off, but new wells were dug inside the compound and the crisis averted. Reinforced by Legio XXXVII, composed of former Pompeians, Caesar became bolder and attempted to seize the whole of the Pharos Island, on which the great lighthouse, one of the Seven Wonders of the World, was built.

The skill of his Rhodian captains and sailors prevailed in a naval action fought within the Great Harbour, and allowed Caesar to land troops on the mole joining the Island. However, things began to go wrong as the enemy rushed reserves to the spot. Panic began with the crews of some ships who had landed to plunder and then spread to the legionaries. The boat carrying Caesar away was swamped by fugitives, forcing him to dive into the water and swim to safety, at the cost of abandoning his general's cloak.

Ptolemy had been held hostage by Caesar from early in the siege, and after this reverse Caesar decided to release him. The lad claimed to be reluctant to go, then promised to end the war, but, once he joined the army, promptly led it back to fight the Romans. The balance of power had shifted in his court by this time; Pothinus, assisted by Ptolemy's other sister Arsinoë, had murdered Achillas and these two were the real powers behind the throne. In the meantime an army led by Caesar's ally, King Mithridates of Pergamum, had marched overland from Asia Minor to Egypt. Leaving only a small garrison, Caesar took the bulk of his 5,000 or so men, and sailed out of Alexandria's harbour to join his ally. Ptolemy's forces heard of this and attempted to prevent their juncture, but failed. In open manoeuvring, Caesar showed the superiority of his men over the enemy and in a rapid campaign trounced the Egyptian army. Ptolemy fled but drowned when the boat carrying him to safety capsized. Arsinoë was exiled to Italy. Caesar returned to relieve Alexandria.

The war in Egypt was over, but for more than half a year Caesar had been out of contact with the rest of the world. The surviving Pompeians had had time to regroup and the Civil War would drag on. Yet, even though the war in Egypt was now complete, Caesar remained there for two months, allegedly spending his time feasting with Cleopatra. At one stage the Queen is supposed to have taken him on a luxurious cruise down the Nile. Militarily and politically, Caesar's inaction for this long period makes no sense. Perhaps he had never had a clear plan for what he should do once he had won the Civil War, or perhaps he was simply exhausted and could not resist a time of rest in fascinating company.

Veni, vidi, vici – the Zela campaign

It was not until late May or early June that Caesar finally stirred himself to move. There was bad news from Syria, and he sailed there with Legio VI, leaving the rest of his army to garrison Egypt. After the suicide of Mithridates of Pontus, his son Pharnaces had been left with only a small fraction of the old kingdom of Pontus. Seeing the disorder caused within the empire by the Civil War, Pharnaces decided to seize once more the lost territory, and invaded the old heartland of Pontus. Caesar's legate Domitius Calvinus had marched to oppose him, but suffered defeat. Pharnaces celebrated his victory in brutal manner, torturing and executing his prisoners, and castrating large numbers of young Romans who fell into his hands.

The forces at Caesar's disposal were small, consisting of the greatly reduced but veteran Legio VI, along with the survivors of Domitius's army. These included a legion of Deiotarus's Galatians which had fled before contact, another raised in Pontus, and Legio XXXVI which, although composed of former Pompeians, had fought well. Though outnumbered, Caesar characteristically chose to advance on Pharnaces, stopping five miles away from the enemy camp outside the town of Zela. In the night Caesar suddenly marched out and began to build a new camp on the opposite side of a valley to the Pontic army. On the next morning, 2 August 47, Pharnaces drew up his army in battle order. However, because the ravine separating them was steep, offering very bad going to any attacker trying to climb it, Caesar thought that this was simply a gesture of confidence, of the type commonly made by armies in this period, and so allowed his men to continue constructing the camp. He was amazed when Pharnaces led his troops down

Another scene from the monument at Adamklissi in Romania shows a legionary slashing with his gladius. Although the Roman army's training emphasised the use of the point rather than the edged of the sword, the gladius was in fact a very well balanced weapon that could be used effectively to cut or thrust. (Author's collection)

across the valley in a full-scale attack. The Romans were unprepared and hastily tried to put together a fighting line. Scythed chariots – all but useless against steady and properly formed troops – caused some losses among the dispersed Romans, before their teams were shot down with missiles. The fighting was long and bitter, but eventually Legio VI on the right flank punched through the enemy line and exploited the success to threaten the remainder of their army in the flank. Finally, the Pontic army dissolved into rout and the fleeing men were massacred by the vengeful Romans. The legionaries were so exhilarated that they crossed the valley and stormed the enemy camp, in spite of the resistance of its garrison.

Although the battle of Zela proved hard-fought, it decided the war within days of the beginning of the campaign. Caesar is said to have commented on how lucky Pompey had been to make his reputation as a commander fighting such opponents. Later, when he celebrated his triumph over Pontus, the procession included placards bearing just three Latin words: '*Veni, vidi, vici*' ('I came, I saw, I conquered').

Africa – December 47–April 46

Although the eastern Mediterranean was now settled, many problems had developed elsewhere during Caesar's absence. Cassius's behaviour in Spain had provoked rebellion, while in Africa, Scipio, Afranius, Labienus, Cato and many other die-hard senators had raised an enormous army supported by King Juba. There were also difficulties in Italy, made worse by the lack of communication from Caesar while he was in Egypt. Several of his supporters, notably the tribune Publius Cornelius Dolabella and Cicero's friend

Caelius Rufus, had tried to rally support by advocating the abolition of debt and had had to be suppressed by Mark Antony, who was suspected of having acted too harshly and was replaced as the dictator's subordinate or Master of Horse (*Magister Equitum*) by Marcus Lepidus.

There was also another mutiny among Caesar's veterans, news made all the more bitter because the ringleaders this time came from his own favourite, Legio X. The older soldiers wanted to be discharged and others complained that they had not received the rewards promised once their labours were at an end. These were their public grievances, but boredom may have played as big a part in provoking the outbreak, for throughout history armies have been more prone to mutiny when they are inactive. Caesar arrived back in Italy just as the mutineers were gearing themselves up to march on Rome. His behaviour amazed them when he rode into their camp and addressed them and asked what they wanted. When they shouted out that they wished to be demobilised, Caesar declared that they were discharged and informed them that he would let them have all that he had promised once he had won the war in Africa with other troops. Already stunned, the veterans were horrified when he addressed them as Quirites – civilians rather than soldiers – instead of comrades. It was an incredible display of Caesar's charisma and self-assurance, for soon the legionaries and especially Legio X were begging him to decimate them and take them back into his service.

Caesar was impatient to embark on the African campaign, and spent the bare minimum of time in Rome before hurrying across to Sicily. Reaching the port of Lilybaeum with just one legion, only bad weather prevented him immediately embarking for Africa. Frustrated, he ordered his tent to be pitched on the beach as a public demonstration of his eagerness and confidence. This was in spite of reliable reports stating that Scipio had formed ten legions, supported by four of Juba's as well as many auxiliaries and 120 war elephants. Even when he finally did set sail on 25 December 47, Caesar still had only six legions and 2,000 cavalry. The operation was not well planned, the ships' captains not having been briefed as to where they should land, and this, combined with unfavourable winds, resulted in the fleet becoming scattered. When Caesar disembarked near Hadrumentum, he had only 3,000 legionaries and 150 horsemen. Perhaps his instinctive – and characteristically Roman – boldness was now verging on recklessness, or maybe the stress and exhaustion of so many years of command were taking their toll.

Yet Caesar proved just as capable at improvisation as he always had in the past. Messengers went back to Sicily and Sardinia and soon he had gathered most of his troops. On 3 January 46 he shifted the army's main camp to Ruspina, deposited his baggage there under guard and sent the rest of the troops out foraging. A few days later he led another similar expedition to gather food, taking 30 cohorts, 400 cavalry and 150 archers. The legionaries marched *expedita*, that is, without packs and ready for battle, although the term is often mistranslated as 'lightly armed'. This time they were intercepted by a strong force of enemy cavalry and light infantry led by Labienus, which was later joined by another force under Petreius. Time and again the Numidian light cavalry swooped down on Caesar's line, throwing javelins before they swung round and retired. The legionaries charged forward to catch their attackers, but the Numidians easily evaded the men on foot. Whenever a cohort attacked it was exposed to more missiles from the infantry skirmishers, especially against the men's unshielded right flank. Casualties slowly mounted and progress was slow as the column moved across the open plain. Worse was the effect on the morale of the mostly young soldiers in the army. Their enemy was wearing them down and they were unable to strike back; some began to lose heart. One story, which probably refers to this fight, tells of Caesar grabbing hold of a standard bearer who was beginning to run, turning him around, and saying: 'Look, that's where the enemy are!'

In the meantime Labienus was riding up and down along the line, hurling abuse at Caesar's soldiers in the rough jargon of the camp. An experienced soldier, who had once served with Legio X but was now with another unit, managed to bring down Labienus's horse with his *pilum*, and Caesar's old subordinate was carried from the field. The situation remained desperate. Now surrounded, Caesar stretched his cohorts out into a single line – a rare formation for a

War elephants were used by Pompeians in the African campaign. They were most probably of the African species rather than the Indian elephant shown here. At Thapsus one legionary of V Alaudae won fame when he cut off the the the trunk of an elephant which had seized a camp follower. (AKG Berlin)

Roman army – and had alternate units face about, so that they could throw missiles or charge in either direction. They then charged and drove the enemy back for some distance. Quickly disengaging, the Caesareans used this temporary advantage to march on towards Ruspina, until they were again attacked by a new force of the enemy. Going round the line, Caesar urged his men to a last effort. As darkness was falling they launched an attack against an enemy-held hill blocking their line of march, driving the Numidians off and giving the whole army time to withdraw. Another version claims that Petreius withdrew because he wanted his commander-in-chief Scipio to gain the glory of defeating Caesar.

Caesar became more cautious after this display of enemy strength, sending to Italy and Sicily for supplies and reinforcements. Later in January two legions, XIII and XIV, arrived, along with 800 Gallic cavalry and 1,000 archers and slingers.

Caesar now moved forward to besiege Uzitta, forcing Scipio to come to its support. In spite of Pompeian naval activity, two more legions – VIII and X – arrived and Caesar felt confident enough to offer battle outside the town, although the enemy declined. He also took the opportunity of making an example of one of the tribunes of Legio X who had been heavily involved in last year's mutiny. This man, Avienus, had brought so many servants and horses, along with copious amounts of personal baggage, that he had required an entire ship simply to transport his household. Such extravagance was shocking at a time when Caesar needed every transport to be crammed with soldiers or supplies, and so he publicly rebuked Avienus and dismissed him from the army, along with another tribune and several centurions who were known to have been ringleaders in the mutiny.

Caesar was still having supply difficulties and sent out several expeditions, one of which provoked a large-scale cavalry action in which Labienus was again defeated. The enemy was also sending out detachments to gather food, and Caesar attempted to intercept two legions

isolated from the rest. The operation failed and as it retired his army was harassed by Labienus and a strong force of Numidian light cavalry and infantry skirmishers. Once again his own shortage of cavalry and light infantry made it difficult for Caesar to deal with such attacks. He gave orders that in future 300 soldiers in each legion should march *expedita*, without their packs and ready for action. These troops operated in close support of the cavalry, forming a dense block behind which the horsemen could rally, rest and reform after a charge and so prepare to advance again. This tactic surprised the enemy and caused them to become more cautious. After a period of manoeuvring failed to provoke the enemy to battle and left Caesar camped in an area without an adequate supply of water, on the night of 4 April he led his army out and marched back to Thapsus. The town was still held by the enemy, and the threat prompted Scipio to come to their support, dividing his army into two camps some eight miles from the town.

Thapsus was not easy for an enemy to approach because a wide salt lake permitted access only across a relatively narrow plain from the west or south. Such restricted battlefields offered an effective counter to the numerous and fast-moving Numidian cavalry which might otherwise slip round the flanks of Caesar's army. Even so, when Caesar observed that Scipio had deployed his army with elephants in front of each wing, he took care to strengthen his own flanks. The legions deployed in the usual three lines, with the veteran II and X on the right and equally experienced VIII and IX on the left. He then divided Legio V Alaudae (or 'Larks'), the legion recruited from Gauls, into two sections of five cohorts apiece and stationed each group in a fourth line behind the flanks. His cavalry and light troops were divided into two and stationed on the wings.

The enemy advance was sudden, and Caesar busily rode around marshalling his army and encouraging the soldiers. They could see that the enemy army appeared confused, and the more experienced soldiers urged Caesar to attack immediately, confident that the Pompeians would not stand. Reluctant to enter a battle before his army was ready, Caesar rebuked them for their impertinence and tried to finish drawing up the lines. However, a trumpeter on the right with the veteran legions gave in to the soldiers and sounded the advance. The call was quickly taken up by the musicians in the other cohorts and the whole line began to surge forward. Centurions desperately turned about and tried to restrain the legionaries, but Caesar quickly realised that it was now too late, so he gave the watchword for the day – 'Good Luck' (*Felicitas*) – and spurred his horse towards the enemy. This at least is the version presented by whichever of Caesar's officers wrote the *African War*. Another tradition claims that Caesar began to suffer an epileptic fit and this was the reason why the battle started in such a disorganised way.

However the battle began, it proved to be one of the swiftest of Caesar's victories. The enemy elephants were specially targeted by his archers and slingers, panicking the animals who fled, trampling their own troops. Elsewhere the Pompeian legions gave way with very little fighting. The attack of the Caesarean legionaries was ferocious and they mercilessly cut down even those enemies who tried to surrender. The veterans seemed determined to end the war once and for all. Caesar's casualties were very slight, compared to an enemy loss of many thousands. Cato committed suicide, as did Juba after he had fought a gladiatorial bout with and killed Petreius in a strange suicide pact. Scipio fled by sea, but drowned when his ship sank. Afranius, pardoned once before, this time was captured and executed. However, Labienus and Pompey's two sons escaped to Spain to continue the struggle.

Caesar went back to Rome. In the past he had held the dictatorship for long enough to hold consular elections, but now the Senate voted him into the office for ten years. He held four triumphs over the Gauls, Egyptians, Pharnaces and Juba respectively. Yet, in November 46, he had to leave for Spain to fight the final campaign of the Civil War.

Spain – November 46 – September 45

Cassius had proved both corrupt and incompetent as governor of Spain, alienating both his own troops and the local population. By the time he was replaced by Caius Trebonius, the situation was almost beyond redemption and the new governor was expelled by mutinous soldiers. Pompey's elder son Cnaeus arrived and was rapidly acclaimed as commander of the rebellious legions. He was soon joined by other Pompeians, including his brother Sextus and Labienus. A huge army of 13 legions and many auxiliaries was raised, although the quality of most of the new units was highly questionable.

Caesar travelled rapidly as was his wont, covering the 1,500 miles to Corduba in just 27 days, and whiling away the trip by composing a long poem, *The Journey*. He had eight legions – the best probably being Legio V Alaudae which was experienced but still eager – and the old soldiers of Legio X, and 8,000 cavalry. The early stages of the fighting included a number of fierce skirmishes, but Cnaeus Pompey was reluctant to risk a battle. It was already proving the most brutal campaign of the entire conflict.

The Pompeians were suffering a continual trickle of deserters. Men accused of publicly stating that they thought Caesar would win were arrested. Of these soldiers 74 were executed and the remainder imprisoned. In the middle of March Pompey reached the hilltop town of Munda. Caesar followed in pursuit and camped nearby. The next morning, 17 March 45, he prepared to march after the enemy, but then saw that they were forming up in battle order on the high ground. Pompey had the bulk of 13 legions, a strong force of cavalry, and some 12,000 Spanish auxiliaries, half of them skirmishers. There was a level plain between this rise and the hill on which the Caesarean camp was located. His army marched out to deploy in the usual three lines, Legio X on the right and III and V

The battle of Thapsus

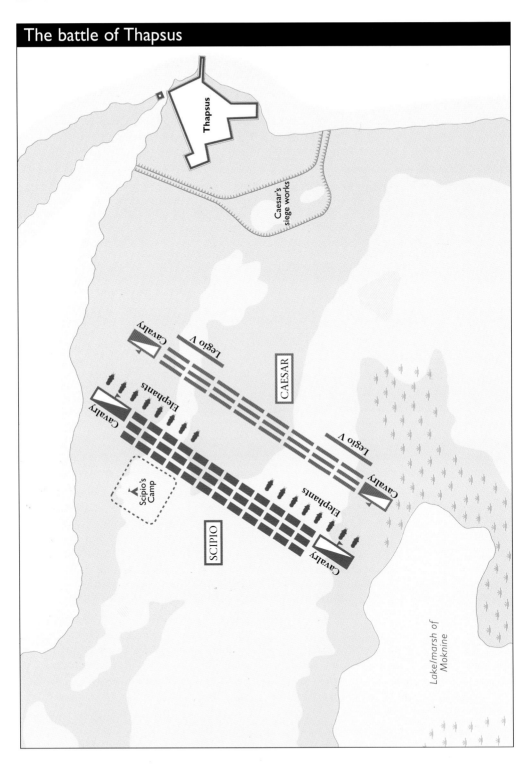

Thapsus

Caesar's siege works

Cavalry

Legio V

CAESAR

Cavalry

Elephants

Legio V

Cavalry

Scipio's Camp

SCIPIO

Elephants

Cavalry

Lake/marsh of Moknine

Alaudae on the left, each flank guarded by cavalry. Once formed, the Caesareans marched down onto the open ground, expecting the enemy to do the same. The Pompeians did not move, keeping to the high ground so that the enemy would have

The battle of Munda

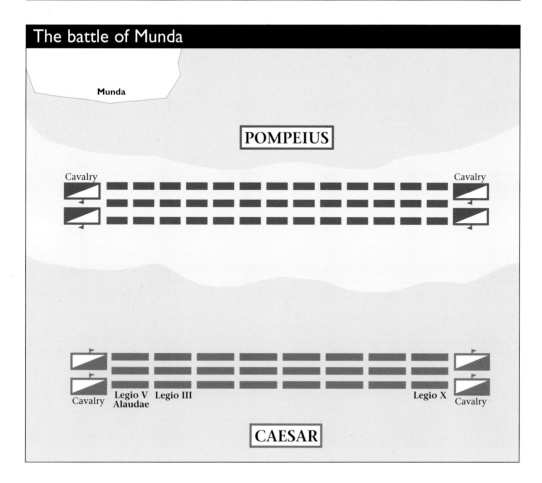

to attack uphill. Caesar's men were as eager as they had been at Thapsus and he attacked anyway, in spite of the disadvantage. The fighting was fierce and determined. One tradition claims that the Caesareans began to waver and that he dismounted and charged alone against the enemy, rallying first his officers and then the remainder of the army. In the end, the veterans of Legio X started to drive back the enemy left. Pompey tried to shift troops from his right to plug the gap, but Caesar's cavalry renewed the pressure on that flank and pinned the legions there. At last the

Pompeians broke and were slaughtered in great numbers. All 13 eagles were taken, and most of the enemy leaders, including Cnaeus Pompey and Labienus, were killed in the next few days. Some 1,000 Caesareans had fallen, a heavier loss than in any of the earlier victories and testimony to hard fighting. Munda was blockaded, the legionaries grimly fixing the severed heads of Pompeians to spikes topping their rampart. The mopping-up took several months. Caesar had won the Civil War, but now it remained to be seen whether he could win the peace.

Caesar's legionaries

No personal account written by an ordinary soldier or junior officer survives for the Civil War. In the surviving narratives only a handful of men from the ranks are even mentioned by name, usually because they performed some conspicuous act of heroism. We know that soldiers were primarily recruited from the poorer classes. In normal circumstances most, if not all, were volunteers, but during civil wars many were probably unwilling conscripts. Soldiering had become a career, but the wages were low, lower than a man could earn as a labourer on the land or as a casual worker in the city. When Caesar doubled the pay of his soldiers, an ordinary legionary still received only 225 denarii (1,000 sesterces) a year. We do not know whether or not there were fixed terms of service, and the traditional maximum of 16 years may still have been in force, although during the civil wars some men served for more than two decades. Active campaigning, especially in a prosperous area, might bring greater rewards in the form of plunder, either taken individually or as the soldier's share in the booty acquired by the entire army. The most successful generals rewarded their soldiers lavishly. Conditions in the army were basic and the discipline brutal. At the whim of his centurion a man could be flogged, and many other crimes were punishable by death. At the end of their service, soldiers hoped to be provided with some source of livelihood. Usually this meant the grant of a plot of land, which suggests that many recruits were still coming from rural areas.

Legionaries were men who had received little from the Republic or the Senate and had small interest in maintaining it. They identified far more strongly with their legion, the community in which they lived for many years. The legions of this period had a far greater sense of corporate identity than the temporary militia legions of the Middle Republic. They kept a number, and sometimes a name, for many years, marching

under their eagle standard. Even at Munda, and in spite of earlier mutiny and indiscipline, it was the depleted veterans of Legio X who made the critical breakthrough. In fact these men would go on to play a prominent role in the civil war after Caesar's death. A good commander could inspire incredible devotion in his men. Caesar had been lavish with his plunder in Gaul, although during the Civil War he was less willing to permit his men to profit from

defeating fellow citizens. Yet it was not simply financial self-interest that bonded his soldiers so closely to him. Caesar's army developed almost a cult of heroism, especially bravery performed in the sight of all. Their commander shared the rigours of campaign

This figure from the altar of Domitius Ahenobarbus shows a figure – sometimes indentified as the war god Mars – dressed in the uniform of a senior officer. Many of the senatorial and equestrian officers during the Civil War may have looked very similar. (AKG Berlin)

with his men, leading them on marches and in battle. In his speeches he called them comrades and spoke of their shared efforts. Even if our sources exaggerate a little when they claim that no Caesarean soldier ever deserted to the enemy, it is certainly true that defections were far more common from Pompey's legions. In his *Commentaries*, Caesar repeatedly claims that he explained to his soldiers the wrongs done to him and the ill-treatment of the tribunes of the plebs. It is hard to know how far such concerns swayed his soldiers, and whether their prominence in his accounts has more to do with the intended audience for these works.

By no means all the soldiers fighting in the Civil War were Romans. Many non-citizens were swept into the legions, although each side tended to accuse the other of doing this. There were also large numbers of foreign auxiliaries, often serving under their own tribal leaders. The chieftains of Gallic, German and other tribal peoples displayed their status by the number of warriors in their personal following. They supported these men, some of whom might come from outside the tribe, feeding them and rewarding their courage, and in turn the warriors were obliged to fight for them. Their loyalty was to the person of the chieftain, rather than a tribe, nation or cause. Therefore the warriors fought for one of the sides in the Civil War simply because their chief had chosen to do so, and if the leader chose to stop fighting or change sides, then his warriors followed. When the Allobrogian brothers Roucillus and Egus defected, the warriors of their household automatically went with them. The bond between chieftain and warriors was exceptionally close and similar relations could develop even if the commander was not a native chieftain. Caesar had a bodyguard of 900 German and Gallic cavalry, and Labienus was followed by another unit of tribesmen who proved just as loyal to him. Later Cleopatra received a bodyguard of Gauls.

While the ordinary legionaries receive little individual mention in our sources, a far more prominent role is reserved for the

centurions. Time and again Caesar explains the success of his legions as being due to the courage and leadership of these officers. Even in disasters, the heroism of his centurions often provided the one bright note. It has often been assumed that the vast majority of centurions were promoted from amongst the ranks of the ordinary soldiers after long and distinguished service. Sometimes they are compared to the sergeant-majors who provide the backbone of many modern armies. There is virtually no evidence for this view, and certainly Caesar never once mentions a centurion promoted from the ranks, although he frequently refers to centurions being promoted to higher grades. It is far more likely that many centurions entered the army in that capacity, or as one of the junior officers within the century, and that they were recruited from the better-educated and reasonably well-off classes, rather than from the very poor who provided the mass of the ordinary legionaries. Both in Cicero and Caesar centurions appear as far more politically significant than the ordinary soldiers. Centurions were professional officers, rather than professional soldiers.

The deeds of several centurions are recorded in some detail in our sources. One such man was Scaeva, who made a name for himself at Dyrrachium. He was a centurion in one of the three cohorts holding an isolated fort that was attacked by an entire enemy legion supported by many archers and slingers. Fighting ferociously, Scaeva's shield is supposed to have been hit by 120 missiles. In the end, like many of his colleagues, he was struck by an arrow in the eye. Wounded, he called out to the enemy as if to surrender. When two men sprang forward to take such a distinguished prisoner, Scaeva killed one and sliced the arm of the other. His stubbornness inspired his men to continue the struggle. Caesar promoted him to the post of *primus pilus*, along with a bounty of 50,000 denarii, and publicly praised him. Although he is not mentioned again, there is some evidence to suggest that Scaeva continued to have a distinguished military career. The tombstone of a former cavalry trooper from Gallia Narbonensis, which probably dates to the 30s BC, records his unit as the Ala Scaevae (cavalry regiment of Scaeva). Thus it seems that Scaeva went on to command a unit of Gallic auxiliary cavalry. The bold centurion described by Caesar would certainly seem an ideal candidate to act as chieftain for a group of such warriors.

A former *primus pilus* of Legio X figures prominently in Caesar's account of Pharsalus. This man, one Crastinus, had rejoined the army and now commanded a unit of 120 other veterans who had returned to service. He is supposed to have addressed the men, telling them that this battle would win back

Caesar's position and allow them to retire again, their duty to him fulfilled. Turning to Caesar as he rode past, marshalling the army, he called out: 'Today, general, I shall earn your thanks whether I live or die.' Crastinus and his men led the charge, hacking their way into the enemy ranks. He was finally killed when a sword was thrust into his mouth and came out at the back of his neck. Caesar ordered men to search for him after

This tombstone from Capua commemorates the brothers Canuleius, both of whom served in Caesar's Legion VII. Quintus was only 18 when he was killed during the campaigns in Gaul, but it is possible that Caius, who died at the age of 35, served in the Civil War. Military tombstones from this period are very rare.

The tombstone of Publius Gessius was found at Viterbo in Italy and is thought to date to the middle of the first century BC. The inscription makes no mention of any military service, but Gessius is shown wearing a cuirass and with the hilt of a gladius just visible. (Boston Museum of Fine Arts)

the battle and after laying military decorations on his corpse – a rare thing, for the Romans did not usually give posthumous awards – buried him in a special tomb away from the massed grave of the other casualties.

In the army of the imperial period, it became very common for soldiers to erect engraved monuments recording the details of their military career, but this practice was only just beginning in the Late Republic. One of Pompey's centurions, a man called Granonius, from Luceria in Italy, died at Athens and was commemorated on a tombstone, probably sometime in 49–48. One man who may have served at the very beginning of the Civil War and had certainly fought under Caesar in Gaul, was Caius Canuleius of Legio VII. He was commemorated by his father on a monument, along with his brother who had been killed in Gaul at the age of 18 while serving with Legio VII. Some other men who are commemorated on tombstones and memorials from the late first century BC may well have fought in the Civil War, but little or no detail is given as to their length of service, so such information must remain conjecture.

A Mediterranean war

The Civil War affected the entire Roman world and ultimately destroyed a centuries-old political system. Many ordinary citizens were swept up into the armies, to serve in brutal conditions. Some died in battle, many more probably through disease and privations, while others were permanently crippled. At least some soldiers, especially auxiliary troops such as Gauls, were accompanied on campaign by their wives and children, who in turn suffered from the rigours of hard journeys and poor food. Yet it was not just soldiers and their families who were caught up in the conflict, for many civilian communities also suffered. An extreme case was a town like Gomphi in Thessaly, which Caesar permitted his soldiers to sack in an effort to restore their spirits after the retreat from Dyrrachium. In such circumstances Roman soldiers were extremely brutal, impossible for their officers to restrain even had they wished to do so. Caesar deliberately did not march into Corfinum at night in 49 because he did not trust his men to keep their discipline once they slipped off into the dark streets, and he did not wish to begin the campaign by plundering an Italian city. In 46, it was also considered a considerable achievement when Caesar's men were camped outside Hadrumentum and he was able to prevent them from plundering it.

Communities within the area of any of the campaigns were likely to suffer even if they were not subjected to a sack. The armies needed food in vast quantities. Most hoped to gain as much of this as possible from willing allies or to ship supplies in from elsewhere, but this was not always possible, especially as operations became more protracted. The needs of the local population mattered little when the armies sent out foraging expeditions to gather up all the grain and cattle they could find. There were also cases when the armies clashed within urban areas, often causing damage. The siege of Caesar's small force in Alexandria brought considerable destruction on the city, as buildings were demolished or set on fire.

The Civil War pitted legion against legion and made Rome vulnerable to foreign enemies. The most spectacular success was enjoyed by Pharnaces, until his army was destroyed at Zela. Other threats failed to materialise. Parthia had already invaded Syria once after its victory over Crassus, and seemed on the brink of doing so once again in late 50. Internal problems, during which the victorious commander at Carrhae was executed by the king as a potential rival, absorbed Parthia and delayed a new offensive. In the west, Caesar's conquest of Gaul had been quick and spectacularly successful, but the new province had not yet been properly consolidated. In fact there were no repeats of the rebellions that had broken out between 54 and 51 during Caesar's lifetime, but it did take another generation and further unrest before the province was fully pacified. Other allied countries sought to benefit from involvement in the Civil War. Deiotarus sent troops to aid Pompey in part because he was his client but also in the hope of securing his kingdom. Juba's attitude was similar. In Egypt the rivals in their own civil war tried to win favour from victors in the Roman conflict, Cleopatra gaining greatly from this and preserving some measure of independence for an area that had been in something of an anomalous position between ally and province for some time.

'Sulla did not know his political alphabet' – Caesar's dictatorship

In the first years of the Civil War Caesar spent little time in Rome. In 46 he spent the greater part of the year there, having just been appointed dictator for ten years, and then after his return from Spain in October 45 remained there until his assassination on 15 March 44. The rest of the time Caesar was busy on campaign and ruled Rome through deputies. He was planning to leave once again to fight a war in the Balkans against Dacia and then to move east and confront Parthia in spring 44, a task which at the very least would have kept him away from Italy for several years. Yet, although he spent little time in the city, the period of Caesar's rule profoundly and permanently changed the nature of Roman political life. Caesar is supposed to have declared frequently that Sulla showed his political illiteracy when he resigned his dictatorship. Evidently, Caesar did not plan to withdraw from politics and so the Republic would inevitably be dominated by a single all-powerful individual on a permanent basis, the very thing Rome's constitution was supposed to avoid.

However, it is much harder to say precisely what sort of position Caesar envisaged for himself in the long term. Civil war was renewed within months of his death, as his supporters sought vengeance against his murderers, and it was obviously in the interests of both sides to distort the record of what Caesar had done and, even more, what he planned to do. The conspirators needed to show that Caesar was bent on becoming an autocratic monarch who would have denied freedom to the rest of the Senate. Therefore he had to be killed because of what he would become. Caesar's heirs and supporters maintained the opposite view, pointing out that Caesar's rule had been and would have continued to be benevolent and that he had not wanted to become anything as un-Roman as a king. We have very few contemporary sources for details of the last months of Caesar's life, since most of Cicero's letters from that period were not preserved, and virtually all our accounts are later and inevitably influenced by the propaganda of both sides. Eventually Caesar's adopted son Octavian (Augustus) would make himself Rome's first

emperor after his defeat of Mark Antony and Cleopatra in 31. As part of the adoption, his name became Caius Julius Caesar Octavianus. Therefore if either Caesar himself or Octavian passed a law, it would be recorded as a Julian law *(lex Julia)*, and if they founded a colony it would be a Julian colony *(colonia Julia)*. This makes it very easy to confuse the actions of the two men, and it is not always clear when Augustus actually implemented a measure that Caesar had planned.

Initially Caesar was given a ten-year dictatorship with the additional title of *praefectus morum* (prefect of morals). This was an invention that seems to have given him most of the powers of the censors, in particular the ability to appoint and expel senators and add names to the roll of citizens. In effect his power was greater than the consuls and, not only did he sit among the magistrates, but his opinion was always called for first. Even more importantly, he appointed all the significant magistrates. This provided him not only with control of the important offices of state, but also with the ability to reward the loyalty of his followers during the Civil War. The Senate grew enormously in size as Caesar's partisans were rewarded. By his death it had almost 1,000 members, compared with the 600 established by Sulla. Many of the new appointments were considered utterly unsuitable by traditionalists, for throughout the war Caesar's party had been seen as a haven for all the disreputable men and failures in the state. As Cicero joked grimly, how could you expect such men to guide the Republic when they could not even manage their own fortunes for a couple of months? Rumours circulated that in former years Caesar had gone round recruiting such wastrels by telling them that what they really needed was a civil war to restore their fortunes. Other appointments were unpopular, less because of the reputation of the individuals in question, but because of their nationality, for there were many aristocrats from the towns of Italy. In addition, Caesar, who had as consul granted citizenship to Cisalpine Gaul and during his campaigns extended the franchise to many noblemen north of the Alps, appointed several Gallic senators. This move again prompted caustic comments about barbarians, only recently bereft of their trousers and put into a toga, wandering aimlessly around the city as they failed to find the forum. Throughout his career Caesar had taken pride in always rewarding those who assisted him, and his actions as dictator simply confirmed this.

Sulla had filled his enlarged Senate with his partisans. Caesar to a great extent did the same thing. However, although most of the older and more famous senators who had sided against him were now dead, other, younger, men who had received Caesar's clemency were taken back and given honours and magistracies. Brutus and Cassius, the two main leaders in the conspiracy that would murder Caesar, had both fought against him in 49–48. Caesar appointed both men to the praetorship in 45. Yet all such honours were devalued by the freedom with which he doled them out to his supporters. The number of praetorships was increased to accommodate the number of men whose loyalty demanded a magistracy. The number of consuls was not increased from two, but Caesar encouraged men to resign before their year of office, allowing him to appoint others as suffect or replacement consuls. Such men were entitled to all the insignia of the full rank. An extreme case was Caius Caninius Rebilus, who had served as an officer with Caesar throughout much of the Civil War. When one of the consuls for 45 died on the last day of his office, Caesar appointed Caninius to hold a suffect consulship for less than 24 hours. Cicero quipped that he proved one of the Republic's most dedicated magistrates, never sleeping a wink while he held power, and that everyone needed to rush and congratulate the new consul before he had to relinquish it. In spite of this he, and many other senators, resented Caesar's disdainful treatment of the hallowed offices of the Republic.

At first Caesar was assisted by the dictator's traditional subordinate, the Master of Horse (*Magister Equitum*), a post held by Antony and later Lepidus. In 45 eight prefects were appointed to aid the Master of Horse, marking another stage between Pompey's indirect rule of his Spanish provinces and the use of legates and prefects by the later emperors to govern the empire. Though large, the Senate lacked any real freedom of debate and was becoming distanced from the main decision-making processes that tended to occur in private and involved only Caesar and his trusted advisers. If senators had, in 59 and afterwards, resented the need to go to one of the triumvirs if they wanted to secure any post or favour for a client, now the situation was much worse. It is possible that Caesar had become too accustomed to supreme military command to adapt his style of leadership to the more tactful needs of political life. He had spent most of his life for more than a decade issuing orders, which had always ultimately resulted in success. Caesar knew his own abilities, trusting them far more than he trusted the capacity of anyone else. His manner often suggested impatience with display and the feelings of others whom he did not respect.

On one occasion he caused offence when he failed to rise from his work and greet the consuls as soon as they came into his presence. The people loved the lavish games and spectacles he staged in Rome, but did not like his habit of listening to and answering correspondence while he sat in his box.

Caesar certainly displayed all the energy he had shown as an army commander during his dictatorship and the range of reforms he initiated during such a short time is truly remarkable. In some cases this consisted of tidying up an existing situation, as when he reformed the constitutions of the towns in Italy. The provinces too were affected, with renewal of the taxation system, usually in favour of the provincials. Plans were drawn up for a massive programme of colonisation throughout the provinces. This was to include

This coin was minted by Caesar during his dictatorship and shows him wearing the laurel wreath of a triumphant general. The right to wear this on all public occasions was especially attractive to Caesar, who had lost much of his hair. (AKG Berlin)

not only the vast number of soldiers enrolled during the Civil War and now nearing retirement or no longer required, but also a significant number of the urban poor. Caesar had resisted pressure to abolish debt completely, the habitual desire of many citizens who lacked regular employment and lived in rented apartments, and arranged a more equitable system of repayment, but this measure would have eased the plight of many as well as adding to the number of prosperous citizens. It is uncertain just how many of these colonies were actually founded, for as mentioned above they are easily confused with the more numerous Augustan foundations. However, the programme was certainly already underway in Transalpine Gaul by the time of Caesar's death and had probably also begun elsewhere. Perhaps as many as 100,000 colonists were settled in Spain, Gaul and Africa.

The removal of part of Rome's population, which by this time was close to the one million mark, helped to relieve some of the city's problems. Laws were passed banning the trade guilds which men like Clodius and Milo had turned into gangs of thugs, although this measure may not have achieved much, as it still allowed 'legitimate' organisations. The number of poor citizens receiving a handout of wheat purchased and distributed by the state was reduced by more than half to only 150,000 recipients, many of those removed from the list being sent out as colonists. As a further measure to improve the food supply to the city, Caesar ordered the construction of a massive new harbour at Ostia, but this does not appear to have moved beyond the planning stage. A major building programme was begun in Rome, with older temples and public buildings being heavily restored and new monuments built. An entire forum complex, the Forum Julium, containing a new Senate House or curia to replace the one burnt down by Clodius' supporters, was begun. Occupying a prominent place within the complex was a grand temple dedicated to his divine ancestor, Venus Genetrix. Apart from making the city more splendid, projects such as this provided work for large numbers of the urban poor who might otherwise be a source of instability.

Apart from the grand parades that marked Caesar's triumphs in 46 and 45, he held many spectacular public entertainments, and in particular gladiatorial displays. On a more cultural note, a large public library was planned, supervised by the polymath (wide-ranging scholar) Varro. Caesar seems to have interested himself in practically everything, and probably his most enduring measure was the reform of the calendar. The traditional Roman calendar required constant attention from the priests, and had long since ceased to conform to the natural season, creating problems for Rome's political year. Caesar replaced this with a calendar of twelve 30-day solar months. In 46, 67 days were added to the year so that the new calendar would begin at the right time. The modern Gregorian calendar, created in the late sixteenth century and slowly adopted throughout the world, modified Caesar's system but left it substantially intact. The month of July still bears the name of the Roman dictator.

Cicero and the Civil War

The Civil War presented the vast majority of Romans with a dilemma, for it was clear that joining either side or remaining inactive all had their perils. As we have seen, only a minority even among the Senate actually wanted war. The letters written and received by the great orator Cicero during these last months of peace and the years of war provide us with a remarkable insight into these times and the impact of the war on one man, his family and friends. The majority of these letters were to his long-time friend and correspondent Atticus, an equestrian who remained outside formal politics and yet seemed to know, and have friendly relations with, every prominent Roman in this period.

Marcus Tullius Cicero was a 'new man', the first in his family to reach the consulship. His rise was almost entirely due to his skill as an orator, for his fame came more from winning famous cases in the courts than military achievements. Almost an exact contemporary of Pompey, Cicero had advanced his career through the same turbulent decades of civil war, dictatorship and attempted coups and revolutions. His great moment came as consul in 63, when he presided over the defeat and punishment of Catiline's conspirators. In spite of his fame, Cicero did not have the wealth, influence and client-base of a Pompey, Crassus or Caesar and would never be more than one of a number of distinguished senators. His vulnerability had been made all too clear in 58, when Clodius had forced him into exile for alleged illegal behaviour during his consulship. Although this was only temporary, it had proved that he could not rely on the support and protection of men like Pompey.

On 24 November 50 as tension grew in Rome, Cicero arrived back at Brundisium after a year-long tenure as proconsul of Cilicia in Asia Minor. This in itself was an indirect consequence of the machinations of Caesar's opponents, for the law decreeing a five-year interval between magistracy and governorship had created a shortage of provincial governors. As a result, men like Cicero, who had been consul over a decade before and had no real ambition to go to a province, were required to fulfil their obligations. In Cilicia he did his best to govern well, preparing the defences in case the Parthians, flushed with their success at Carrhae, launched the expected invasion. When this did not materialise he conducted a minor campaign against the tribesmen of Mount Amanus, for which he hoped to receive a triumph. In spite of the continuing Parthian threat, Cicero left at the first legal opportunity, arriving back in Rome just in the last period of peace. As a governor he still had *imperium*, which he could not lay down if he wanted to be granted a triumph. In fact in the end he was only granted the lesser honour of a 'supplication', which was probably more in keeping with the scale of his success.

Cicero's correspondents had kept him well informed about the impending crisis. He had always been closer to Pompey than Caesar, though Pompey's failure to protect him from Clodius still rankled. When Pompey had been allied with Crassus and Caesar, Cicero had aided them, for instance, delivering a powerful speech in favour of extending Caesar's initial command in Gaul, while his brother Quintus had served as one of Caesar's legates in Gaul. Even before he reached Rome, Cicero was writing to Atticus saying that, publicly, he would vote with Pompey, although in private he would urge him to strive for peace. Caesar's supporters he saw as wastrels, most of them young and

Cicero was the greatest orator of his day and was also a prolific author. His letters, which were published after his death, provide a very vivid picture of the period of the Civil War. (AKG Berlin)

already associated with criminal activity. Yet he realised their strength, claiming that the only thing Caesar's side 'lacked was a good cause, since they had everything else in abundance'. Yet already Cicero could not help wondering why this situation had been allowed to occur. Would it not have been better to have opposed Caesar when he was weaker, rather than waiting until the Senate itself had granted him honours and power, making him a far more dangerous opponent. Caesar had been allowed to win office because the Senate had not effectively opposed him when he was weak and vulnerable.

By the middle of December Cicero was outside Rome and began to realise just how divided the Senate was over the issue. The vast majority, both in the Senate and the equestrian order, wanted peace. Most were also dubious about Pompey's intentions and what would happen once he defeated Caesar. As Cicero put it, 'from victory (for Pompey and the Senate) will come many evils, and certainly a tyrant.' Seeing just how strong was the desire for peace, he again wondered why they had allowed Caesar so much power if they were only going to fight him in the long run. When war finally came, Cicero's correspondence became filled with the rumours that circulated among the nervous citizens. He could not understand Pompey's decision to leave Rome and then not to make any effort to defend the city, seeing this as an open admission of weakness. He remained there for a few days, before retiring to the country. He corresponded with Pompey and Caesar as well as many other friends, most of whom urged him to declare himself more openly.

Marcus Caelius Rufus was one of that wild, irresponsible generation that figured so heavily in the radical politics of the Late Republic, but he remained very friendly with Cicero, who had successfully defended him in court. During his tenure in Cilicia, Caelius had sent a series of gossipy letters packed with news and scandal from the city. Now he had joined Caesar, feeling that even if Pompey might have the more honourable cause, then Caesar certainly had the better army, which was what counted as soon as a political dispute spilled over into open war.

Pompey's decision to abandon Italy and instead build up his power in the east dismayed Cicero along with many others. It also added to his own uncertainty, made worse because he had still not laid down his *imperium* as proconsul and therefore had the power to command troops. During these months his letters to Atticus were probably more frequent than at any other time in his life, and on some days he wrote more than one. Pompey's strategy seemed misguided, and yet still he felt a loyalty to him and gratitude, even if he did not really believe in his cause. Both Caesar and several of his associates begged Cicero to return to Rome, for he wanted to summon a legitimate

Senate, and the presence of a distinguished ex-consul would add greatly to its authority. There is a strange, almost unreal quality about some of these letters, as Caesar's associates quote their commander's letters reporting that his army has cornered Pompey in Brundisium and telling of the progress of the siege. At the end of March, as Caesar returned to Rome, he called on Cicero and in person assured him of his respect and tried to persuade him to go back to Rome. Cicero said that if he came, he would say that the Senate could not approve of Caesar taking his legions to fight in Spain or Greece, and then lament Pompey's fate. When Caesar replied that he did not want such sentiments expressed publicly, Cicero explained that he could not go to Rome and speak under any other circumstances, which was why he chose to remain in the country.

Caesar left soon afterwards for the Spanish campaign, and Cicero began to wonder about belatedly following Pompey, or perhaps travelling simply to stay out of the conflict. Caelius marched with Caesar and in April wrote to Cicero during the march, telling him that he ought not to join the enemy, for Caesar was already gaining a marked advantage. Around the same time Curio stopped at Cicero's villa en route to Sicily. Cicero found him as boastful and unrestrained in his speech as ever, and was disturbed to hear that Curio also believed that Caesar's clemency was a temporary ploy and that his true nature would eventually assert itself. In the end, after continued heart-searching, he decided to embark for Macedonia and join Pompey's army. His teenage son, also called Marcus, was already there, having volunteered to serve as a cavalry officer. What Cicero found in the Pompeian camp dismayed him, for the senators had become increasingly extreme, and spoke of extreme punishments not simply for Caesar's partisans, but also for anyone who had remained neutral. Pompey seemed to lack his old confidence and purpose and there was little sense of unity among the commanders. Illness kept him from the field at Pharsalus where the defeat confirmed his low opinion of the army. In the aftermath as an ex-consul still possessed of proconsular *imperium*, Cato is supposed to have offered him command of the survivors, but Cicero declined and returned to Italy.

Caesar's long stay in Egypt, and the lack of communication from him for months on end were incomprehensible. All Cicero wanted was for the war to end, and for at least some semblance of normality to return to Roman politics, but now that Caesar had won the war, he failed to end it utterly. Cicero waited near Brundisium for the victor to return, nervously wondering how he would be treated. In the event, Caesar proved extremely friendly, but even so Cicero spent increasingly little time in formal politics and more writing philosophical works. Part of him hoped that Caesar could guide the state and allow a gradual return to the proper institutions of the Republic. Yet the reality of Caesar's supremacy, and the dictator's continued reliance on the dubious individuals who had proved loyal to him in the past, steadily alienated him. Cicero was not involved in the conspiracy, although since the letters to Atticus for the months before Caesar's death were not published it is possible that his friend was implicated in some small way, but wished to conceal this by the time that the letters were published. He had high hopes of better things after the deed and, for almost a year, once again took a leading role in politics. His respect for Brutus was considerable, even though he had seen the ruthless and unscrupulous side of his character during his own governorship of Cilicia, where Brutus' agents had demanded four times the legal rate of interest on a loan given to the city of Salamis. Even so, he was not persuaded by Brutus when the latter argued that he should not encourage Octavian's ambitions, lest they raise up another Caesar. Cicero saw Antony as the real enemy, and was willing to deploy any means to destroy him. He failed, and himself perished, leaving his letters, speeches and philosophical books as a permanent memorial.

The Ides of March

On 15 February 44, Caesar's dictatorship and other powers were extended for life. A month later he was stabbed to death by a group of senators that included men who had served him for years, as well as pardoned Pompeians. Before discussing why the conspirators acted in this way, we must consider the difficult question of Caesar's own long-term aims – a subject of continuing scholarly debate and little agreement. It has often been stated that the Roman Republic failed and was replaced by the rule of emperors because the system, designed to regulate the public affairs of a city-state, could not cope with the changed circumstances of governing a world empire. There is some truth in this as we have seen, for during the last years of the Republic it became increasingly difficult to accommodate and regulate the competition between a few overwhelmingly powerful individuals. At the same time the Senate failed to acknowledge the emergence of a professional army or to do anything to provide for discharged soldiers who were no longer men of property, encouraging them to a closer bond with generals who offered them more. Yet, even under the empire, the institutions of Rome were to a great extent those of a city-state, but the emperors imposed more control of the system and encouraged the integration of first Italy and then the provinces. Institutions developed to support a permanent army, kept loyal to the emperor alone. Senators still held most of the senior positions in imperial government, although usually with authority delegated from the emperor, but the number of people, both citizen and non-citizen, benefiting from the regime was greatly increased. The empire, or Principate as it is more often known, gave Rome and the provinces a remarkable level of stability, broken only

twice by civil war in the first two centuries of its existence, in comparison to the period from 133 BC to 31 BC.

Augustus was Caesar's adopted heir, had risen to power as his father's avenger, and copied some of Caesar's innovations to create the Principate, although in other respects he learned from the dictator's mistakes and did things very differently. The Roman Republic faced many political, social, economic and military problems in the first century, and it is worth considering to what extent Caesar was aware of these. He had fought the Civil War to maintain his own honour and political status. Had a compromise been reached that permitted him to stand for a second consulship and go on to a further provincial command, the future would have been very different, with Rome dominated by two great men, Caesar and Pompey, instead of just one. This did not occur and, whether or not Caesar had long aimed at supreme power, he did achieve it through his victory. His reforms as dictator were wide ranging, but did they have the coherence of a clear plan to solve Rome's problems, whether or not the solutions in themselves were practical?

There are essentially two ways of viewing Caesar. The first is to see him as a man perceptive enough to understand that the Republican constitution could no longer function. Throughout his career he had taken considerable interest in the conditions of the poor in Rome and the native population in Rome's provinces, and realised that the territories could not be run simply for the selfish benefit of a tiny élite in Rome. Observing the incompetence and weakness of the Senate as a group and of individual senators, and contrasting this with his own abilities, Caesar knew that the state needed to be guided by a single individual who could discern the general good and act accordingly. In this way he tried to bring to Rome the stability it would gain from the Principate, and failed only because the Romans were not yet ready for this revolution; and perhaps because he let his impatience show. If Caesar thought in this way, then he may not have been entirely unique. On several occasions Cicero had talked of the need for the Republic to have a rector, a powerful leader who would help to guide the Senate and magistrates in making decisions for the common good. He had hoped that Pompey might fulfil this role, but even at his most optimistic had lower expectations for Caesar. Cicero's rector was certainly a less powerful figure than the dictator Caesar had become.

The alternative is to see Caesar more as an aristocrat steeped in the traditions of the Senate than as a visionary. Caesar, like all

This coin bears the head of Marcus Junius Brutus, one of the principal leaders of the conspiracy which murdered Caesar. Brutus was highly respected for his learning and conduct and was a particular favourite of Caesar, who pardoned him even though he fought for Pompey at Pharsalus. Brutus committed suicide after the Second Battle of Philippi in 42. (Barber Institute of Fine Arts)

This coin was also minted by the conspirators during their war with Caesar's heirs. it shows two daggers and in the centre the cap traditionally worn by a slave after he had been given his freedom. Beneath is the simple date, the Ides of March (EID Mars). (Barber Institute of Fine Arts)

men of his class and upbringing, wished to have a distinguished public career, holding high office and winning fame and glory on the state's behalf. Perhaps because his family had for generations been removed from the inner circle of the Senate, or perhaps just because he was aware of his own great gifts, his ambition was especially great, and he not only wished to succeed, but to achieve more than anyone else. This is the man who is supposed to have said that it would be harder to push him down from first to second place in the state than from second to last. He pursued his ambition with relentless purpose, adopting any radical measure to achieve his ends, even to the extent of fighting a civil war. By 45 Caesar had achieved his objective, for all potential rivals were dead and he was able to celebrate more and greater triumphs than any other Roman, permanently commemorating his achievements in a massive building programme. That he now had supreme authority in the state and the ability to reform the Republic were largely incidental. There was no grand plan for solving Rome's problems, for Caesar was either unaware of them or could not think of any way of solving them. Instead he wasted his energy with huge numbers of unconnected initiatives and reforms, tinkering with minor problems rather than confronting the real issues. It was not long before he wished again for the simple objectives of an army commander, and so decided to leave his political problems behind and instead to go and fight long wars in Dacia and Parthia.

We do not know what Caesar's long-term plans were, and the contradictory propaganda of both sides after his death will probably forever make these uncertain. Perhaps he was a mixture of the two extremes. Certainly there is no evidence that he planned ever to resign his considerable powers, but whether he thought of these as personal, or planned to create a permanent position of dictator, emperor or king and to pass this on to a successor is impossible to state with certainty. At the time many Romans certainly feared that this would happen, and at least some of the conspirators thought that they were striking a blow for liberty, in the sense of desiring that Roman aristocrats had freedom to pursue their political careers without the supervision of one all-powerful individual.

Brutus, one of the leaders of the conspiracy and the man felt by all to have had the most altruistic motives, certainly acted because he feared what Caesar might become. Married to the daughter of Cato, and a learned and serious student of philosophy himself, Brutus objected to the idea of a dictator or king, but did not hate Caesar himself. Caesar was indeed very fond of Brutus, and had once had an affair with his mother, the lively and intelligent Servilia, whom he appears to have regarded far more highly than any of his other mistresses with the exception of Cleopatra. This relationship prompted rumours, undoubtedly false but no less persistent for all that, that Brutus was in fact Caesar's illegitimate son. Others among the conspiracy acted more from personal hatred, or in the case of his former officers, who included Decimus Brutus and Caius Trebonius, disappointment with their rewards.

Caesar had already been voted many exceptional honours, not unprecedented but usually on a grander scale than any of his predecessors. Caesar's link with the goddess Venus seemed to be more public and was represented as closer than the claims of past commanders, such as Sulla and Pompey, to be especially favoured by the gods. A temple was dedicated to Caesar's Clementia, the clemency with which he had pardoned so many of his bitter enemies. In public Caesar was granted the right always to wear a laurel wreath – an honour which is said to have especially pleased him for he was concerned over his growing baldness – as well as the other robes of a triumphing general, and he sat on a gilded chair instead of the magistrate's simpler seat. Rumours abounded that he wished to go a stage further and become a king, perhaps after the model of the Hellenistic world where the monarch was considered to be a god. When a crowd hailed him as rex (king), he replied that he was 'Not Rex, but Caesar' for Rex was also a family name in Rome. Later he made great show of refusing a crown offered to him by the mob.

Yet his behaviour gave sufficient grounds for doubting his long-term intentions. He dressed in the long-sleeved tunic and high boots of the kings of Alba Longa, a long-vanished city that had been a rival of early Rome, and from the royal family of which the Julii Caesares claimed descent. Caesar, having lost his only legitimate child, Julia, had already adopted his nephew Octavian as his heir, sending the teenager to Greece to prepare for the eastern expedition, but it was not clear whether he was to inherit just his private possessions or also his position. Even more worryingly, Cleopatra had come to Italy and been openly installed in a big house as Caesar's mistress. A statue of the Egyptian queen was placed next to that of the goddess in Caesar's great temple to Venus. Wild rumours circulated about special

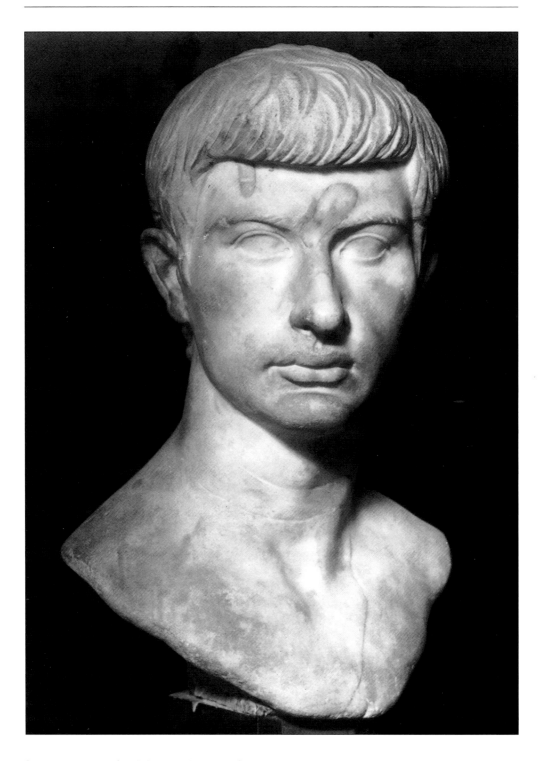

Persistent, although unfounded rumour claimed that Brutus was
in fact Caesar's illegitimate son. More than any of the other
conspirators he was believed to have been motivated by his
sense of the common good rather than personal ambition or
vindictiveness. (AKG Berlin)

legislation being planned to permit Caesar to marry her. After Caesar's death a boy was produced by the queen and Mark Antony, who claimed that he was Caesar's illegitimate son and named him Caesarion, claiming that the dictator had acknowledged him. There is no contemporary record of the child dating to before March 44, and considerable doubt must exist as to his actual paternity. Another rumour current at the time spoke of an ancient prophecy, part of the Sybilline Books that had often guided the Republic at times of crisis, which declared that Parthia would only be conquered by a king. The Senate is supposed to have been planning a decree that would grant Caesar the title throughout the empire but not in Italy itself. Yet, whatever his ambitions Caesar made no attempt to rule by force, dismissing his personal bodyguard and travelling through the streets of Rome just like any other senator.

Caesar planned to leave Rome on 18 March 44 and, given the scale of his planned campaigns, would be most unlikely to return for several years. Brutus, Cassius and the more than 60 other conspirators decided that they must act. They were a disparate group, but had preserved their secret for several months. On the morning of 15 March (a date known as the Ides) there was some dismay when Caesar did not arrive at the Senate on time. Eventually he came and the Senate rose to greet him. The conspirators clustered round his chair, using the excuse of pleading for the recall of Publius Cimber. For a while the charade went on, but when Caesar stood to leave and tried to shake them off, the conspirators drew their knives, Casca striking the first blow from behind. Caesar died of multiple stab wounds. There was a final irony about his death, for Caesar's own Senate House had not been completed and the old *curia* still lay in ruins from its destruction by Clodius's men. As a result, the Senate had assembled in a temple attached to Pompey's theatre complex. When Caesar fell, his body lay at the foot of a statue of Pompey.

Civil wars and the end of the Republic

At Brutus' insistence the conspirators killed only Caesar. Mark Antony threw off his senator's toga to escape, not realising that he was not in danger, mingling with the crowd as the senators fled in panic. No one seems to have had much idea of what was going to happen next. Slowly and cautiously, apparently realising that there were not gangs of supporters bent on revolution and pillage, the Senate went back to the Capitol and spoke to the conspirators. The value of Brutus' reputation to the conspirators was now proved, for the vast majority of the senators were ready to listen to him. The more distinguished members, including Cicero, stood with the conspirators, signifying their support and after a few hours even Antony and Lepidus, Caesar's most important subordinates, appeared to be reconciled to the deed. The reaction of the population as a whole was less certain, for Caesar had always been popular with the poorer citizens, and there was some open protest when Brutus made a public speech explaining their motives.

Perhaps the conspirators simply expected everything to return to normal. The dictator was dead, so the Senate and properly elected magistrates could resume their guidance of the state. The problem was that virtually no one could remember a time when the traditional institutions of the Republic had functioned properly. Even the oldest, and there were few enough of these left after the Civil War, had grown up with a world of dictators like Sulla and Caesar, the dominance of informal triumvirs and the ever present threat of revolution from men like Lepidus, Catiline and Clodius. Caesar's former supporters seemed willing to agree to a general amnesty for the conspirators. The latter made no demands for personal power, and although the leaders were soon given

provinces, this was no more than their due as ex-magistrates. Brutus even granted Antony's request to hold a public funeral for Caesar. At this ceremony Antony read out Caesar's will, which included sizeable benefactions to the ordinary citizens, and, sensing their growing hostility to the conspirators, roused the mob to demand vengeance against the murderers of their hero. Some of Caesar's soldiers were making similar demands and most turned to Antony or Lepidus to lead them. The uncertain truce between the two sides continued for some months.

A new factor arose when Octavian, formally taking the name Caius Julius Caesar Octavianus now that his adoption had been confirmed in the will, returned to Italy. Moving from Brundisium to Rome, he rallied a few of Caesar's veterans. He was just 19, but incredibly self-confident. Mark Antony failed to take him seriously, and anyway saw him as a rival for the loyalty of Caesar's supporters rather than as a useful ally. It was round about this time that he and Cleopatra brought the child Caesarion into the public eye, presenting an actual son of Caesar to counter the adopted heir. Antony soon left for Cisalpine Gaul, taking charge of an enlarged army – for part of the garrison of Macedonia was posted there – with which he was in a position to threaten Rome. To those senators who hoped for a return to peace and stability and were broadly sympathetic to the conspirators, Antony was clearly the greatest threat to peace, for Lepidus was cautious by nature and unlikely to act of his own accord, even though he had command of the legions in Transalpine Gaul and Nearer Spain. Cicero had his last great moment of glory, emerging as one of the most distinguished of the surviving senators to dominate the debates in the House. At this time he delivered a series of speeches attacking Antony in a way that was vitriolic even by the standards of Roman politics. The speeches were known as the Philippics, for he modelled them on the tirades directed at Philip II of Macedon (Alexander's father) by the great Athenian orator Demosthenes. Octavian was seen as a useful figurehead, who would help to draw support away from Antony. Cicero is supposed to have said that they would 'praise the young man, decorate him, and discard him' (*laudanum aduluscentem, ornandum, tollendum* – there is a rhythm and double meaning to the Latin which does not easily translate). Yet Octavian was building up his power and rallied a force of veterans from Legio VII and VIII, and was soon joined by two more legions which were nominally under Antony's command but answered the call of Caesar's heir.

At the beginning of 43 Antony reached Cisalpine Gaul, but was resisted by the governor from the previous year and one of the conspirators, Decimus Brutus. Antony's army was superior in both numbers and quality and Brutus was soon besieged at Mutina. The Senate resolved to send the two new consuls for 43, Hirtius – one of Caesar's old officers and the man who had completed his Gallic *Commentaries* and possibly also written some of the books continuing the *Civil War Commentaries* – and Pansa to relieve Brutus. Cicero and the other senators decided to employ Octavian and his legions to aid them, giving the youngster, who was not even a senator, proconsular *imperium*, just as an earlier Senate had chosen to make use of Pompey and his private army in the 70s. The armies clashed in a confused battle at Forum Gallorum on 14 April 43, and after a hard struggle the arrival of fresh units forced Antony back with the loss of two eagles. Pansa was wounded by a missile during the fighting and died some days later. The army moved on to Mutina and attacked Antony's camp. At first things went well and they broke in, but then Hirtius was killed in the fighting near Antony's tent and Octavian and his men forced to retreat. Decimus

Brutus was released from siege, but Octavian had no desire to welcome one of his father's murderers. Brutus began to journey to join the other conspirators in the east, but was killed during the journey.

Both consuls had died within a matter of days, and Octavian was now, effectively, in control of three armies, altogether some eight legions, plus cavalry and other auxiliaries. Rumours circulated at the time and later claiming that Octavian had had a hand in the deaths of both his colleagues. He moved south and stood successfully for election to the consulship for the next year, though he was probably very aware that the Senate was attempting to use him only as a short-term measure. Now that Antony was for the moment checked, they could begin to discard him, and rely instead on the conspirators. Letters began to pass between Antony, Lepidus and Octavian. After a while the first two joined forces, and later in the year all three met at Bononia. Together, at the head of a huge army – altogether nearly 43 legions, though not all were present – they seized Rome and on 27 November 43 had a tribune pass a law by which they became triumvirs with consular power to restore the state (*triumviri rei publicae constituendae consulari potestate*) for five years. The wording was almost the same as the dictatorships adopted by Sulla and Caesar, save that this time there were three men instead of one. The need to avenge Caesar figured heavily in their propaganda, and the dead dictator was formally deified and a temple constructed for his cult. A comet seen in 44 was proclaimed as a clear sign that Caesar had ascended to heaven after his murder, and from now on Octavian was regarded as the son of a god.

There was far more of Sulla than Caesar about the triumvirs' behaviour, for this time there was no talk of clemency, and the lists of the proscribed were again posted. Some 200–300 senators and several thousand equestrians suffered death as a result. Among them was Cicero, caught by Antony's horsemen as he fled in his carriage. His head, along with the hand that had penned the

Philippics, was nailed to the speaker's platform in the forum. Many of these men were killed for political reasons, but the triumvirs needed money to support their huge war effort and plenty of names were added to the list simply to confiscate their property. In spite of this they still had to levy extraordinary taxation. What was left of the Senate was packed with the triumvirs' supporters and simply confirmed, often in advance, their actions. Preparing for war, and also keen to cement their own power, they took provinces. Antony received Gallia Comata (long-haired Gaul), the area conquered by Caesar, Lepidus had Transalpine Gaul and Spain, and Octavian was given Sicily, Sardinia and Africa. Octavian was also betrothed to Antony's step-daughter Claudia.

Meanwhile, Brutus and Cassius had had time to prepare a large army, drawing on the provinces around the eastern Mediterranean just as Pompey had done. In the end they amassed some 17 legions, including some such as Legio XXXVI which had fought first for Pompey and then for Caesar in the last Civil War, and would now fight against Caesar's heirs. Cicero's son was with them, serving as a cavalry officer. Antony and Octavian brought 22 legions to oppose them in the summer of 42. They met in the twin battles of Philippi. In the first Antony routed the wing commanded by Cassius, who committed suicide without realising that Brutus had in turn smashed Octavian's legions. Various stories claimed that the latter had either fled in terror or been ill in his tent during this battle. A few weeks later the second battle was fought and, on this occasion, the Caesarean cause won an outright victory, Brutus emulating the action of his colleague. Most of the credit for the victory went, probably rightly, to Antony.

After this victory Octavian and Mark Antony began gradually to ease out Lepidus, who was transferred to the province of Africa, while Octavian took Spain and Antony Gaul. Afterwards Antony went to the east to ensure the loyalty of the region and to secure provinces still threatened by the

Parthians, who had begun to become more aggressive again. The son of Labienus had gone into exile at the king's court, and led a band of followers as part of a Parthian invasion of Syria. At the same time Pompey's younger son Sextus, who had escaped after Munda, had built up a considerable fleet in Sicily and was actively opposing the triumvirs. He was a problem most of all for Octavian, whose task it was to supervise Italy. One of Octavian's greatest tasks was to arrange the demobilisation of nearly 100,000 soldiers, a mixture of captured enemies and men whose service was up or who were no longer needed after the victory at Philippi. In 41 he began confiscating land throughout Italy to provide farms for these veterans, evicting many farmers, including the poet Virgil. Capitalising on the resentment this caused, while at the same time hoping to win over as many veterans as they could, Antony's formidable wife Fulvia and his opportunistic brother Lucius publicly rallied support against Octavian. In the autumn they raised an army, but were besieged at the town of Perusia. Excavations on the site have produced many moulded-lead sling bullets fired by both sides, which often contain political slogans and even more frequently extremely crude insults. It was not until the beginning of the next year that Lucius was forced to surrender, but during this time most of Antony's commanders in the west showed their allegiance to Antony.

It looked as if an open breach had occurred between the triumvirs which could only be solved by yet another civil war. Fighting began at Brundisium, but at the last minute the two leaders patched up their alliance. Fulvia had died of disease, so Antony married Octavian's sister Octavia. They confirmed the division of the empire, so that effectively Antony controlled the eastern Mediterranean and Octavian the west. A short-lived treaty was agreed at Misenum with Sextus Pompey, granting him pardon and acknowledging his power, but this was soon in ruins, since neither Sextus nor Octavian adhered to its terms. Antony busied himself with a Parthian expedition, while Octavian built up his naval power to confront Sextus. In 36, aided by squadrons sent by Antony, Octavian's admiral and close friend Marcus Vipsanius Agrippa defeated the Pompeian fleet at the battle of Naulochos fought off the coast of Sicily. Sextus fled to the east, where he was captured by one of Antony's officers and executed.

Octavian's military resources had been built up considerably to undertake this conflict and were now markedly superior to Antony's. An abortive rising by Lepidus in Italy was swiftly defeated, and Octavian for once emulated his adoptive father's clemency. Lepidus was spared and allowed to live out the rest of his life in comfortable r tirement, retaining his post as *Pontifex Maximus*, Rome' senior priest. In the meantime Antony had launched a major invasion of Parthia, beginning the war which Caesar had planned. Despite initial success, his offensive bogged down as the enemy harassed his supply lines. During the subsequent retreat the Romans suffered heavy casualties. The war had been a costly failure, but Antony refused the aid sent to him by his wife Octavia, and instead publicly praised Cleopatra for her assistance. His affair with the Egyptian Queen became more open, and they paraded both Caesarion and their own children. Over the next years the fragile alliance between Octavian and Antony broke down altogether. Antony's obsession with Cleopatra made it easy for Octavian's propagandists to depict him as a man so dominated by a sinister eastern seductress that he had betrayed his Roman origins. His scornful treatment of the respectable, and Roman, matron Octavia only made this task easier. Octavian portrayed himself as the champion of all Italy (*tota Italia*) against the eastern menace. War finally came in 31, and culminated in Antony's defeat at the naval battle of Actium. He and Cleopatra both escaped to Egypt, and commited suicide shortly afterwards.

Octavian was now unrivalled master of the Roman world, commanding an enormous army of some 60 legions. Militarily, he was more secure than either Sulla or Caesar, but

his actions soon showed that he had learned from the failures of both. When he returned to Rome in 29 he formally laid down his powers, dissolving the triumvirate. Eventually he created the system known as the Principate, but this evolved gradually and there were more than a few false starts along the way. At first his power was still too blatant, for he held the consulship each year, and there was resentment, especially

This coin was minted by Mark Antony to pay his army during the war that culminated in the Battle of Actium. On the face is a picture of an oared warship, for Antony was relying heavily on Egypt's fleet in this campaign. On the reverse are three signa. These coins have a low silver content, which probably reflects the difficulty of paying such a large number of troops. (AKG Berlin)

whenever he left the city. It was at this time that he appears to have been planning to build an enormous palace on the Palatine Hill, with a monumental entrance approached along a new road from the opposite side of the hill to the forum and Rome's political centre. In time, Octavian's public position was made to seem less monarchic. He made considerable effort to disassociate himself from Octavian the triumvir, the man responsible for the proscriptions and other cruel and violent acts. Eventually he became, instead, Augustus, a name with deeply traditional associations, and the Father of his Country (*pater patriae*). When it was finally built, his palace was less grand, in appearance more like an ordinary aristocratic house, and was approached through the forum along a road lined with the houses of other senators. To all intents and purposes Augustus was a monarch, for his power could not be opposed by any constitutional means. From the beginning the Greek-speaking eastern half of the empire referred to him as king (*basileus*). Yet he managed to maintain the illusion that he was not the master of the state, but its servant, a magistrate like all other magistrates save that his authority, and his continued services to the state, were greater.

In its final form Augustus' powers rested on two chief elements. The most important, though the least public, was his 'power greater than any proconsul' (*maius imperium proconsulare*). Pompey had enjoyed similar, though not quite as extensive, power during his brief command against the pirates in 67. During his second consulship he had been granted a massive province embracing all of Spain and yet been allowed to remain in Rome and govern through representatives. Augustus was granted the same privilege, but his province was truly vast, including most importantly Syria, Egypt and the frontier zones on the Rhine and Danube. Like Pompey and others who had dominated the state, Augustus's power was ostensibly given to him by the Senate, and renewed every five or ten years, but there was clearly never any possibility of its being withdrawn. Every

province garrisoned by a legion, with the sole exception of Africa, formed part of the Emperor's province and was governed by his representative or legate. In most cases these were senators, but Egypt, the supplier of a high proportion of the grain consumed by the city of Rome, was governed by an equestrian, for it was too risky to grant such a command to a potential rival. A new senatorial career – and soon also an equestrian one – emerged in which traditional magistracies, which remained prestigious even if they lacked real power, were mingled with posts such as the emperor's legate. Like Caesar before him, Augustus effectively controlled elections to all significant posts.

The other, far more public, element of Augustus' formal power was the 'power of the tribunate' (*tribunicia potestas*). The Roman people, especially the poorer citizens, had strong emotional attachment to the tribunes of the plebs, who had originally been created to defend them from the misuse of power by other magistrates. In this guise Augustus was the people's champion. Through it he was able to summon the Senate or the Popular Assemblies and could impose his veto. In fact Augustus made little use of these powers, but he referred to them frequently, even numbering the years of his reign from the time this title was granted to him.

Ultimately Augustus' powers rested on military force. For the first time Rome received a permanent garrison. The emperor had his Praetorian Guard, and also formed a police force (the Urban Cohorts) and fire brigade (the Vigiles). All of these troops were kept directly under his personal control. He also took great care to ensure the loyalty of the army. Service conditions were fixed, as were the soldiers' legal status and rights. On honourable discharge each soldier was entitled either to a plot of land or a lump sum of money. This, along with the soldiers' pay, was funded by a special Military Treasury (*aerarium militare*) which was supervised, and often subsidised, by Augustus. The problem of veterans looking to their commanders to provide them with some form of livelihood was at long last

averted, and Augustus also took care that the legionaries' loyalty was focused on him and no one else. The men were paid by the emperor, swore an oath of loyalty to him, and, when they performed any feat of gallantry, received medals awarded by him.

Military power lay behind the Augustan regime, but attention was rarely drawn to this. Most of the Republic's institutions persisted. The Senate was reformed and reduced in size to remove many of the less suitable men who had been enrolled in

This famous Prima Porta statue of Augustus shows Rome's first emperor at the height of his power. He is depicted as a military leader, but in fact possessed only moderate ability as a commander. However, he possessed the knack of finding reliable subordinates, most notably Agrippa, who won his victories for him. (AKG Berlin)

Caesar celebrated four triumphs during his dictatorships, each of them more spectacular than any that had been seen before. This relief from the Arch of Titus dates to the first century AD and shows Titus riding in his chariot in celebration of his capture of Jerusalem. The rituals of the triumph changed little during Rome's history. (Ancient Art and Architecture Collection)

reward for dubious favours to the various sides in the civil wars. More Italians were included and in time senators would come from the aristocratic families of many of the provinces. Augustus attended the Senate as simply another member, if a highly distinguished one, pretending to be merely the 'first in the senate' (*princeps senatus*) an old and thoroughly republican title. He encouraged the members to debate freely and to vote with their conscience. Augustus may have genuinely desired them to do this, but in practice this was a sham. Every senator knew that his future career depended on the emperor's favour, and so the vast majority said what they felt he wanted them to say. Both the senators and emperor wished publicly to pretend that Rome had not become a monarchy, politely ignoring the obvious reality. From early in his reign

Augustus began to groom a successor, although the appallingly high mortality rate within the imperial family meant that quite a few individuals filled this role. When Augustus finally died in AD 14, his successor, Tiberius, had his powers formally voted to him by the Senate and at first feigned reluctance to take on the role. By this time scarcely anyone could conceive of, or remember, life without an emperor.

Augustus succeeded where Caesar had failed. He had learned from his father's murder and tried to veil his power behind more acceptable titles. By 31 the population of all classes was also far more willing to accept the rule of anyone who could put an end to the chaos of continuing civil war. The Augustan regime was a very Roman form of monarchy. Through the success of his adopted son, Rome was to be ruled by 'Caesars' for centuries, for the name became synonymous with supreme power. Even at the beginning of the twentieth century there was a tsar in Russia and a Kaiser in Germany, emperors whose titles derived from the family name of a Roman aristocrat who had made himself dictator and was murdered in 44 BC.

Roman provinces c. 27 BC–AD 200

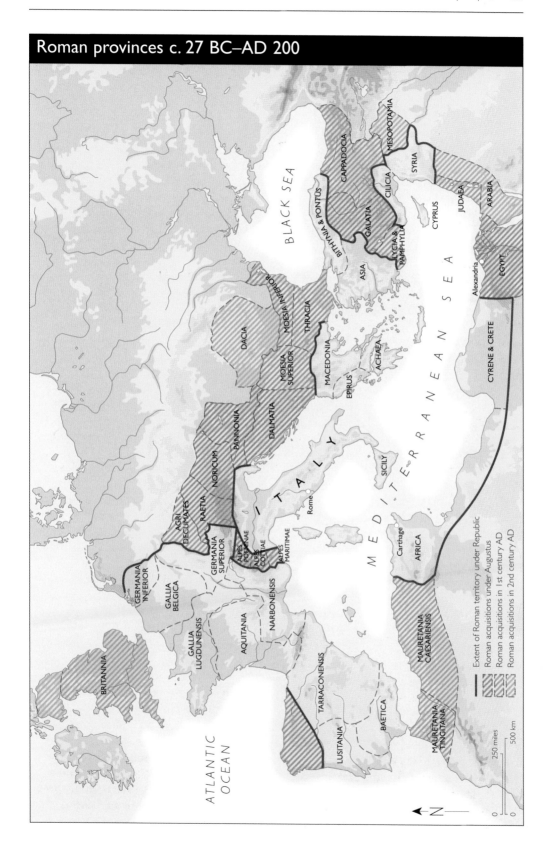

BLACK SEA

MEDITERRANEAN SEA

ATLANTIC OCEAN

MESOPOTAMIA
CAPPADOCIA
SYRIA
GALATIA
CILICIA
ARABIA
BITHYNIA & PONTUS
LYCIA & PAMPHYLIA
JUDAEA
CYPRUS
ASIA
ACHAEA
EGYPT
Alexandria
MOESIA INFERIOR
THRACIA
DACIA
MOESIA SUPERIOR
MACEDONIA
EPIRUS
CYRENE & CRETE
PANNONIA
DALMATIA
NORICUM
RAETIA
ITALY
SICILY
AGRI DECUMATES
GERMANIA SUPERIOR
ALPES POENINAE
ALPES COTTIAE
ALPES MARITIMAE
Rome
Carthage
AFRICA
GERMANIA INFERIOR
GALLIA BELGICA
NARBONENSIS
MAURETANIA CAESARIENSIS
GALLIA LUGDUNENSIS
AQUITANIA
BRITANNIA
TARRACONENSIS
LUSITANIA
BAETICA
MAURETANIA TINGITANA

Extent of Roman territory under Republic
Roman acquisitions under Augustus
Roman acquisitions in 1st century AD
Roman acquisitions in 2nd century AD

0   250 miles
0   500 km

N

The early Empire

Octavian's victory over Antony at Actium concluded two decades of almost constant internal conflict, but it did not entail even a pause in Roman military activity. Although the new civilian controller of Rome, the *princeps* Augustus, proudly proclaimed that he had on three occasions shut the gates of the Temple of Janus, the action which traditionally commemorated the cessation of all hostilities, he also oversaw and organised the most substantial expansion of Roman territory: these far outstripped the conquests of his adopted father Julius Caesar and were presented to the Roman people with great pride in the statues and temples which adorned the newly-constructed Forum of Augustus. These contrasting propaganda displays reflect the conflicting demands on Roman leaders, the desire for peace and stability on the part of the civilian inhabitants, especially the propertied classes and those in the more central provinces, and the expectations of military success, fuelled in part by historical tradition, in part demanded by the existence of a powerful military machine which could not remain inactive indefinitely.

The Roman public expected Augustus to complete two items of unfinished business from Caesar's life, the conquest of Britain and the punishment of Parthia for the humiliation of Carrhae, but in fact neither happened: the Parthians succumbed to diplomatic pressure to return the three captured legionary eagles and the Britons were left to their own devices for the time being. Instead Augustus undertook important but unspectacular campaigns to annex north-western Spain and the Alps, difficult work of consolidation whose lack of easy booty would have deterred republican commanders. In the 20s BC Augustus participated himself, although the main work of command was executed by his son-in-law Agrippa; thereafter he relied entirely on other relatives, principally his two step-sons Drusus and Tiberius. In the East there were expeditions into Arabia and against Ethiopia, which may have been preliminaries to conquest, though nothing came of these possibilities; elsewhere Augustus tinkered with client kingdoms, turning Galatia into a full province and doing the same in Judaea after first bolstering the authority of King Herod, and manoeuvring against Parthia for influence in Armenia. Augustus also pushed Roman frontiers north to the upper and middle Danube, enhancing the security of northern Italy and safeguarding the main land route between western and eastern parts of the Empire. New provinces of Pannonia, Noricum and Raetia were created, and these came to play a pivotal role in the Empire's defence. Roman armies followed Caesar's lead across the Rhine to campaign as far as the Elbe. By AD 4 the surrender and partial resettlement of the German tribes appeared to create the conditions for the formation of another province, but disaster soon struck. First the new Danubian provinces were rocked by a massive revolt which took three years to subdue (AD 6–9), and just as order was being restored in the Balkans the governor of the new province of Germany, Quinctilius Varus, was ambushed in the Teutoberger Forest near Osnabruck and three whole legions were wiped out. Augustus' long reign ended in AD 14 on a gloomy note, with the despairing emperor said to wake at night begging Varus to give him back his legions; on his deathbed he gave conservative advice to his designated successor Tiberius, urging him to keep the Empire within its boundaries.

The arrival of Roman provincial government was a profound shock to many newly-incorporated societies. The Caledonian chief, Calgacus urges his followers to resist expansion into Scotland by Roman armies commanded by Agricola, father-in-law of the Roman senatorial historian Tacitus (Agricola 30.5).

'To robbery, butchery and rape they give the name 'government'; they create a desolation and call it peace.'

The expansion of the Empire

Augustus' immediate successors in the Julio-Claudian dynasty carried on his work of internal pacification and consolidation with occasional external activities. The handover provoked mutinies in the armies of the Rhine and Danube, who were discontented by the longer service which had been introduced after Varus' disaster but also concerned that only Augustus could guarantee the terms and conditions which they had enjoyed; in each case rapid action defused the situation and the leading mutineers were abandoned to their punishments, which in one legion involved decimation, the killing by their former colleagues of one man in every ten. Under Tiberius (AD 14–37) there were substantial revolts in the Balkans and Gaul, while in Africa, the only part of the Empire where the Senate was still responsible for selecting the commander of a provincial army, a native uprising proved difficult to quash; in the East the annexation of client kingdoms continued with the transformation of Cappadocia into a province, while Armenia was temporarily reduced to a protectorate. Claudius (AD 41–54) oversaw the integration of Thrace and North Africa into the Empire and the continuing assertion of Roman authority over the tribes along the Rhine, but the greatest achievement of his reign was the initiation of the long-delayed conquest of Britain. Claudius himself, a thoroughly unmilitary man, travelled north to be present at the moment of symbolic

victory. Nero (AD 54–68), another ruler with little taste for military endeavour, had to confront challenges in Armenia where the Parthians attempted to reassert control; Britain, where harsh methods of tax-gathering and other consequences of annexation provoked Boudicca's uprising; and Judaea, a province where religion intensified the standard grounds for complaint found in other relatively new provinces. In each case Nero was fortunate to have good commanders to overcome the threats, Corbulo in Armenia, Paulinus in Britain and Vespasian in Judaea, but his own lack of interest in the armies meant that few were prepared to defend him when his unpopularity with the Senate led to challenges to his rule.

The Year of the Four Emperors (68–69) revealed to legions as well as senators what Tacitus described as a 'secret of imperial rule': that emperors could be created outside Rome. Galba with support from Spain, next Otho with the backing of the Praetorian Guard at Rome, and then Vitellius with the legions he commanded in upper Germany all briefly fought their way to power, but it was Vespasian, commander of the largest army group in the Empire at the time, who

The Roman ability at sieges was a major asset. No place could be confident of resisting capture, as the massive earthworks outside Masada in the Judaean desert reveal from the siege of AD 70–73. Here the Roman attack on Jotapata earlier in the same war, as described by Josephus, the commander of the Jewish garrison, illustrates the awesome power of a Roman bombardment (Jewish War 3.166-7).

'Vespasian now posted his artillery, of which he had 160 pieces, around the place and gave orders to shoot at the defenders. In one great barrage the catapults fired bolts, the stone-throwers hurled stones weighing nearly 50 kilos, there were firebrands and showers of arrows, making it impossible for the Jews to man the ramparts.'

triumphed; the support of the Danubian legions, which had supplied many detachments for the army assembled in Judaea to deal with the Jewish revolt, gave him an overwhelming advantage. Ironically Vespasian had been chosen as commander of this powerful force because Nero had reckoned that his undistinguished background in provincial Italy meant that he could not pose a serious political threat. Vespasian's position was legitimated, retrospectively, by a senatorial decree which sanctioned all his actions since the day on which his rebellious troops had acclaimed him as emperor.

The new Flavian dynasty (AD 70–96) inaugurated by Vespasian faced similar problems to those of the previous dynasty. The Jewish Revolt was eventually crushed and the Temple of Jerusalem destroyed, the annexation of Britain was advanced with campaigns pushing up into north-eastern Scotland, the process of taking over client kingdoms in the East continued with the annexation of Commagene, and the pressure of German tribes on the upper Rhine and

Troops crossing a river by pontoon bridge, from a section of Trajan's column. (AKG Berlin)

Danube was relieved by the creation of a new frontier to cut off the re-entrant angle between the two rivers. Success, however, bred further challenges and Domitian (81–96) found the Dacians beyond the lower Danube, united under the inspirational leadership of Decebalus, impossible to subdue. Trajan (97–117) inherited the challenges. He was, after Augustus, the greatest conqueror and empire-builder of Roman rulers, and for most of his reign he was personally engaged in expansionist campaigns. In North Africa he pushed Roman authority south to the Aures mountains, a considerable achievement but one which was promptly eclipsed by his activities elsewhere. Between 101 and 107 he campaigned repeatedly beyond the Danube, which was crossed by a long pontoon bridge, first forcing Decebalus to capitulate and then, after a failed rebellion, cornering him so that he committed suicide. A substantial new province, roughly the area of modern Romania, was established. On the eastern frontier, the client Nabataean kingdom was annexed to create the province of Arabia, and then further north Trajan crossed the Euphrates to re-impose Roman authority over Armenia, established a new province of Mesopotamia and finally campaigned down

the Tigris to capture the Parthian capital of Seleucia. Trajan may have been inspired by dreams of emulating Alexander the Great, but the diversion of substantial military resources to the eastern provinces had provided opportunities for rebellions elsewhere; even before his death the eastern expansion was looking shaky and thereafter Mesopotamia was promptly abandoned.

Trajan's two successors, Hadrian (117–138) and Antoninus Pius (138–161), though both competent commanders, pursued a policy of cautious consolidation. This is epitomised most solidly by their respective walls in north Britain, the stone-built Hadrian's Wall which ran from the Tyne to the Solway and the turf Antonine Wall which blocked the Forth-Clyde neck. Comparable though less monumental works were undertaken in southern Germany and along parts of the frontier in North Africa. At the same time there were internal revolts, most seriously in Judaea where up to half a million provincials may have perished in the restoration of Roman authority and the religious centre

Impressive defences reinforced Rome's psychological superiority along the frontiers. Taken from Trajan's column in Rome. (AKG London/Hilbich)

> *Most emperors had direct experience of military campaigns which served to strengthen links between ruler and soldiers, provided that the emperor behaved appropriately and was reasonably successful. Here the third-century historian Herodian praises the behaviour of Septimius Severus (History 2.11).*
>
> 'He shared the hardships of the soldiers, using a basic tent, sharing the same food as everyone else and not displaying the trappings of imperial luxury. Therefore he won even greater approval from his fellow-soldiers, who respected him because he joined personally in all their labours.'

of Jerusalem was transformed into a standard Roman colony called Aelia Capitolina.

One feature of the imperial succession in the second century was that emperors did not have sons to succeed them; instead they adopted individuals of proven talent. This process culminated in the reign of Marcus Aurelius (161–180), whom Hadrian had required his immediate successor Antoninus to adopt, in order to arrange the succession

at one remove. Marcus Aurelius is regarded by many as the best Roman emperor, partly it is true because he was a reflective intellectual whose introspective *Meditations* appeal to modern minds, and it was from his reign that Gibbon chose to measure the 'Decline and Fall of the Roman Empire'. In spite of his philosophical preferences Marcus had to spend much of his reign on campaign. There was the usual round of provincial unrest with Egypt and Mauretania being affected, but a Parthian invasion of Syria reignited hostilities on the eastern frontier; the Romans, under the command of Marcus' co-emperor Lucius Verus, were successful and re-established a province in Mesopotamia. Much more serious were the various tribal threats to the upper Danube, where Marcus had to spend most of his last decade resisting incursions by the Marcomanni, Quadi and Sarmatians, all of whom were under pressure from Gothic groups which had been shuffling

southwards from near the Baltic towards the Black Sea and Danube.

Marcus' death broke the habit of adoptive succession since he had a son, Commodus (180–192). Although he acquired the reputation of a playboy emperor, who could not stomach the hard work of ruling and preferred to cut deals with enemies rather than fight, his reign witnessed continuing campaigns along the Danube. It was not lack of action which led to his downfall but the failure of his praetorian prefect to ensure that legions received their pay on time which provoked insurrection. Two years of civil war were won by the commander of the largest and toughest army group in the Empire, the Danubian legions, and Septimius Severus (193–211) established a new dynasty. Internal strife inevitably created problems on frontiers, with units being withdrawn for action against fellow Romans, and the protracted campaigns won by Septimius were no exception. In the East, where he had defeated Pescennius Niger and the Syrian legions, not only were substantial cities such as Byzantium sacked but the balance along the frontier had been upset; here Septimius achieved some victories

The triumphal arch built in the forum at Rome to commemorate the victories of Septimius Severus (AD 193–211). (Michael Whitby)

Most attention to Roman warfare
naturally focuses on the armies, but the
following words attributed to the Caledonian
chief Calgacus attest the contribution of
the navy to the conquest of Britain and the
security of northern Gaul; imperial fleets
also protected the Mediterranean from
pirates and reinforced defences along the
Rhine and Danube (Tacitus, Agricola 30.1).

'Even the sea is no longer safe with
the Roman fleet near at hand.'

but chose not to extend Roman territory, relying instead on the construction of a client kingdom of Osrhoene based on Edessa (Urfa). At the other end of the Empire, in Britain, Septimius' second main rival, Clodius Albinus, had depleted the garrison to pursue his ambitions and frontier defences were overrun. First there were substantial works of restoration along and around Hadrian's Wall, after which Septimius spent the last three years of his life beyond the wall in Caledonia. A massive double legionary fort at Carpow on the river Tay and harbour works at Cramond on the Forth suggest that the Romans were intending to stay, and they may have attempted the systematic depopulation of Strathmore beyond the Tay in order to safeguard their presence.

On his deathbed at York Septimius urged his two sons, Caracalla and Geta, 'to look after the soldiers and ignore the rest', advice which did not prevent Caracalla from rapidly disposing of his younger co-ruler. The constant campaigning of Septimius continued under his dynastic successors, with Caracalla (211–217) engaged in Britain, the upper Rhine and the East and Severus Alexander (223–235) active in the latter two sectors. Under Severus Alexander there occurred one of the significant shifts which separates Roman imperial history into earlier and later periods. This was when the Arsacid Parthian dynasty was replaced as Rome's eastern neighbour by the more aggressive Sassanids. His eventual fate also foreshadows the imperial turmoil of the next half-century since inconclusive campaigning on the

Rhine prompted soldiers to complain about their leader, who hid behind his mother's skirt: he was murdered along with his mother Julia Mamaea, to be replaced by the rough soldier Maximinus the Thracian.

The frontiers of the Empire

What should be apparent from this rapid survey of 250 years of warfare is that emperors had to consider a variety of external threats, while remaining alert to the dangers of provincial revolt and the presence on the fringes of settled society of bandits, who would be encouraged by any loss of official authority or reduction in vigilance to extend their depredations. It is argued that generals and emperors were more interested in the rewards of external conquest than in routine defence of the Empire's inhabitants, and that from the military perspective provinces more often required subjugation than protection. Exchanges across frontiers, the significance of military glory, and the preservation of law and order are all valid considerations, but the ideology of *pax Romana* was also important: emperors were believed to have a duty towards the civilian members of the Empire, or at least their performance of this role was an issue which might be picked up in speeches of praise or defamatory tracts. In many years internal policing and repression tasks probably absorbed as much military manpower as action on or beyond the frontiers, but their recurrent and small-scale nature made them less newsworthy; along the frontiers we are better informed about grand campaigns than the run-of-the-mill patrolling and surveillance which will have occupied much of the garrisons' time.

Roman imperial frontiers can be divided into three main sectors, the Rhine, Danube and Euphrates with Britain as the fourth area of significance. It is no accident that in the first three instances a river accorded the frontier sector its basic structure. Although the defensive value of rivers has been debated, that they constituted some sort of barrier is demonstrated by the greater

Roman provinces c. AD 200 – 700

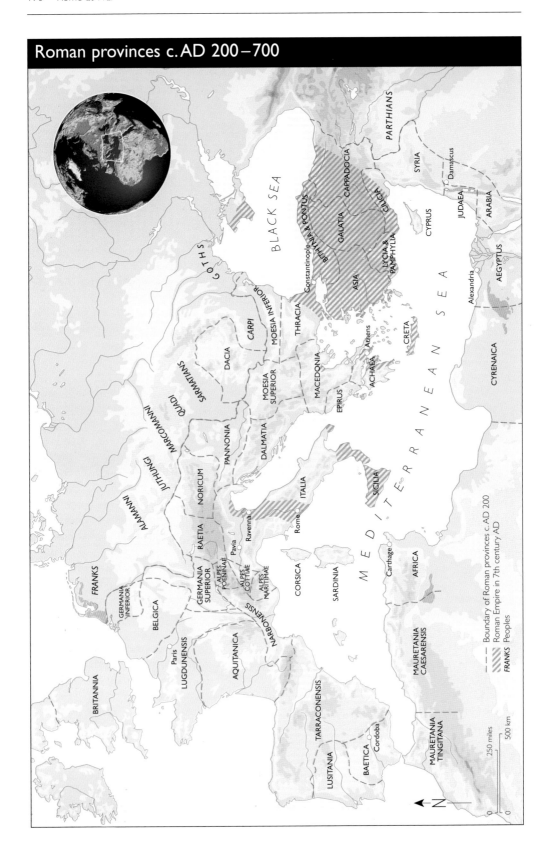

PARTHIANS

BLACK SEA

GOTHS

Constantinople

BITHYNIA & PONTUS

GALATIA

CAPPADOCIA

CILICIA

SYRIA

Damascus

LYCIA & PAMPHYLIA

ASIA

CYPRUS

JUDAEA

ARABIA

AEGYPTUS

Alexandria

CARPI

MOESIA INFERIOR

THRACIA

CRETA

CYRENAICA

DACIA

SARMATIANS

MOESIA SUPERIOR

MACEDONIA

ACHAEA

Athens

EPIRUS

QUADI

PANNONIA

DALMATIA

M E D I T E R R A N E A N   S E A

MARCOMANNI

JUTHUNGI

NORICUM

ITALIA

SICILIA

Rome

ALAMANNI

RAETIA

Ravenna

Pavia

FRANKS

GERMANIA SUPERIOR

ALPES POENINAE

ALPES COTTIAE

ALPES MARITIMAE

CORSICA

SARDINIA

Carthage

AFRICA

GERMANIA INFERIOR

BELGICA

NARBONENSIS

Paris

LUGDUNENSIS

AQUITANICA

MAURETANIA CAESARENSIS

BRITANNIA

TARRACONENSIS

MAURETANIA TINGITANA

LUSITANIA

BAETICA

Cordoba

N

- - - Boundary of Roman provinces c. AD 200

/// Roman Empire in 7th century AD

FRANKS Peoples

250 miles

500 km

A view along part of Hadrian's Wall (showing Cawfields milecastle), another defensive structure which combined protection and propaganda. (Ancient Art and Architecture)

ease with which enemies breached European frontiers, at least, either in the depths of winter when the rivers were frozen or at the height of summer when they might become fordable. They could certainly be crossed, but often at identifiable points which could be watched by Roman guards, with the fleets to supplement this protection. Where rivers did not exist to demarcate different territories, the Romans tended to create visible alternatives, though these were not necessarily a continuous structure: in face of the north African desert the Romans constructed various linear earthworks, whose purpose seems to have been to channel the natural movement of the inhabitants of marginal lands along observable routes, but not to prevent it altogether.

At the same time Roman frontiers are rightly no longer seen as simple barriers, best represented by what appears to be the solid obstacle of Hadrian's Wall, but zones of communication and integration, with the Romans always keen to push their influence out beyond their defensive installations while their neighbours regularly crossed over. It is ironic that the best-studied Roman defences, the salient between the Rhine and Danube in south-western Germany and the walls of north Britain, are not typical of Roman frontier areas overall; but even in the case of an apparent barrier, scrutiny of the installations along Hadrian's Wall reveals its purpose was to control, but not completely prevent, movement. Rivers were both obstacles and important lines of communication, providing the Romans with a reasonably secure means of supplying their forward posts, as well as allowing the inhabitants beyond the frontier to benefit from the Roman presence through trade or from employment, either directly in the army or indirectly through supplying some of the numerous services on which military life depended. Roman garrisons had considerable wealth, by local standards, to spend on slaves, women, furs or basic foodstuffs, while the Romans were a source of luxury goods such as wine or spices. A symbiotic relationship could emerge in which the Romans wanted tribal manpower and supplies, while tribal leaders relied on the Romans for the wealth and display goods which demonstrated superiority over their rank and file and reinforced their power as patrons through the local distribution of the benefits of civilisation. A cyclical pattern to relations on the frontier can be seen: the Romans bolstered the authority of compliant leaders whose expanding following generated greater demands; when these expectations became too excessive for a leader to satisfy through the rhythm of normal exchanges, conflict ensued between Rome and a major tribal grouping; Roman victory led to a reshuffling of tribal groups and the cycle would begin again.

In the first century of empire the Rhine was the premier frontier, the area with the potential for expansive conquests as well as threatening tribes. Out of the Empire's 29 legions, the establishment after the loss of three with Varus, eight were stationed close to the river at camps from Nijmegen and Xanten in the north to Strasburg and Windisch in the south, with Moguntiacum (Mainz) the home to a powerful double legionary group. Once grander Roman visions to incorporate Germania were renounced, the temporary military installations of mobile warfare were replaced by stone, permanent camps which attracted settlements of veterans, traders and other camp-followers; prosperous sites were honoured with colonial status, for example Colonia Agrippina (Cologne). But the stabilisation of structures did not entail static defensive strategy: active defence was needed to remind neighbours on a regular basis that the Romans deserved respect, and energetic commanders like Corbulo under Claudius were keen to demonstrate their talents. By the second century the military establishment had been halved to four legions, supported by about 40 auxiliary units; the latter were recruited from provincials rather than citizens, and supplemented the heavy infantry legions with a variety of smaller units, including numerous cavalry *alae*, wings, as well as flexible 'part-mounted' units. In military terms there was nothing inferior

about the auxiliaries, and indeed they were often used for the toughest fighting, for example in Agricola's victory over the Caledonians at Mons Graupius, since their casualties did not involve the shedding of Roman blood.

The military force on the Rhine in the second century was roughly equivalent to that stationed in the new province of Britain which was home to three legions and over 50 auxiliary units. By now the premier region was the Danube which was held by nine legions stationed from Vienna in the west to the Delta, with one further legion in Trans-danubian Dacia and two new legions being added to the river defences in the 160s; these citizen troops were supported by over 220 auxiliary units, a massive deployment which reflected the diversity of threats to this long frontier. On the upper Danube the external triangle of territory which linked its defences to the Rhine frontier near Argentoratum (Strasburg) was always a sensitive area, while further downstream the Romans had to cope with not only the normal cyclical pressures of

Although Hadrian's Wall provides the most spectacular remains of a Roman frontier, other areas where there was no major river to demarcate formal Roman authority received comparable attention. In southern Germany, in the angle between the upper Rhine and Danube, Domitian stabilised the military position in the AD 90s by constructing a military road and palisade to mark off Roman territory. The circumstances are recorded in a second-century collection of military advice (Frontinus, Stratagems 1.3.10).

'When the Germans in their usual way kept emerging from woods and other hiding-places to attack our soldiers, Emperor Domitian, by extending the frontier along a length of 120 miles, changed the nature of the fighting and dominated the enemy since he had uncovered their places of ambush.'

evolving tribal groups but also the consequences of the destabilising movement of
peoples from northern Europe or across
the south Russian steppe. The Danube was
also the strategic centre of the Empire and
its units were best placed to respond to
demands for reinforcements on the Rhine
and eastern frontiers.

On the eastern frontier Roman dealings
were in part haunted by the memory of the
Parthians' annihilation of three legions at
Carrhae (Harran) in Mesopotamia in 53 BC,
in part tempted by the renown of Alexander
the Great's achievements which lured
successive western rulers to emulation. For
the Romans the East was the most prestigious
area for conflict, and ideally for expansion.
Until the mid 1st century AD small client
kingdoms constituted buffer states for
Roman territory in Anatolia and the Levant,
but thereafter the upper Euphrates became
the frontier and two legions were quartered
at Satala near Erzerum and Melitene
(Malatya); further south Syria and Palestine
were garrisoned by four legions, all based in
or near major cities. In the second century
two of the legions in Syria were moved up
to the Euphrates at Samosata and Zeugma
(Birecik), while the ferocious Jewish revolts
ensured that Palestine now had two legions
of its own with a third east of the Jordan
in the former Nabataean kingdom. Overall
there were now eight legions in the region,
supported by about 65 auxiliary units. The
progressive incorporation of client kingdoms
during the first 150 years of empire did not
mean that this strategy for safeguarding
Roman territory was neglected: to the north
in Armenia the normal Roman aim was to
secure the status of patrons of that kingdom,
while in the south where desert provided
a buffer zone between the Euphrates and
Arabian Gulf, it was essential to maintain
the support of Arab tribes who knew how to
operate in this inhospitable terrain. As Roman
concern for developments in southern Russia
grew during the second century, attention
was increasingly attracted to Transcaucasia
where, again, client arrangements proved
an effective means of securing influence.

The development of the Imperial Roman Army

The origins of the soldiers who defended the
Empire evolved over the first three centuries,
though they were always predominantly
from rural backgrounds. Under Augustus
Italy, especially the colonies of the Po valley,
was the prime recruiting ground for the
legions, to be joined by the colonies and
other veteran settlements of southern Gaul
and Spain; in the Greek-speaking east where
colonies were fewer, legionary recruitment
among the provincials began under Augustus,
with citizenship being the reward for
enlistment. By the end of the 1st century
AD the proportion of recruits from Italy
was already in decline, and there is evidence
for imperial interest in supporting the
population in several areas, but veteran
settlements in the Danube provinces now
emerged as an important resource to
supplement other provincial suppliers of
manpower. One important factor which
encouraged recruitment from veteran
families was the prohibition, until the reign
of Septimius Severus, on marriage for serving
soldiers. This meant that the children of the
soldiers' inevitable liaisons were illegitimate
and hence excluded from Roman citizenship, which, however, they could secure
by joining the legions. The same incentive

*Roman soldiers were regularly involved
in military constructions such as camps and
siege-works; they constituted the largest body
of expert manpower in the Empire, and so
were often used for other projects such as
roads, bridges or, as recorded in the following inscription of AD 75 from south-east
Turkey, a canal by the river Orontes north
of Antioch.*

'Emperor Vespasian ... arranged for the
construction of a channel 3 miles long
for the river Dipotamia, with bridges,
by the soldiers of four legions, the III
Gallica, IV Scythica, VI Ferrata, XVI
Flavia, and also of 20 auxiliary cohorts.'

operated for the auxiliaries; originally these were raised among particular ethnic groups, whose name would be preserved in the unit title, for example Batavian, Sarmatian or Thracian, but such connections would be diluted when the unit was deployed away from its point of origin and recruits would tend to be found wherever a unit was stationed.

If citizenship was one important incentive to enlist, the terms and conditions of life were another. Legionary pay was reasonable, 9 *aurei* (225 *denarii*) in the 1st century AD and 12 in the 2nd century AD, a good wage for an unskilled workman, especially considering that it was regular. Troops received in addition occasional bounties or donatives, at accessions between Claudius and Vespasian and again consistently from Marcus Aurelius, sometimes for service on particular campaigns when booty was also a powerful lure, and occasionally by bequest at an emperor's death. On the other hand there were compulsory deductions for food, including fodder for cavalry mounts, clothing, and boots, so that any residue to be deposited for safe-keeping at the shrine of the legionary standards was likely to be small unless an individual had struck lucky with booty. On discharge veterans received 3,000 *denarii* in the first century, which had increased to 5,000 by the early third, with a sizable allotment as an alternative where land was available. Auxiliaries undoubtedly received less favourable terms than legionaries, but there is insufficient evidence to chart how these changed over the centuries. Soldiering was tough, but there were other benefits from belonging to the most powerful institution in the Roman world. Soldiers could overawe ordinary civilians to supplement their official rewards, relying on military camaraderie to protect them if things went wrong; food was probably better and more varied than that enjoyed by the average peasant, and medical treatment was certainly organised more professionally. The writing tablets preserved at the fort of Vindolanda in north Britain, dating

> *Soldiers were permitted, in certain circumstances, to demand support or services from the civilian population, a practice which inevitably gave rise to abuses. This is the context for the Biblical injunction 'to go the second mile' when a civilian was required to assist with military transport. Here the philosopher Epictetus gives analogous advice (Discourses 4.1.79).*
>
> 'If a requisition is taking place and a soldier takes your mule, let it go and do not complain: for if you do, you will get a beating and lose your mule all the same.

to the decades before the construction of Hadrian's Wall, reveal an auxiliary unit engaged in defence of a new frontier, but also active in the hinterland to secure its supplies of essentials and luxuries, while the wife of the commander could invite other suitable ladies in the vicinity for a birthday party.

Regular payment, especially in coins minted with the emperor's head and bearing a suitable slogan on the reverse, was one important mechanism for ensuring military allegiance. New recruits swore an oath of loyalty to the emperor and Rome; this was renewed annually, and attention to the emperor and his ancestors was sustained by regular commemorations of significant dynastic days and by the presence of imperial images next to the standards which focused the military cohesion of units. Most emperors also had some experience of command and so could genuinely refer to soldiers as 'fellow-campaigners', thereby creating an important bond of shared memory. Such positive measures were reinforced by the harsh punishments which indiscipline would incur, at least from strict commanders, with the result that mutiny was rare: discontent undoubtedly existed, but it usually required a particular catalyst to erupt into serious trouble, such as the death of Augustus or the arrival of a very lax commander. Most serious threats came not from the rank and file but from

Coin showing Constantius II on the obverse, and on the reverse a Roman soldier spears a fallen enemy horseman, and the slogan 'Happy days are here again' reflects the Roman attitude to warfare and expectation of victory. (Dr Stan Ireland)

A papyrus discovered in the record office of the 20th Palmyrene auxiliary cohort, stationed at Dura on the Euphrates under Severus Alexander (AD 222–235), records over 50 religious celebrations for the troops during the year; the festivities cemented loyalties to the ruling Severan dynasty, but also linked the troops to the idea of Rome and its imperial tradition from Augustus through all subsequent approved emperors.

'3 January Because vows are fulfilled and undertaken both for the welfare of our lord Severus Alexander Augustus and for the eternity of the empire of the Roman people, to Jupiter best and greatest a cow, to Queen Juno a cow, to Minerva a cow, to Jupiter Victor an ox, to Juno Sospes a cow, to Father Mars a bull, to Mars the Victor a bull, to Victory a cow.

24 January For the birthday of the divine Hadrian, to the divine Hadrian an ox.

21 April For the birthday of the eternal city of Rome, to the eternal city of Rome a cow.

1 July Because Alexander our Augustus was designated consul for the first time, a supplication.

23 September For the birthday of the divine Augustus, to the divine Augustus an ox.'

ambitious generals. Augustus had acted to limit potential competition from other generals, ensuring that the aristocratic Crassus was denied credit for personally killing an enemy commander in battle and denying triumphs to anyone outside the imperial family after the celebration by his supporter Balbus in 19 BC terminated the long Republican tradition of competitive displays; Balbus was also the last 'outsider' allowed to construct and name a major public building in central Rome. Thereafter many important campaigns were led in person by the emperor or a close relative. Careful attention was devoted to the selection of the governors of frontier provinces with substantial armies under their command, they were personally chosen by the emperor from among former consuls. In most reigns generals were monitored quite carefully, even at a distance, and inappropriate actions might be countermanded or the culprit removed in disgrace.

Life within the Empire

Within the frontier Roman territory was divided into provinces, of which there were 25 at the end of Augustus' reign; numbers gradually increased with the conquest of new territories and the incorporation of client states, but also more importantly by the subdivision of larger units or provinces with particular problems, so that there were about 60 in the early 3rd century AD. Most provincial governors were drawn from the senate, which retained considerable authority even after the demise of the Republic since it was easiest for emperors to govern with its support, although the limits to its power are revealed by accounts of craven discussions in which individual senators vie with each other to foresee or support imperial wishes. In the 'interior' provinces the governors' primary functions were to maintain imperial control and ensure the smooth collection of taxation. They suppressed brigandage, which subsisted at a low level in many parts of the Empire, regulated disputes between provincial cities and ensured their internal stability, and oversaw communications between the province and Rome, including the important annual expressions of allegiance to the emperor.

Taxation was the lifeblood of the Empire, which depended upon a regular cyclical flow of wealth. The areas of greatest consumption were Rome, where the imperial court and senatorial households spent lavishly, and the frontier armies whose salaries had to be paid at the risk of mutiny. Most frontier provinces could not support the full costs of the legions based in them, and so tax surpluses had to be transferred from 'interior' regions, for example Gaul or Asia Minor, whose inhabitants generated cash to meet tax demands by selling produce: the Empire thus evolved quite a complex system which locked different areas together. The two most important taxes were a poll tax and a land tax. The former was simpler, although its coverage and rate varied. The latter was based on an assessment of land value as determined by agricultural use, for example arable as opposed to vineyard or pasture-land, and was levied as a fixed percentage of the valuation. These taxes were not progressive, which meant that financial

burdens fell more heavily on small-holders than grandees, who would also have greater influence to secure exemptions. In addition there were customs duties at both imperial and provincial boundaries, and a 5% tax for Roman citizens on inheritances and the freeing of slaves.

Movement of produce, as both trade and tax revenue, was an important aspect of the Empire's economic system. Massive amounts of grain from Egypt and other parts of North Africa, and of oil and wine from Spain, were transported to supply Rome as taxation or the produce of imperial estates; similarly senators' provincial estates supported their palatial households in the capital. Supplies for the army might also seem to be located within this command economy and to an extent they were, but the Vindolanda writing tablets reveal that army units were also supported by their own supply networks.

The best evidence for Roman trade inevitably relates to the exceptional needs of the elite, who had an enormous appetite for eastern 'luxuries' – spices from eastern Africa, and silks, gems and spices from India. Eastern trade was a substantial enterprise which enriched both the imperial exchequer through customs revenues, and middlemen whose profits were invested in Petra and Palmyra. The current view of the Roman economy, based in part on the increasing evidence from shipwrecks, is that trade played a minor but significant role in the Empire's prosperity: trade in luxury items was the tip of the iceberg, beneath the surface were networks of local, intra- and inter-regional exchange which were greatly facilitated by the existence of the roads, ports and other installations established to service the crucial elements of the imperial system, namely the capital and the armies.

The Empire was, overall, prosperous during the first two centuries AD, as can be seen from the archaeological remains of provincial cities where local elites competed to beautify their home towns. Wealth did flow out of the Empire, but this was balanced by the substantial production of mines, such as the silver mines of Spain, imperial properties

The colonnaded streets of Palmyra were evidence of the wealth derived by the city from its trading activities. (Ancient Art and Architecture)

which were exploited under the protection of military units. In spite of the inflexibility of the tax system, imperial revenue tended to exceed expenditure during peace time and wars could be supported, especially if they were of limited duration and generated some booty: the agricultural production of the provinces sustained both the imperial machine and the demands of local cities.

On the other hand, there were already ominous signs of strain in the 2nd century AD, the golden age of imperial prosperity. The purity of the basic silver coin, the denarius, was reduced from about 90% to 75%, and then to 50% under Septimius Severus. Prolonged warfare was expensive, especially along the European river frontiers where booty was unlikely to offset costs: troops had to be moved to the area of conflict, imposing demands on communities along their lines of march, and extra resources were demanded to make good losses. Civil war was even worse, partly because such conflicts

were, at best, a zero-sum game (and at worst ruinously expensive to ravaged provinces and all who supported the losers), but more significantly because any attempt to secure the throne required lavish promises of donatives and higher pay for armies, which would also be expanded to meet the crisis. The plague brought back from the east by Lucius Verus' army in 167 was also a significant factor, and the consequences of the loss of agricultural population can be traced in papyrus records of land leases in Egypt: in some areas the impact seems to have lasted for a generation, in others three generations.

The Empire functioned best when rulers survived for reasonably long reigns with the support of both senate and provincial armies, when conflicts remained localised and did not coincide with challenges on other frontiers, and when climatic and other conditions permitted a reasonable level of agricultural production; this was the case for much of the 2nd century AD. The accession of Septimius Severus in 193 provided a severe jolt, since this was followed by three years of internal conflict across much of the Empire. His son Caracalla, who succeeded in 211, had

Cassius Dio, historian, twice consul and experienced provincial governor, writing about 230, assesses the change in the Empire's fortunes in 180 (72.36).

'[Marcus Aurelius] encountered a host of problems practically all through his reign ... he both survived himself and preserved the Empire in extraordinary and untoward circumstances. One thing alone marred his personal happiness: his son [Commodus] ... our history now falls away, as affairs did for the Romans of that time, from a realm of gold to one of iron and dust.'

to buy favour with the troops by awarding a 50% pay increase, which he financed by issuing a new overvalued silver coin and by doubling the 5% inheritance tax: to increase the revenue from the latter, he gave Roman citizenship to all the free inhabitants of the Empire and so brought them into the tax net. The Empire survived Caracalla, but if the balance of imperial prosperity was delicate during the 2nd century AD it now become precarious, with a major external threat or significant internal upheaval likely to generate a crisis.

Coin minted in AD 201. The obverse shows the head of Caracalla, and on the reverse are two captives seated either side of a trophy. (Dr Stan Ireland)

Part III
Rome at War
AD 293 – 696

Introduction

In the early 3rd century AD the Roman Empire stretched confidently from Scotland to the Sahara and the upper Tigris, an enormous imperial enterprise and the most powerful state in the world. The following four centuries saw the Romans pitted against enemies in the traditional three main frontier sectors: along the Rhine against the Alamanni, Franks and other Germanic tribes; on the Danube against first the Sarmatians and Goths, then the Hunnic tribes, and finally the Avars and manifold Slav groups; in Armenia and Mesopotamia with the Sassanid Persians; eventually, towards the end of the period, Arab tribes erupted from the Arabian peninsula to sweep through the Levant.

By the late 7th century AD Rome had shrunk to a rump consisting of Anatolia, the Aegean fringes of the Balkans and limited territories in Italy around Rome and Ravenna, still strong in Mediterranean terms but now forced to confront and interact with a variety of new powers. In the east Arabs inspired by Islam had overrun the Levant and Egypt, as well as the Persian kingdom; more than a millenium of conflict between Islamic east and Christian west had been introduced as Arab warriors pushed westwards through north Africa and into Spain and regularly raided towards Constantinople. Slav tribes had established themselves throughout much of the Balkans, with

The Emperor Theodosius and his family receive tokens of submission from barbarians while seated in the imperial box at the hippodrome. From the base of the obelisk at the Hippodrome in Constantinople. (Ancient Art and Architecture)

specific leaders emerging in certain areas – Bulgars in the north-east, Serbs and Croats in the north-west. In Italy the Lombard kingdom based in the Po valley fragmented authority in the peninsula, as it remained until reunification in the 19th century. Franks controlled Gaul, though it was usually split between different branches of the ruling Merovingian dynasty. In the Iberian peninsula the Visigoths had established authority, sometimes tenuously, over the groups who had settled during the 5th century; their switch from Arian to Nicene Christianity in the 7th century, however, provided a force for unity which would survive centuries of conflict with Muslim invaders. The British Isles presented another mosaic, with Saxons increasingly dominant in the south and east, Britons holding on in the west, and rival Pictish and Scottish kingdoms in control of southern Scotland; here again religion offered hope for future unity, with the Saxons progressively converted through the Roman mission based at Canterbury and the Celtic Church which was dominant in Ireland, Scotland and the north-west then reconciled with Roman traditions.

Thus, by the end of the 7th century many of the important elements of the modern European political landscape were in place, or at least in evidence, but the stages whereby Roman hegemony fragmented are complex. It is essential, above all, to remember that there was nothing inevitable about this process: Europe did not have to be organised into the territorial units and dominated by the national groups with which we are familiar today. 'Decline and Fall' has been a powerful model for analysing this transition, from the composition of Edward Gibbon's masterwork in the late 18th century, and before, but the vitality of the Roman system, especially when reinvigorated by Christianity, the commitment of peoples to the Roman ideal, and the sheer power of Roman arms also need to be stressed in opposition.

Identification of turning points is an understandable temptation, and acceptable provided that the qualifications for each

Bronze head of Constantine with eyes characteristically gazing to heaven. (Ancient Art and Architecture)

particular date are not forgotten. The conversion of Constantine to Christianity in 312 initiated the Empire's transformation from polytheism to Christianity, and prompted the development of the Church as a powerful and wealthy institution; for some scholars the Church was yet one more substantial group of idle mouths for Roman tax-payers to support, with unfortunate long-term consequences, but the Church also served imperial goals beyond the frontiers and reinforced loyalties within. In 363 Julian's grand invasion of Persia ended in death for himself and near disaster for the Roman army, but this set-back ushered in 140 years of almost unbroken peace in the east. In 378 the eastern emperor Valens was killed in battle at Adrianople in Thrace, and many of his Gothic opponents had to be allocated lands for settlement, but thereafter successive eastern emperors generally managed the 'Gothic problem' to their advantage. In 395 the last sole Roman ruler, Theodosius I, died, the Empire was split between his young sons, and emperors ceased to campaign regularly in person, but such divisions had occurred in the past, often beneficially, and there were advantages in withdrawing the emperor from the battlefield. 'Immortal' Rome was captured by Alaric's Visigoths in 410, but it had long ceased to be an imperial capital so that the event was largely of symbolic importance: Augustine in Africa wrote *City of God* to demonstrate the superiority of the heavenly over the terrestrial city, but in Italy the Visigoths withdrew and emperors continued to rule from Ravenna. In the 440s Attila challenged imperial authority in both east and west, threatening even to reduce emperors to vassal status, but his Hunnic federation disintegrated after his death in 453 so that within a decade his heirs were seeking Roman help. In 476 the last Roman emperor in the west was deposed by a 'barbarian' general, but the authority of the eastern emperor was still acknowledged, a western consul was annually nominated to share the chief titulary magistracy with eastern colleagues, and under Theoderic the Ostrogoth a regime which carefully maintained a Gotho-Roman façade dominated the western Mediterranean from Ravenna.

Individually the significance of each of these 'key' dates must be qualified, but cumulatively they contributed to diminishing imperial authority and undermining the fiscal and military structures which permitted the imperial machine to function. By the late 5th century an emperor had become irrelevant in the western Mediterranean, although the eastern ruler was accepted as a figurehead by some. The East's continuing power was revealed by its ability to organise the reconquest of the Vandal and Ostrogothic kingdoms, which extended to the recovery of parts of Spain and the exercise of intermittent influence in Gaul. Even if the cumulative impact of recurrent bubonic plague and the demands of western warfare

One of the more accurate assessments of the Empire's demise occurs in a conversation between Jews in prison at Carthage in the 630s. They discuss the state of the Empire and the news of a new prophet among the Saracens in terms of the vision of Empire in the Book of Daniel (Doctrine of the Newly-baptised Jacob 3.8).

'Jacob asked him: "What do you think of the state of Romania? Does it stand as once, or has it been diminished?"

Justus replied uncertainly, "Even if it has been somewhat diminished, we hope that it will rise again."

But Jacob convinced him, "We see the nations believing in Christ and the fourth beast has fallen and is being torn in pieces by the nations, that the ten horns may prevail."'

left the Empire economically and militarily weaker in 600 than it had been in 500, in comparative terms it might have been stronger since its greatest rival, the Persian kingdom, also suffered heavily during a century of conflict; its current ruler, Khusro II, had only secured the throne with Roman help. In the early 7th century internal dissension and foreign invasion seemed to have forced the Romans to the brink of destruction, symbolised by the arrival of a Persian army on the Bosporus and its co-operation with the Avar Chagan in the attack on Constantinople in 626, but the city and its Empire survived: within two years Heraclius had defeated the Persians, and overseen the installation of friendly rulers on the Persian throne, including, briefly, the Christian Shahvaraz, and during the 630s the Avar federation was disintegrating as the reduced prestige of its leader permitted subordinate tribes to assert their independence. For the East the decisive blow came out of the blue when a new religion transformed long-standing manageable neighbours into a potent adversary.

Inside and outside the empire

Army of the Roman Empire

The Roman Empire depended on the power of its armies, which had always been composed of a combination of citizen and non-citizen troops. Before the universal extension of citizenship in AD 212 citizens were recruited into the legions, while non-citizens traditionally entered the auxiliary units. Remarkably little is known about the process of recruitment:

Late Roman cavalry. Artwork by Christa Hook. (Osprey Publishing)

Late Roman infantry. Artwork by Christa Hook. (Osprey Publishing)

conscription was probably always a feature, with manpower needs being apportioned in line with census records of citizens, but there was also some element of hereditary service as units drew on veteran settlements. At times, perhaps often, military service offered a reasonably good and quite safe career for the young provincials, especially if they served close to home.

In the later Empire it is often alleged that the balance of the armies changed, with citizens being outnumbered by foreigners, the traditional infantry backbone eclipsed by cavalry units, and frontier units (*limitanei*) relegated to an inferior status. Romans were progressively demilitarised and the increasingly un-Roman armies declined in discipline and loyalty. These theories reflect developments in the later army, although they are all ultimately misconceptions.

Roman armies did continue to rely on substantial units of non-citizens, especially when troops had to be recruited quickly, as in civil war and after military defeat, or for special expeditions. These 'outsiders' were often excellent troops who provided reliable bodyguards for emperors and generals, whose personal retinues of *bucellarii* (biscuit-men) might represent the elite part of an army. There were also several senior non-Roman commanders who played important political roles, especially during the fragmentation of the western Empire in the fifth century, but it is invalid to infer from their prominence that non-Romans also dominated the ranks of the army.

Infantry had always been the particular strength of the Romans, and it is true that cavalry units performed a more important role in late Roman armies, but there is little evidence to support the popular notion that the Romans switched to reliance on heavy-mailed cavalry, an anticipation of medieval knights. The Romans had a few units of mailed lancers (*clibanarii* or boiler-boys) in imitation of Parthian and Persian units, but mounted archers on the Hunnic model were probably more common. The sixth-century historian Procopius chose

a horseman equipped with a composite bow to represent the ideal contemporary soldier. But infantry remained the basis for most armies, and Roman foot-soldiers, when properly trained and led, were capable of defying all opponents.

Another development in the late Roman army was that, from the fourth century, distinctions were drawn, in terms of status as well as rewards, between *limitanei* and troops of the *comitatus*, i.e. between more static provincial units and those which accompanied the emperor or senior generals. It is often claimed that *limitanei* became soldier-farmers, losing their military quality along with their professionalism, but that misrepresents the nature of the estates which helped to support them and ignores their continuing use in conjunction with mobile troops on major eastern campaigns. It is noticeable that the *limitanei* included more cavalry units than the *comitatus*, a reflection of the usefulness of horses for local patrolling and of the greater ability of infantry to retain fighting strength when required to move long distances quickly.

There had been a gradual change in the deployment of Roman armies. In the early empire legions were quartered in major bases near the frontier (e.g. Cologne), but military need dictated that units were detached for specific duties as frontier garrisons or in the interior. Later this ad hoc dispersal was consolidated so that troops were spread across provinces in numerous forts and cities. Emperors, however, also needed mobile forces for more rapid deployment. In the east there came to be two armies 'in the presence' stationed near Constantinople, and others in the Balkans and the east; in the west Gaul and Italy had their own armies until imperial authority contracted from the former.

Overall, Roman armies changed between the third and seventh centuries, but the majority of troops were drawn from the Empire's inhabitants. Specific upland regions had the reputation for producing good recruits: the Balkan highlands,

Late Roman parade helmet. (AKG London)

mountainous Isauria in southern Asia
Minor, and Armenia. Goths, Germans and
Huns also made important contributions,
but such soldiers often came from groups
who had been accepted into the Empire and
given lands with the explicit purpose of
providing recruits. To educated observers
from the cities, the people who wrote most
of our evidence, Roman armies undoubtedly
looked quite barbaric and undisciplined,
but the same could often have been said
about early imperial armies.

The size of late Roman armies is a complex
game for which most of the pieces are missing.
In the third century army units probably
numbered upwards of 350,000, with a further
40,000 in the navy. Numbers increased
significantly under Diocletian (284–305) and
Constantine (306–37), so that the total
military establishment exceeded 500,000 –

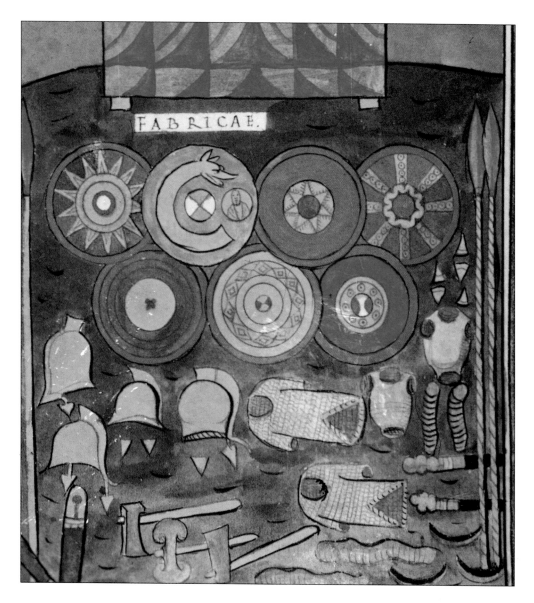

FABRICAE.

Folio from the *Notitia Dignitatum*, depicting the responsibilities of the Master of Offices which included the imperial weapons factories (*fabricae*). (MS Canon Misc. 378, f. 141r, Bodleian Library)

perhaps even 600,000. But paper strength will always have surpassed disposable strength, and many troops were committed to particular assignments so that only a small proportion of the total establishment could be deployed for individual campaigns. In the fourth century an army of 50,000 was large, and by the sixth century mobile armies rarely exceeded 30,000.

In spite of complaints about discipline, Roman training appears to have remained tough. A succession of military manuals indicates that attention was devoted to training and tactics, at least in the eastern Empire, although it is probably correct that organisation, rather than basic military skill, increasingly emerged as the way in which Romans surpassed their opponents. The Romans had the capacity to co-ordinate troops over long distances to build up complex armies, with artillery units as well as infantry and cavalry, and then keep these supplied on campaign: the infrastructure of roads, warehouses, granaries, arms factories and the billeting arrangements generated a complex body of law, and enabled the Romans to move their men wherever they were needed.

Persian arrangements

Only in the East did the Romans face an enemy with a sophistication comparable to their own. The Iranian Sassanids supplanted the Parthian Arsacids during the 220s, imposing themselves as a new military elite on a heterogeneous population, which included substantial groups of Jews and Christians in densely populated lower Mesopotamia. Persian armies are not clearly understood, since almost all our knowledge comes from Roman informants reporting Persian actions during the repeated conflicts. One important strategic point to bear in mind is that, from the Persian perspective, their north-eastern frontier, the sector in which they confronted the nations of central Asia, took priority; we occasionally glimpse Persian action in this area, as when King Peroz led his armies to disaster against the Hephthalite Huns in the late fifth century, or during the service of the Armenian Smbat Bagratuni in the early seventh, but there is a substantial gap in our appreciation of Persian might.

The career of Smbat
The Armenian Smbat, a member of the noble Bagratid house, commanded cavalry for the Romans in the Balkans in the 580s, but was exiled to Africa for instigating revolt. In the 590s he reappears in Persian service, being appointed provincial governor by King Khusro II; he was trusted to suppress awkward rebellions in the east and received the nickname 'Joy of Khusro', but Khusro was reluctant to allow him to return to Armenia and Smbat was kept at court as an honoured advisor.

The Greek historian Theophylact preserves rare information on Persian military arrangements.(3.15.4)
'For, unlike the Romans on campaign, Persians are not paid by the treasury, not even when assembled in their villages; the customary distributions from the king, which they administer to obtain income, are sufficient to support themselves until they invade a foreign land.'

Persian kings did not maintain a large standing army until at least the sixth century: there were garrisons in frontier cities and fortresses, but for major campaigns kings instructed their nobles to mobilise provincial levies. Minor gentry of free status served as mounted warriors providing a backbone, and they probably brought along their own retinues. The system was feudal, with royal land grants carrying an obligation to serve or send troops on demand; campaigns inside the Persian kingdom seem to have been unpaid, on the assumption that soldiers could support themselves from their estates, but payment was given for foreign expeditions. Feudal arrangements could be extended to attract troops from outside the kingdom – who worked for specific terms – but mercenaries were also recruited, sometimes from the Hunnic and Turkic tribes beyond the north-east frontier, sometimes from specific internal groups such as the Dailamites who inhabited the mountains south of the Caspian.

Persian armies are often associated with heavily mailed cavalry, but their most potent element were mounted archers: Roman tactical writers advised that the Persians could not withstand a frontal charge, but that any delay in engaging at close quarters would permit them to exploit their superiority at archery. The Persians were heirs to a long Middle-Eastern tradition of siege warfare and they had a formidable capacity to organise sieges, dig mines and deploy a variety of engines to capture even the most strongly fortified positions. In the sixth century there was a substantial overhaul of the tax system as well as a redistribution of land, which was intended to bolster royal power by permitting the payment of some permanent units, an imitation perhaps of the Roman *comitatus*. But the feudal link between king and nobility remained crucial, dictating that military prestige was essential for royal authority: kings might embark on foreign campaigns to acquire booty and prestige for internal consumption.

Enemies in Europe

The personal prestige of the war leader was also vital for Rome's various tribal enemies in Europe. These groups ranged from small war bands from an extended family or single village, through more complex clan and tribal bands into which the family units would be subsumed, to the occasional but mighty international federation. At the bottom of the scale were the Slav raiders who crossed the Danube in the sixth century; these might operate in groups of 200 or 300, perhaps accompanied by their families in wagons as they sought land for settlement.

Most of the German and Gothic groups who challenged the Empire were collections of such smaller clan or village units, united under the authority of a king. The right to lead depended ultimately on success, especially in warfare; although leading families (such as the Gothic Balthi and Amali) attempted to create dynasties, these could not survive the shock of prolonged failure or the absence of a suitable war-leader. There was some instability in these groups, and units – such as the Carpi, who were prominent down to AD 300 – might disappear permanently; others such as the Lombards are absent from our sources for several generations before re-emerging in the sixth century. Such changes did not represent the elimination of these people but their subjection to a different elite which imposed its identity on its followers. Powerful German kings might be able to

mobilise 10,000 warriors, and larger forces – such as those that confronted Julian at Strasburg in AD 357 – could be produced through alliances. On rare occasions German leaders commanded larger numbers – the Amal-led Ostrogoths fielded 25,000–30,000 warriors after subsuming a rival Gothic group in the Balkans – but this was exceptional, the product of Roman power which forced tribes to coalesce or face defeat.

The most powerful Roman enemies were the supranational federations, represented by the Huns in the fifth century and the Avars in the sixth and seventh. These groupings swallowed the variety of smaller tribal units within their sphere of action, with terror and booty providing the cement; their existence required regular warfare, and their ruthless leaders had the manpower to overrun the defences of even major cities. Both Huns and Avars posed serious challenges to Roman authority, but their inherent instability was their undoing: Attila's death in 453 led to fatal dissension among his potential heirs, while the Avars never recovered from their failure at Constantinople in 626, since weakness at the top permitted constituent sub-groups to rebel. The image of the Huns is of nomadic warriors whose attachment to their horses was such that they could scarcely walk, and it is true that the various warrior elites will have fought as cavalry, but all these groupings could also field substantial infantry forces which would have been provided by less prestigious elements, for example the Slavs within the Avar federation.

Collectively Rome's enemies rivalled, or surpassed, its military strength, but the Romans could usually hold their own, partly through superior organisation and training, partly through strong defences, but above all by the strategy of trying to avoid simultaneous conflict on different frontiers. Along the Danube or Rhine tribal groupings might co-operate in the short term, but Roman diplomacy was adept at exploiting potential splits. Wider collaboration was extremely rare, the only real instance

Movement of Goths across Europe

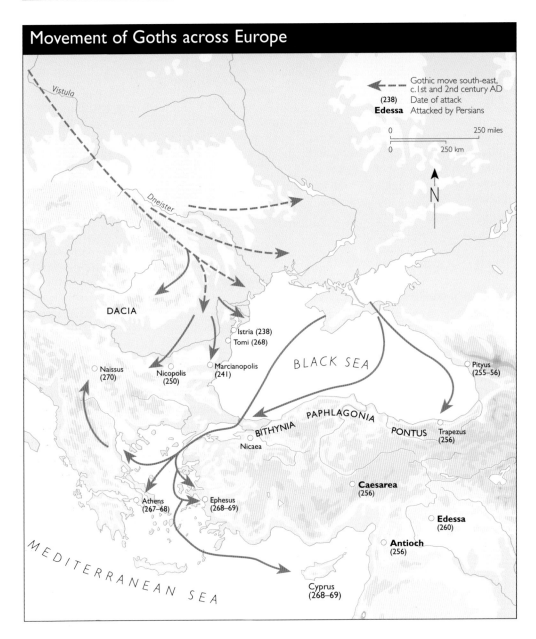

occurring in 626 when Persian troops encamped on the Bosporus attempted to join the Avar attacks on Constantinople, only to be thwarted by the Roman fleet. Possession of a small but powerful navy was a factor which distinguished the Romans from all their opponents, with the exception of Saxon raiders in the North Sea and the Vandal kingdom in North Africa which took over part of the western Roman fleet.

Creating crisis

After the murder of Severus Alexander in 235 the Roman Empire experienced 50 years of instability, commonly termed the Third-century Crisis, a period which marks the transition to the later Empire. The 'crisis' can be viewed from a number of interlocking aspects – frontier pressure, usurpers, religious change, financial shortages – but it is reasonable to begin from the frontiers: here developments can be identified which then arguably prevented the Empire from controlling change in other areas.

Beyond the eastern frontier a new dynasty was inaugurated when the Sassanid Ardashir was crowned in Ctesiphon in 226. The change was significant since the Romans had generally dominated the Parthians, and indeed repeated Roman successes had contributed to undermining royal prestige, but the Sassanids propagated a dynamic nationalism, including links with the Achaemenids, who ruled Persia before Alexander the Great's conquests. Embassies demanded the return of their ancestral property, with war as the consequence of the

The Greek historian Herodian records demands of a Persian embassy to Alexander Severus in the 220s (6.4.5).

'The mission declared that by order of the Great King the Romans and their ruler must abandon Syria and the whole of Asia opposite Europe, allowing Persian rule to extend as far as Ionia and Caria and the peoples within the Aegean-Pontus seaboard. For these were the traditional possessions of the Persians.'

inevitable refusal. Gordian's attempt to discipline Ardashir's son Shapur I ended in humiliation in 244, with Gordian defeated and murdered and his successor Philip the Arab forced to purchase the withdrawal of his army. Shapur's invasions in 253 and 260 resulted in the capture of Antioch, the major city of the eastern provinces as well as

The ruined walls of Dura by the River Euphrates. (Ancient Art and Architecture)

The Valerian Wall at Athens, cutting across the agora. (Author's collection)

numerous lesser places such as Dura on the Euphrates, and the transport to Persia of massive booty; Emperor Valerian was captured in battle at Edessa (Urfa) in 260 and taken back to Persia. For the next decade imperial authority in the east was limited, with the most effective resistance to the Persians being provided by the ruler of Palmyra, Odaenathus. The east had become an expensive military arena for the Romans, and the substantial tax revenues of its provinces were jeopardised.

The problem was compounded by events on the Danube, where the Romans also had to face a new enemy. Here change had been slow, the result of the gradual movement of Gothic peoples from northern Poland. The first attested Gothic incursion came in 238, when they sacked Istria near the Danube

mouth; a decade later they swept across the north-eastern Balkans, and Emperor Decius was killed and his army annihilated while trying to force them back across the Danube in 251. Further ravaging occupied the 250s, with the Goths commandeering shipping on the Black Sea to cross to Asia Minor and sail into the Aegean where they sacked Athens in 268. Mining operations in Macedonia and Thrace were inevitably disrupted.

This great movement of Goths naturally displaced other peoples who might find themselves squeezed against the Roman frontier; this process could trigger the formation of substantial federations as different tribes steeled themselves for the ultimate challenge of attacking the Romans. On the upper Danube the Vandals, Quadi and Marcomanni breached the frontier, and on the upper Rhine the Alamanni increased their strength to the extent that they twice invaded Italy in the 260s. On the lower Rhine

Porchester Castle. One of the late third-century Saxon shore fortifications, built to protect southern and eastern Britain from raids across the North Sea. (Ancient Art and Architecture)

the Franks gradually came to dominate another large federation which threatened frontier defences during the latter half of the century, and Saxon pirates began to raid across the North Sea and down the Channel.

Of the Roman world only Africa, the Iberian Peninsula and, to a lesser extent, Britain, were spared invasion. The cumulative nature of the frontier pressure is evident, with emperors unable to divert troops from one sector to another and instead constrained to confront invaders in conditions which led to defeat. The consequences for imperial prestige are obvious, and by the late 260s the Empire was virtually split into three units which attended separately to their own security. Trouble began in 235 when Severus

Alexander, who had just campaigned unsuccessfully in the east, was overthrown by the Rhine armies who feared his leadership. They proclaimed as their leader Maximinus the Thracian (allegedly an uneducated peasant risen from the ranks). Maximinus made no attempt to conciliate the senate, his control of the armies, especially those in the east, was shaky in spite of a promise to double military pay, and the extensive confiscations needed to provide funds for his promises damaged his reputation further. Maximinus survived until 238 when his failure to deal with rivals supported or proclaimed by the senate caused his troops to mutiny. Seven emperors within one year, fighting in North Africa and northern Italy, and disturbances in Rome were a foretaste of the anarchy to come; such substantial internal upheavals naturally afforded external enemies a chance to invade, which then increased the problems for whoever happened to occupy the throne.

The rapid turnover of emperors is best illustrated by a simple list – with the proviso that it is difficult to include all the shorter-lived local claimants to the throne.

235–38	Maximinus
238	Gordian I & Gordian II
238	Balbinus & Maximus
238	Pupienus
238–44	Gordian III
244–49	Philip the Arab
249–51	Decius
251–53	Trebonianus Gallus
251–53	Volusianus
253	Aemilianus
253–60	Valerian
253–68	Gallienus
268–70	Claudius II Gothicus
270	Quintillus
270–75	Aurelian
275–76	Tacitus
276	Florianus
276–82	Probus
282–83	Carus
283–85	Carinus
283–84	Numerian

Each new emperor meant another donation to the troops; each bout of civil war more loss of life, physical destruction and distraction from the frontiers. Ironically, in 248 Philip celebrated the millennium of Rome's foundation in spectacular fashion, but the military reverses of the 250s effectively split the Empire into three. Odaenathus' defence of the east fuelled ambitions for imperial authority, which were inherited by his wife Zenobia in 268/9, while in Gaul, the Rhine armies proclaimed their successful general Postumus. The air of crisis generated apocalyptic literature in the east (for example, the *Thirteenth Sibylline Oracle*), and a circuit of walls for Rome, 11.8 miles (19 km) in length, was rapidly constructed in 271. The Empire was only reunited by Aurelian in a series of energetic campaigns, which were helped by instability in Gaul following the murder of Postumus in 269 and by the death of Odaenathus; also, he was prepared to abandon the exposed province of Dacia and redeploy Roman troops along the lower Danube. Perhaps most significantly, the energetic Shapur died in 270 and it was to be 50 years before the Persians had a comparable leader. If military failure guaranteed overthrow, success did not ensure survival: both Aurelian and Probus, who continued Aurelian's re-establishment of the Empire, succumbed to plots in military camps, and Carus died while invading lower Mesopotamia, allegedly struck by lightning.

Aurelian's wall at Rome. (Ancient Art and Architecture)

Prolonged warfare inside the frontiers, regular defeat, and the rapid turnover of emperors cumulatively had major economic consequences. Emperors required more money to pay donatives and salaries to their troops, and the available supplies of bullion had to be squeezed in order to produce the necessary precious metal coins. Under Gallienus this resulted in the silver content of the *denarius*, the standard coin for military pay, declining to 5 per cent; subsequently there were issues of bronze washed in arsenic to provide a short-lived silvery brightness. The declining value of coinage triggered an offsetting rise in prices which resulted in an inflationary spiral, particularly during the last third of the third century.

One victim of inflation was the government, whose tax revenues declined in value; granted the inflexibility of the tax system, it was difficult to raise large new sums of cash. A consequence was an increasing reliance on taxation in kind: troops needed to be supplied and, rather than extracting increasingly worthless coin from rural taxpayers to permit units to purchase food and other necessities, the cycle was short-circuited by the transfer of goods directly to the troops. This development might have been accidental and haphazard, with armies gradually adopting the practice of securing their own supplies and leaving provincial administrations to acknowledge that their appropriations could be offset against tax demands. Other victims of inflation were the cities, where the spectacular building developments of the previous 150 years ceased.

Gold medallion of Valerian I and Gallienus Salonim proclaiming Concordia Augustorum. (© R Sheridan Ancient Art and Architecture)

Coin with legend *Carausius et fratres*, c. AD 286.
(Ancient Art and Architecture)

Another consequence of crisis was the marginalisation of the senate and a professionalisation of military command. In 238 the senate and armies had contested the imperial succession, but under Gallienus senators were effectively removed from military commands. This development had begun earlier, since the Severans had sometimes preferred trustworthy non-senators for important commands, but the insecurity of emperors furthered the change while troops also demanded reliable leaders rather than aristocratic amateurs. When Aurelian came to power with the backing of the upper Danube legions and then used these troops to restore the Empire, it transpired that Pannonians, and other officers of Balkan extraction, became prominent. These were professional soldiers, at whom civilian intellectuals might sneer for their lack of culture, but they proved to be solidly committed to the idea of Rome and its traditions, as well as effective generals.

The crisis also had a religious impact, since a natural inference from repeated misfortune was that the gods had to be placated. At first this took the form of intensified supplication to traditional deities: in 249 Decius issued a general instruction to all citizens to offer prayers and sacrifices on his behalf. A consequence, probably unintended, of this order was that Christians were faced with the choice of disobedience or apostasy; some abandoned the faith, many more probably

Radiate coin of Aurelian (AD 270–275). (Barber Institute of Fine Arts)

found means to evade or connive in the ruling, but there were enough martyrs to identify Christians as traitors to the Empire. Persecution lapsed with Decius' death, but was restarted in 257 by Valerian who specifically targeted the Christians, with attention focused on the priestly hierarchy; his defeat in battle terminated proceedings. The successful Aurelian advertised his devotion to the traditional divinities, especially Victoria, Mars, Hercules and Jupiter who were all connected with success in war, and to these he added a special devotion to the cult of the Unconquered Sun, *Sol Invictus*, after the defeat of Palmyra in 273. Devotion to the correct divinity did bring success, as Diocletian and Constantine would continue to demonstrate in their different ways.

A papyrus of AD 250 demonstrates the consequences of Decius' demand for sacrifice: everyone needed a receipt to prove compliance.

'To those superintending the sacrifices of the village of Theadelphia, from Aurelia Bellias, daughter of Peteres, and her daughter Capinis. We have sacrificed to the gods all along, and now in your presence according to orders I have poured a libation and offered sacrifice and eaten of the sacrificial offering; we ask you to sign below to this. Farewell.

Signatures: We Aurelius Serenus and Aurelius Hermas saw you sacrificing. Signed by me, Hermas.

Year 1 of the Emperor Caesar Gaius Messius Quintus Traianus Decius Pius Felix Augustus, Payni 27.'

Challenges to empire

Diocletian's stabilisation

Aurelian reunified the Roman Empire, but Diocletian re-established imperial stability through a reign of 20 years which ended in planned retirement. The secret of success was an imperial college, since one factor promoting earlier disunity had been the desire of major armies to have their own emperor. Power-sharing had worked in the second century when Marcus Aurelius co-opted Lucius Verus to command his Parthian campaign, and was tried in the third century by the families of Valerian and Carus. Family control might enhance loyalty, but perhaps at the expense of ability. Diocletian elevated a long-standing colleague, Maximian, to the rank of Caesar in 285 and dispatched him to Gaul to quell an uprising of *bacaudae*, rebels who have been variously interpreted as Robin Hood-style brigands or supporters of local warlords. In 286 Maximian was promoted to Augustus, with the relationship between the Augusti represented by their divine companions, Jupiter king of the gods

---

An orator in Gaul addresses Maximian in 289, praising his co-operation with Diocletian (Latin Panegyrics 10.11).

'Your harmony has this result, invincible princes, that even Fortune responds to you with an equally great measure of success. For you rule the State with one mind, nor does the great distance which separates you hinder you from governing, so to speak, with right hands clasped. Thus, although your doubled divinity increases your royal majesty, by your unanimity you retain the advantage of an undivided Empire.'

---

for Diocletian and Hercules his son for Maximian. After six years of joint reign, rebellion in Egypt prompted Diocletian to increase his imperial resources by appointing two junior colleagues as Caesars, Galerius for the east and Constantius for the west. Marriage between the Caesars and daughters of the Augusti united the Tetrarchy.

The energetic campaigning of Diocletian and his colleagues is reflected in the victory titles which precede his Edict on Maximum Prices of 301:

'The emperor Caesar Gaius Aurelius Valerius Diocletianus, pious, fortunate, unconquered, Augustus, pontifex maximus, Germanicus maximus six times, Sarmaticus maximus four times, Persicus maximus two times, Britannicus maximus, Carpicus maximus, Armenicus maximus'.

Constantius was sent to recover Britain, which permitted Maximian to leave the Rhine frontier and move to Africa to deal with Moorish incursions. In the east the major achievement was Galerius' success against the Persians in 298, after initial defeat in the previous year. The decisive action was Galerius' capture of King Narses' womenfolk, although he also ravaged lower Mesopotamia. Narses sued for peace and surrendered territory east of the Tigris to recover his women.

Almost as important as the victories was Diocletian's administrative overhaul, which doubled the number of provinces – where governors were expected to keep closer control of their areas – and introduced dioceses which grouped provinces and provided a judicial buffer between the governor and the praetorian prefect at court. The tax system was reformed perhaps to distribute the burdens of land and poll tax more fairly, perhaps to improve efficiency. Provision was made for regular reassessment; for the first time it was theoretically possible to construct an imperial budget. Diocletian also attempted to stabilise the coinage, with new issues of gold, silver and bronze, but he seems to have lacked the bullion to issue enough precious metal coins to convince people. As a result inflation continued, and in 301 Diocletian issued an Edict on Prices, a law for display in all towns and markets of the Empire on which was listed the maximum prices for a wide range of goods and services. In terms of military organisation, Diocletian may have been less innovative than in other areas, although the evidence for his actions is indecisive. His concern for frontiers was reflected in the strengthening of defensive installations, the construction of new roads – for example the Strata Diocletiana which ran from the Gulf of Aqaba to the Euphrates – and the deployment of troops near the frontiers. The army most probably increased in size during his reign, though there are no precise figures.

Diocletian explains the need to control prices. (Preamble to Edict on Maximum Prices.)

'Who does not know that wherever communal safety requires our armies to be sent, profiteers insolently and covertly attack the public welfare, not only in villages and towns, but on every road? They charge extortionate prices for merchandise, not just fourfold or eightfold, but so that human speech cannot find words to characterise their profit and practices. Indeed, sometimes in a single transaction a soldier is stripped of his donative and pay. Moreover, the contributions of the whole world for the support of armies fall as profits into the hands of these plunderers, and our soldiers appear to bestow with their own hands the rewards of military service and their veterans' bonuses upon the profiteers.'

Constantine and conversion

Diocletian retired in 305, to a specially prepared palace at Spalato (Split), but his succession arrangements faltered because they disregarded the soldiers' strong dynastic loyalties: when Constantius the new

Augustus of the west died at York in 306, his troops promptly acclaimed his son Constantine. Over the next six years Constantine schemed and fought his way to mastery of the whole western Empire, a process which culminated outside Rome at the battle of the Milvian Bridge in 312: his opponent, Maxentius, son of Diocletian's partner Maximian, deployed his troops on the north bank of the Tiber, but they were routed and during the confused flight back to the city the wooden bridge collapsed. The

Towers at Constantina (modern Viransehir, Turkey). The large horseshoe towers of basalt date back to the fourth century. (Author's collection)

most significant aspect of the victory was that Constantine's men fought under the sign of Christ, whose inspiration Constantine proclaimed; after the battle he set about rewarding his new God. In some ways this marked a decisive change from Diocletian (who had initiated persecution of Christians in 303) and Constantine's conversion did eventually lead to the Christianisation of the Empire and so of Europe, but the underlying religious attitude was the same: correct worship of the right divinity provided victory.

A contemporary Christian teacher, Lactantius, records how Constantine had the chi-rho monogram (the first two Greek letters of Christ's name) painted on his soldiers' shields (On the Deaths of the Persecutors *44.5–6*).

'Constantine was advised in a dream to mark the heavenly sign of God on the shields of his soldiers and then engage in battle. He did as he was commanded and by means of a slanted letter X with the top of its head bent round, he marked Christ on their shields. Armed with this sign, the army took up its weapons.'

For the next 12 years Constantine shared the Empire in uneasy partnership with Licinius in the east, but in 324 the two clashed in a decisive naval engagement in the Bosporus, with Constantine emerging as sole ruler of the whole Empire. This victory was marked by the construction of a new capital – Constantinople – on the site of the old city of Byzantium, which gained new walls, a palace and the other appurtenances of an imperial seat. Constantine now inherited responsibility for the Danube and Persian frontiers. During the 330s he campaigned energetically against the Goths, to such effect that the area was quiet for the next generation. Towards the end of his reign tension began to rise in the east, with Constantine probably contacting the

Constantine writes to the king of Persia (Eusebius, Life of Constantine *4.9–13).*

'With God's power as ally I began from Ocean's shores and progressively raised up the whole world with sure hopes of salvation ... I believe that I am not mistaken, my brother, in confessing this one God the Author and Father of all, whom many of those who reigned here, seduced by mad errors, have attempted to deny. But such punishment finally engulfed them that all men saw that their fate superseded all other examples, warning those who attempt the same ends ... With these persons – I mean of course the Christians, my whole concern is for them – how pleasing it is for me to learn that the chief regions of Persia too are richly endowed! ... These therefore I entrust to you, since you are so great, putting their persons in your hands, because you too are renowned for piety.'

Christian population of lower Mesopotamia to raise hopes of 'liberation'; he had already written to the young Persian king Shapur II to inform him of the benefits of Christianity and to warn him not to harm his Christian subjects. In the event Constantine bequeathed the conflict to his successors, since he died near Nicomedia in 337 at the start of the march east.

Although his accession disrupted the Tetrarchy, Constantine was in most ways a true heir to Diocletian's purpose. For half his reign Constantine was involved in civil conflicts, which diverted attention from frontiers: he reorganised the central forces which accompanied the emperor, the *comitatus*, and created two prestigious commands for cavalry and infantry, the *magister equitum* and *magister peditum*. The praetorian prefect lost operational military responsibility, but took overall charge of administration, including military supplies and recruitment; in recognition of this increased role, the Empire was divided into four grand prefectures. At provincial level military command was also separated from civilian duties. Constantine's greatest achievement was the establishment of a stable currency, based on gold *solidi* struck at 72 to the pound: the bullion gained from civil war and confiscations of temple treasures underpinned this coinage.

The eastern Empire

The Empire was divided between Constantine's three surviving sons, Constantine II in Gaul, Constans in Rome, with Constantius II in the east inheriting the war against Shapur. Constantius II has suffered historiographically, since most Christian writers regarded him as heretical, while the major contemporary secular author, Ammianus Marcellinus, misrepresented him because of his clash with the pagan Julian. As a result his dogged conduct of 24 years of war with Persia is underrated, although he managed to preserve the eastern frontier with only limited losses in the face of one of the most dynamic Persian rulers. There was only one pitched battle during the conflict, outside Singara in 344: the Romans had the advantage until a disorderly pursuit and attack on the Persian camp permitted the enemy to recover so that the engagement ended indecisively. Constantius' strategy was to build new forts and rely on the major cities of the frontier to hold up Persian incursions, with Nisibis holding the key to advances across upper Mesopotamia: Shapur besieged the city three times, bringing the full might of Persian siege technology to bear, but the defences held, with divine support provided through the city's deceased bishop, Jacob, whose corpse was paraded around the ramparts as a talisman. Singara, however, was captured in 360 when a newly repaired section of wall was undermined, and Bezabde also fell that year.

The siege of Amida (Diyarbakir) in 359, of which Ammianus was a fortunate survivor, illustrates the dynamics of strategic confrontation. Constantius was engaged on the Danube, when Shapur II planned to strike deep into Roman territory, for once disregarding Nisibis. The Romans implemented a scorched-earth policy and placed strong guards at the Euphrates crossings, but the river was in flood and the Persians turned northwards. At Amida Shapur attempted to overawe the defenders by a display of might, but a Roman artilleryman disrupted proceedings when a bolt aimed at the king struck a member of his entourage. Shapur felt obliged to punish the city, which eventually fell after 73 days of determined resistance, but the combination of delay and heavy casualties terminated the Persian invasion.

Civil conflicts as well as the demands of other frontiers distracted Constantius, especially after he became sole ruler in 353. Between 351 and 353 Constantius co-opted his cousin Gallus to supervise the east, but he proved unsuitable. In 355 Constantius turned to Gallus' younger brother, the intellectual Julian, and used him to control the west, with better results until in 360 Julian's troops – quite possibly with Julian's encouragement – demanded imperial equality for their commander. Constantius stabilised the frontier before turning west to confront his rival, but he died en route; Julian inherited the Empire without a battle.

Julian arrived in the empire of the east in 361 with a reputation as a successful general and a need to demonstrate that he could surpass Constantius. A major factor in this was religion: Julian espoused the old gods and had renounced formal adherence to Christianity when challenging Constantius. Persia offered the great testing ground, where Julian could prove the rectitude of his beliefs and the pusillanimity of Constantius' policies. Preparations were made for a grand invasion in 363: Julian himself would lead an army down the Euphrates while a second army created a diversion in northern Mesopotamia. The campaign began well, with Julian overrunning Persian forts along the Euphrates and reaching the vicinity of the capital Ctesiphon in spite of Persian

The arch of Galerius, Thessaloniki, showing fighting between Romans and Persians. (Author's collection)

attempts to thwart his advance by breaching their irrigation canals. However, he now realised that he had little chance of capturing the city, and resolved to march back up the Tigris; this entailed burning his fleet of supply ships which could not be hauled upstream. Treacherous guides led him astray and then Shapur, whose army had not been tied down effectively in the north, began to harass; Julian was mortally wounded in a skirmish, and his successor, the officer Jovian, could only extricate his army by surrendering territories to the east of the Tigris, plus

Eastern frontier in the fourth century

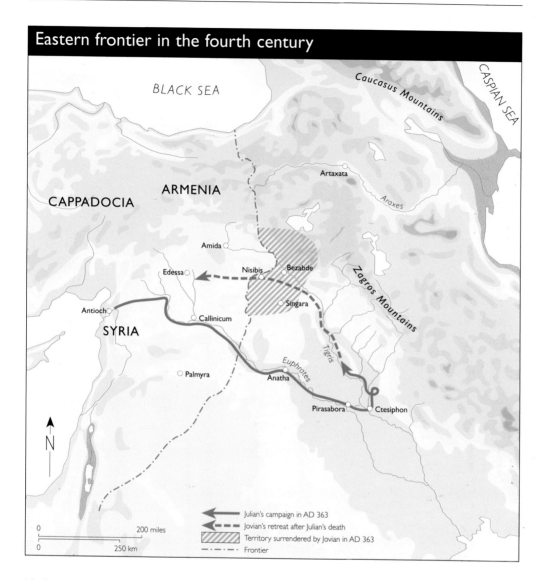

Julian's campaign in AD 363
Jovian's retreat after Julian's death
Territory surrendered by Jovian in AD 363
Frontier

0 — 200 miles
0 — 250 km

Nisibis and Singara. Bitter opposition from the inhabitants of Nisibis who pleaded to continue their battle with the Persians was overruled, and they were resettled in Amida.

Blame for the Roman reverse was allocated in accordance with religious loyalties: for pagans the heroic Julian's success was squandered by the cowardly Jovian, whereas for Christians Jovian's piety rescued the Romans from Julian's folly. The loss of Nisibis rankled, and its recovery was still on the imperial agenda two centuries later, but the agreement of 363 ushered in the most prolonged period of peace which the Roman eastern frontier had ever

experienced, a fact crucial for the eastern Empire's survival during the fifth century. There were moments of tension, and two brief conflicts, but no prolonged warfare until 502. Tension persisted for a time, primarily over control of Armenia, but this was settled in 387 when the Armenian kingdom was suppressed and its territory partitioned between Rome and Persia. In 421/2 war was provoked by the behaviour of Christian activists in Persia against Zoroastrian shrines; the Christians fled west and Theodosius II refused to surrender his co-believers. In 440–42 conflict flared again, this time over Roman payments for the

The Baptistery at Nisibis with the lintels of the original doors just visible. Only a year after the building's dedication Nisibis was transferred to Persian control by Jovian (AD 363). (Author's collection)

defence of the Caucasus; the Romans once more had the better of limited fighting. On each occasion the Romans were prompted to agree peace because of Hunnic activity in the Balkans, while the Persians also had distractions on their north-eastern frontier.

During these years there emerged a system of diplomatic arrangements, which reduced the risks of disagreements spilling over into full-scale war. The rights of minority religions were recognised, which protected the Christians in Persia; their position also became easier when doctrinal questions separated them from Roman Christians. Attempts were made to regulate the transhumant Arab tribes of the frontier, construction of new fortresses was banned, the defence of key fortifications in the Caucasus was accepted as a shared burden, and trade was funnelled through specific markets at Nisibis, Callinicum and Artaxata. Rome and Persia came to see themselves as the two lights of the world, with a mutual obligation to help each other against disruptive and uncivilised outsiders. There was even a story that Emperor Arcadius appointed his Persian counterpart Yazdgard as guardian for his infant son Theodosius.

Khusro appeals to Emperor Maurice, recalling the tradition of collaboration between their states. (Theophylact 4.11.2–3)

'God effected that the whole world should be illumined from the very beginning by two eyes, namely by the most powerful kingdom of the Romans and the most prudent sceptre of the Persian state. For by these powers the disobedient and bellicose tribes are winnowed and man's course is continually regulated and guided.'

European frontiers in the fourth century

After Constantine's death, the crucial factor in the west was civil war: Constantine II was killed while fighting Constans in 340; in 350 Constans was overthrown by Magnentius, an officer on his personal staff, who then dispatched a rival in Rome. Constantius, after seducing the troops of another usurper in Illyria, clashed with Magnentius at Mursa on 28 September 351 in one of the most destructive battles of the century. Once Magnentius was eliminated after a further defeat in 353, the Rhine armies were again disrupted when court intrigues pushed a Frankish general Silvanus into revolt in 354; finally Julian (who had been sent to Gaul in 355 because internal conflict had permitted Franks and Alamanni to breach the frontier) was acclaimed Augustus at Paris in February 360; he marched his best troops east to confront Constantius.

Julian's actions in Gaul are painted in rosy colours by Ammianus, whose surviving books open with the suppression of Silvanus, a daring action in which Ammianus participated. During 356 Julian campaigned energetically and re-established Roman authority along the Rhine. In 357 an ambitious campaign was planned to take the war into Alamannic territory, with the armies of Gaul and Italy operating a pincer movement. Problems of co-ordination

(perhaps compounded by jealousies) unravelled the strategy and the army of Italy was defeated near Basel. But in August Julian confronted the Alamanni on the right bank of the Rhine near Argentoratum (Strasburg): it was a hard-fought struggle. Since Ammianus described it in reasonable detail, it is one of the few battles in late antiquity whose course can be reconstructed. Ammianus commented that superior Roman discipline and training overcame the Alamanni's advantage in physical size, which gave their intitial charge such ferocity; it is also noticeable that the battle was won by the Roman infantry, whereas their cavalry, which included some heavy-armed cataphracts (suit of armour), was forced to flee.

After Jovian's brief reign, the brothers Valentinian and Valens shared the Empire, with the senior Valentinian taking charge of the Rhine and upper Danube and Valens responsible for the lower Danube and east. On the Danube the stability established by Constantine was broken, the reason, as so often, Roman internal conflict. The Goths' relations with Constantius had moments of tension, especially when imperially sponsored attempts to promote Christianity provoked a backlash, but they remained allies of the house of Constantine to the extent that when Procopius, Julian's cousin (and hence distant relative of Constantine) revolted against Valens in 365, he was able to secure help from the Tervingi, the main confederation on the Danube. Thereafter Valens set about disciplining these rebels, but severe flooding and the Goths' ability to disappear into the swamps and mountains prevented a decisive encounter. When Valens halted proceedings in 369, the Tervingi secured better terms, which included a reduction in their obligation to provide troops for the Romans. South of the river Valens embarked on energetic fortification, while the Tervingi returned to persecution of Christians. Further west Valentinian was engaged in similar operations against the Alamanni, Quadi and Sarmatians, while his subordinates dealt with disturbances in North Africa and Britain.

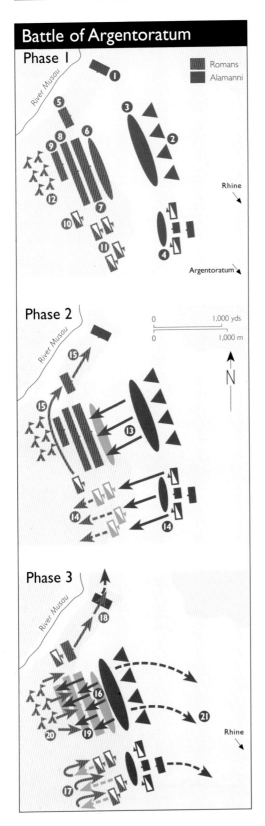

Battle of Argentoratum

Phase 1

River Musau

Rhine

Argentoratum

Romans
Alamanni

Phase 2

River Musau

0		1,000 yds
0		1,000 m

N

Phase 3

River Musau

Rhine

LEFT BATTLE OF ARGENTORATUM

Phase 1: 1 Alamanni infantry in ambush; **2** Main Alamanni infantry in wedge formation; **3** Alamanni skirmishes; **4** Alamanni cavalry; **5** Roman flank guard under Severus; **6** Roman light infantry; **7** Roman front line including Cornuti and Brachiati; **8** Roman second line including Batavi and Reges; **9** Roman reserve including Primni; **10** Julian's personal guards; **11** Roman cavalry; **12** Roman baggage and camp guards.

Phase 2: 13 Alamanni infantry drives Roman light infantry behind front line; **14** Alamanni cavalry routs Roman cavalry on right wing; **15** Alamanni ambush discovered and neutralised by Roman left wing, helped by Julian's personal guard.

Phase 3: 16 Alamanni break through Roman front line, but are held by second line; **17** Julian re-forms Roman cavalry and stabilises right wing; **18** Roman left wing pursues Alamanni ambush from field; **19** Alamanni drive back Roman lines to foot of hill where camp sited; **20** Roman reserve and camp guards push Alamanni back; **21** Alamanni flee towards Rhine, pursued by Romans.

RIGHT BATTLE OF ADRIANOPLE

Phase 1: Roman army deploys from front line of march with cavalry on the right wing and light infantry in lead. **1** Gothic wagon circle defended by infantry; **2** Gothic light infantry; **3** Roman light infantry; **4** Roman cavalry on right wing (*sagitatti* and *scutarii*); **5** Roman heavy infantry; **6** Roman cavalry on left wing; **7** Roman reserves (Batavi); **8** Gothic cavalry (arriving late).

Phase 2: While Goths try to delay the battle to allow their cavalry to return, the two armies come to blows. **9** Gothic infantry withdraws to laager during negotiations; **10** *Sagitatti* and *scutarii* repulsed; **11** Main Roman infantry force attacks laager; **12** Part of cavalry on Roman left wing attacks laager; **13** Gothic cavalry returns, shatters Roman left wing; **14** Roman cavalry on left still forming up.

Phase 3: 15 Most Roman cavalry driven from field; **16** Roman reserves withdraw; **17** Roman army trapped between Goths counterattacking from laager and Gothic cavalry.

In the 370s the position on the frontiers changed. In the west Valentinian suffered a stroke while trying to overawe a delegation of Quadi, and was succeeded by Gratian, whose military experience was limited, and the infant Valentinian II. On the lower Danube masses of Goths arrived to pester Roman officials for the right to cross and settle peacefully. Their desperation was caused by the westward movement of the Huns, who had been displaced from further east and were now approaching the Black Sea with a

Battle of Adrianople

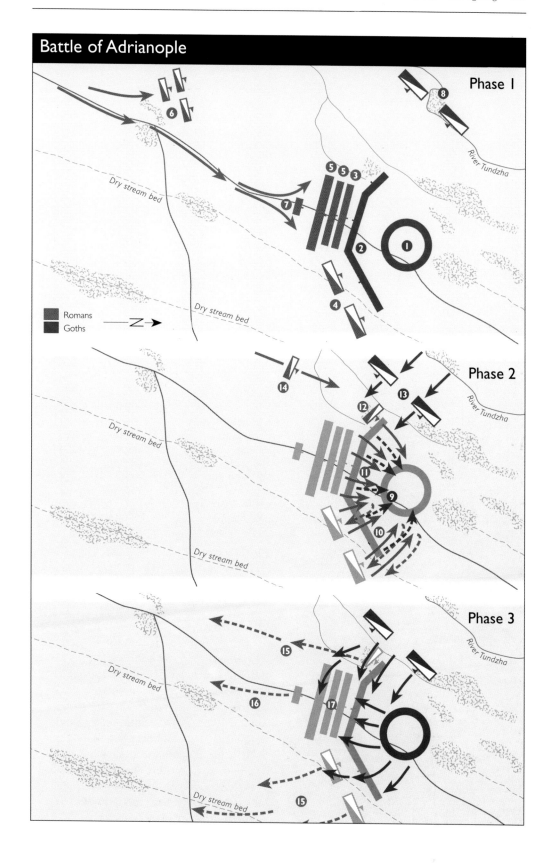

consequent domino effect on the tribes there. The most powerful Gothic group, the Greuthungi, who had been based between the Dneister and Dneiper, was destroyed and the Tervingi were the next to be threatened: the might of Rome appeared less daunting than the Hunnic scourge, and the Danube seemed to offer safety. Roman attempts to control the Goths, by admitting only the Tervingi and removing their leaders failed, but thereafter they managed to contain the Gothic threat quite successfully by exploiting control of food and by harassing the Goths as soon as they dispersed to seek supplies.

In 378 it appeared that the Romans would crush the Goths as Valens returned from Antioch and Gratian marched from the Rhine to co-operate against them. However, Gratian's arrival was delayed when the Alamanni heard about his plans and decided to invade. Valens still felt confident of defeating the Goths, and on 9 August 378 he led his army out of camp at Adrianople towards the Gothic position. The Romans probably outnumbered the Goths, but their deployment from the line of march was confused and the battle was joined haphazardly, with the result that the Roman wings were driven back. At this moment the Gothic cavalry, which had been absent foraging, returned and the combination of their flank attacks, the heavy fire of Gothic archers, and the heat of the long day gradually wore down the Roman centre. Resistance was stubborn, but two-thirds of the army, including Valens, were killed.

Adrianople is often seen as the turning point for the Roman Empire, but it is necessary to remember that the eastern forces survived the destruction of one of its field armies and the Gothic victors were successfully managed by the new eastern Emperor, Theodosius, who gave them lands in Thrace in return for military service. They were a major nuisance, but their inability to capture walled cities limited their impact. Gothic help was fully exploited when Theodosius was drawn westwards to

intervene against usurpers, first in 387 and then in 394: the destruction of these battles, especially at the Frigidus River in 394, certainly weakened the Goths, but more importantly they destroyed the best elements in the western armies. When Theodosius died at Milan in AD 395 the Empire was divided between his young sons, Arcadius in the east and Honorius in Italy. It was the east which was in a much stronger position, as can be seen from the increasingly desperate legislation on recruitment and other military matters issued by Honorius' court over the next dozen or so years.

Ammianus reports the recognition by the victor of Adrianople that his men could not attack cities (31.6.4).

'Fritigern realised that it was pointless for men without experience of siege-works to fight at such a disadvantage. He suggested that the siege should be abandoned and a sufficient force left behind to contain the enemy. He had no quarrel, he said, with stone walls, and he advised them to attack and pillage in perfect safety rich and fruitful regions which were still unguarded.'

Ammianus (16.2.12) made the same point with regard to the Alamanni. 'They avoided the actual towns as if they were tombs surrounded by nets.'

The Huns

The Huns began to arrive along the Danube in the early fifth century, but until AD 395 their epicentre had been further east as they had raided across the Caucasus. In 408/9 a Hunnic chief Uldin crossed the lower Danube but his followers were seduced by Roman diplomacy. By the middle of the next decade the Huns were established on the Hungarian plains, and their approach should probably be connected with the construction of a

Defences at Diocletianopolis (modern Hissar, Bulgaria) showing the characteristic late Roman brick-banded rubble core of city walls. (Author's collection)

The Greek historian Priscus, who served on an embassy to Attila's court, records Hunnic demands. (fr.11)

'Edeco came to court and handed over Attila's letters, in which he blamed the Romans in respect of the fugitives. In retaliation he threatened to resort to war if the Romans did not surrender them and cease cultivating the territory he had won, extending along the Danube from Pannonia to Novae in Thrace; furthermore, the market in Illyria was not to be by the Danube as previously, but at Naissus, which he had laid waste and established as the border between Scythian and Roman territory, it being five days' journey from the Danube for an unladen man. He ordered that ambassadors come to him, not just ordinary men but the highest ranking of the consulars.'

massive new set of walls for Constantinople in 413.

In the 420s Hunnic power expanded through subordination of neighbouring tribal groups and consolidation of authority within a single ruling family, that of Rua, who was succeeded by his nephews, Attila and Bleda. Rua extracted annual peace payments from the eastern Empire, which were 700 pounds of gold in the 430s increasing to 2,100 pounds in 447 (perhaps 5 per cent of total imperial revenue) at the height of Attila's power. During the 440s Attila ravaged the northern Balkans, sacking cities and driving off booty to fuel Hunnic prosperity, but in 450 he turned westwards where Honoria, sister of Emperor Valentinian III, offered herself in marriage.

Hunnic raids and disintegration of the west

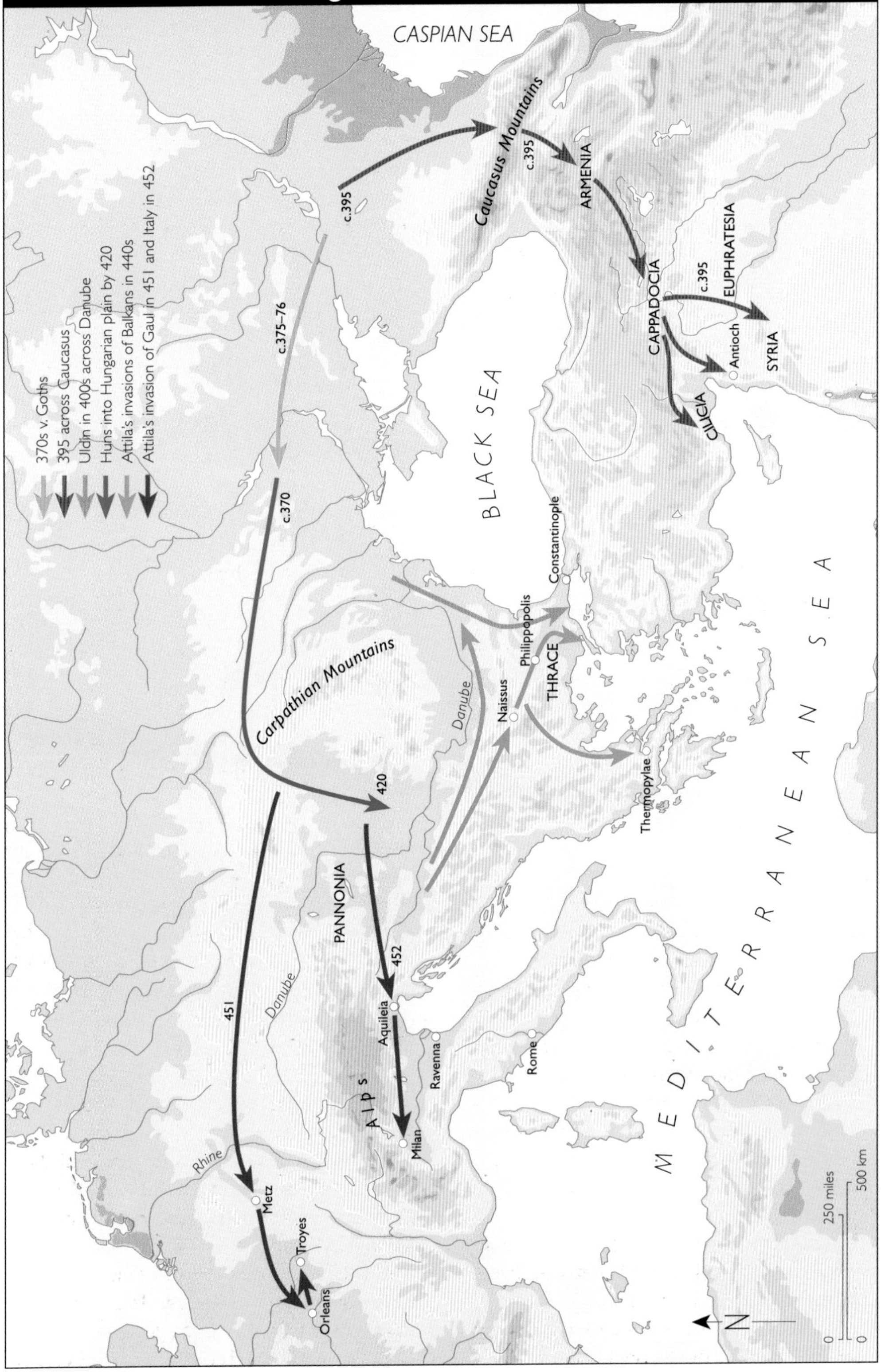

CASPIAN SEA

Caucasus Mountains

c.395

c.395

ARMENIA

c.395

CAPPADOCIA

EUPHRATESIA

Antioch

SYRIA

CILICIA

c.375–76

BLACK SEA

c.370

Constantinople

Philippopolis

THRACE

Carpathian Mountains

Naissus

Danube

Thermopylae

420

PANNONIA

M E D I T E R R A N E A N   S E A

452

Aquileia

451

Danube

Ravenna

Rome

A l p s

Milan

Rhine

Metz

Troyes

Orléans

370s v. Goths
395 across Caucasus
Uldin in 400s across Danube
Huns into Hungarian plain by 420
Attila's invasions of Balkans in 440s
Attila's invasion of Gaul in 451 and Italy in 452

N

250 miles

500 km

Hunnic power depended upon the personal authority of their leader, his ability to dominate all members of his federation. This was achieved partly through the exercise of patronage and the disbursement of the rewards of military victory, but even more by the exercise of sheer terror: Attila repeatedly demonstrated that it was impossible to escape his grasp, and potential rivals were painfully killed. As a result the Romans could not operate their traditional diplomatic strategy of divide and subvert: they were required to hand back Huns, who were probably refugees from Attila's power, and so were denied the chance to cultivate alternative leaders. Attila was also a skilled diplomat, with a wide knowledge of the international scene: he knew the invasion routes into Persia, timed his attacks on the Balkans to coincide with an eastern military expedition to Africa, and exploited tensions between Goths, Franks and Romans in the west; his reception of Roman envoys was a masterful demonstration of psychological pressure. As his federation expanded he came to control vast military resources, which it was in his interest to exploit. His armies, spearheaded by Hunnic cavalry, were capable of rapid movement to anticipate defences, while the masses of expendable subordinates could be thrown at Roman walls to supplement the Huns' considerable skill at siegecraft. The threat was such that Constantinople was provided with a further set of fortifications, the Long Walls, which stretched from the Sea of Marmara to the Black Sea.

Salvation for the Romans lay in the fact that the Hunnic federation could not stand still: military success and booty were regular requirements, and any interruption created tensions within the international conglomeration. Attila's attacks on the west produced only limited success, and this jolt was compounded by his death: his sons fought over the succession, and subordinate tribes rebelled: in 454 the Gepids and then the future Ostrogoths, Lombards, Heruls plus others emerged from the shadow of Hunnic control to confront the Romans along the Danube frontier. For the next generation the northern and central Balkans were repeatedly crossed by Gothic groups in search of land and safety, while the Romans reverted to reliance on fortifications and control of food supplies, plus the incentive of imperial military titles with their accompanying salaries, to hold the balance. The Goths recognised the Roman strategy of playing off different groups, and on occasions tried to counteract this, but the incompatible ambitions of Gothic leaders played into Roman hands. Only the opportune death of one powerful leader permitted his main rival Theoderic the Amal to unite most of the Balkan Goths into an army whose strength was such that the Emperor Zeno commissioned them to invade Italy and reassert imperial control there.

Two Gothic leaders (Theoderic Strabo – son of Triarius – and Theoderic the Amal) reproach each other for playing into Roman hands. (Malchus, fr. 18.2.30–38)
'But the son of Triarius kept riding up to the other's camp, insulting and reproaching him and calling him a swearer of useless oaths, a child and a madman, an enemy and betrayer of his own race, who did not know the Romans' mind or recognise their intentions. "For they remain at peace, while the Goths wear each other down. Whichever of us loses, they will be the winners without effort."'

Loss of the west

In 395 the young Honorius succeeded Theodosius, but the west was controlled by Stilicho, a general of Vandal descent. Stilicho claimed that the dying Theodosius had also instructed him to protect the eastern emperor Arcadius, and that two Balkan provinces should be transferred to western authority. This rivalry drew Stilicho into Balkan affairs, where imperial competition permitted the Goths (who had been weakened by casualties

Ivory plaque depicting Stilicho as defender of the state. (Ancient Art and Architecture)

Edict of Arcadius and Honorius addressed to the provincials (February 406) pleads for more recruits (Theodosian Code 7.3.17).

'On account of our pressing necessities, by this edict we summon to military service all men who are aroused by the innate spirit of freedom. Freeborn persons, therefore, who take arms under the auspices of the country shall know that they will receive 10 *solidi* each from our imperial treasury when affairs have been adjusted.'

in Theodosius' service) to demand a better deal. Alaric, a Gothic commander under Theodosius, emerged as leader of a force capable of withstanding an imperial army, but he still struggled to secure lasting benefits: success only came after other tribal groups breached the western frontiers.

On 31 December, 406 Vandals, Alans and Sueves swarmed across the Rhine, triggering the proclamation of local commanders as emperors. Stilicho's authority crumbled, and his family – which had been trying to marry into the imperial house – was eliminated; with it disappeared the main Roman army in northern Italy, since many of Stilicho's Gothic troops chose to join Alaric. Alaric failed to obtain concessions from Honorius

(who had abandoned Milan for the greater security of Ravenna), established his own emperor, and on 24 August 410 captured Rome.

This brief sack of Rome was of symbolic significance; of greater importance were Honorius' imperial rivals in Gaul and Spain whose ambitions permitted the invading tribes to exploit Roman divisions. Honorius had already demonstrated his inability to protect his subjects in his desperate military legislation of the previous decade. Inevitably local protectors appeared who had to exploit the available military manpower, which was often roaming tribal bands: incompatible objectives emerged, with the policy of crushing invaders at odds with a desire to preserve their manpower for future use.

Alaric died while trying to reach Africa, and his followers, whom it is now convenient to call Visigoths (west Goths), moved to Spain where they helped to subdue the Sueves and Vandals. In 418 they eventually settled in the Garonne valley in south-west Gaul, where Honorius granted them estates with their revenues; in return they were to campaign for Honorius, who sent them back to Spain. Theoderic (417–51) gave essential stability: he challenged the Romans in southern Gaul whenever they seemed weak, and expanded his power in Spain by building links with the Sueves, while appearing co-operative when it suited his interests.

One consequence of Visigothic involvement in Spain was the Vandal crossing to Africa, although the precise cause was, naturally, internal Roman conflict: Boniface, governor of Africa, invited the Vandals to help him to resist pressure from rivals at Ravenna. The Vandals' arrival in 429 condemned the western Empire: within a decade they had taken over the north African provinces, captured Carthage (in 439) and withstood eastern empire attempts to repulse them. North Africa was the most prosperous part of the west, and its wealth had escaped the impact of tribal invasion; its loss decisively reduced the resources on which emperors at Ravenna could call and, to compound the problem, the Vandals used Roman ships at Carthage to dominate Sicily and Sardinia and to ravage Italy; they sacked Rome in 455, a much more destructive event than Alaric's entry in 410.

From the Roman perspective the priorities were to restore battered imperial authority, stabilise the tribal groups, and then gradually weaken their independence. In the latter part of his reign Honorius relied on the general Constantius, who was granted the title of patrician, which thereafter became the designation for the senior western commander. Constantius married Honorius'

daughter (Galla Placidia – the widow of Athaulf), but died in 421. At Honorius' death in 423, Constantius' widow appealed to Constantinople on behalf of her infant son, Valentinian while a usurper at Ravenna sought help from the Huns. Valentinian III was installed in 425, but the dispute brought the Huns into western empire affairs.

Aetius emerged as the new patrician. His greatest achievements were in Gaul, where he contained the Visigoths – often with help from the Huns whom he also used to crush the Burgundians. Aetius had been a hostage with the Huns and so was well connected, but the culmination of his successes was the repulse of Attila's invasion in 451 at the battle of the Catalaunian Plains, with the help of an improbable coalition of Franks, Burgundians and Visigoths (whose king Theoderic died heroically). When Attila turned to northern Italy in 452, Aetius could not prevent the loss of northern cities including Aquileia. He could harass the Huns but without bringing the Visigoths across the Alps he dared not attack directly – instead

The Gallic chronicler Hydatius describes the loss of Spain (Chronicle, 17).

'When the province of Spain had been laid waste by the destructive progress of disasters just described, the Lord in his compassion turned the barbarians to the establishment of peace. They then apportioned to themselves by lot areas of the provinces for settlements: the Vandals took possession of Gallaecia and the Sueves that part of Gallaecia which is situated on the very western edge of the Ocean. The Alans were allotted the provinces of Lusitania and Carthaginiensis, and the Siling Vandals Baetica. The Spaniards in the cities and forts who survived the disasters surrendered themselves to servitude under the barbarians, who held sway throughout the provinces.'

The King of the Visigoths marries a captured imperial princess in 414 in a ceremony intended to signal a rapprochement between Romans and Goths (Olympiodorus, 24).

'Athaulf married Placidia at the beginning of January in the city of Narbo at the house of Ingenuus, one of the leading locals. There Placidia, dressed in royal raiment, sat in a hall decorated in Roman fashion, and Athaulf sat by her side, wearing a Roman general's cloak and other Roman clothing. Amidst the celebrations, along with other wedding gifts Athaulf gave Placidia 50 handsome young men dressed in silk clothes ... Then nuptial hymns were sung, first by Attalus, then by Rusticius and Phoebadius. Then the ceremonies were completed amidst rejoicings and celebrations by both the barbarians and the Romans amongst them.'

Disintegration of the west

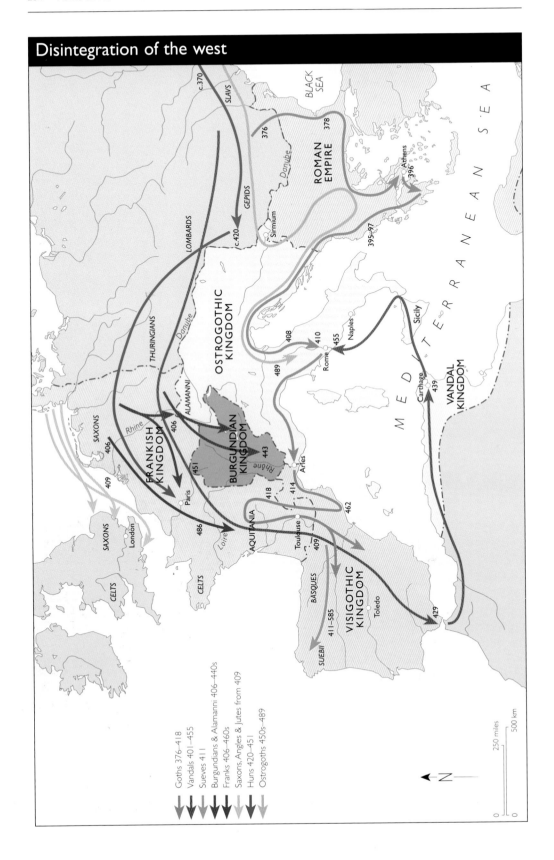

BLACK SEA

ROMAN EMPIRE

MEDITERRANEAN SEA

c.370

SLAVS

376

378

Danube

Athens
396

395–97

GEPIDS

c.420

Sirmium

LOMBARDS

OSTROGOTHIC KINGDOM

THURINGIANS

Danube

408

410   455

Naples

Sicily

489

Rome

ALAMANNI

406

Rhine

FRANKISH KINGDOM

BURGUNDIAN KINGDOM

443

Rhône

Arles

Carthage
439

VANDAL KINGDOM

SAXONS

406

451

Paris

418

414

462

409

486

Loire

AQUITANIA

Toulouse

409

SAXONS

London

CELTS

CELTS

BASQUES

VISIGOTHIC KINGDOM

Toledo

411–585

SUEBI

429

Goths 376–418
Vandals 401–455
Sueves 411
Burgundians & Alamanni 406–440s
Franks 406–460s
Saxons, Angles & Jutes from 409
Huns 420–451
Ostrogoths 450s–489

N

250 miles
500 km

0
0

Mosaic in S. Apollinare Nuovo, Ravenna, depicting the palace of Theoderic. (Ancient Art and Architecture)

Pope Leo was deployed to encourage Attila to leave.

Like Stilicho and Constantius before him, Aetius schemed to link his family to the emperor by marriage, but this contributed to his downfall. In September 454 Valentinian personally assassinated Aetius, only for Aetius' bodyguards to take revenge in March 455. For the next two decades control was contested between the different power blocks with interests in the western state: the Visigoths, Vandals, the eastern Empire and the Italian army under the patrician Ricimer, backed a rapid succession of rulers. The problems are illustrated by the reign of Majorian (457–61), Ricimer's appointee, who curbed Vandal raiding in central Italy and reasserted Roman authority in Gaul and Spain; he appears to have been too successful for when an attack on Africa was foiled, Ricimer had him executed.

One final attempt to crush the Vandals and restore western resources was made in 468 when a massive naval expedition was

An appreciative assessment by a Latin author of Theoderic the Ostrogoth's regime in Italy (Anonymus Valesianus 59–60).

'Theoderic was a man of great distinction and of good-will towards all men, and he ruled for 33 years. Italy for 30 years enjoyed such good fortune that his successors inherited peace, for whatever he did was good. He so governed two races, Romans and Goths, that although he was an Arian, he nevertheless did not attack the Catholic religion; he gave games in the circus and amphitheatre, so that even by Romans he was called Trajan or Valentinian, whose times he took as a model; and by the Goths, because of his edict in which he established justice, he was judged in all respects to be their best king.'

sent from Constantinople, but this was thwarted by Vandal fireships. Failure was ruinous for the eastern state – which spent 64,000 pounds of gold (more than a year's revenue) – and fatal for the western state: in 476, after a rapid turnover of rulers, the army of Italy under Odoacer deposed the young Romulus, who was derisively nicknamed Augustulus ('little Augustus'), and returned the imperial insignia to Constantinople. Odoacer controlled Italy until Theoderic the Amal took Ravenna in 491 and established the 'Ostrogothic' (east Goth) kingdom. Theoderic in his long reign (491–526) created a successful Romano-Gothic realm during which Italy prospered and a ruler at Ravenna secured considerable power in southern Gaul and Spain and intermittent influence in Vandal Africa.

Sixth-century wars

While the western Empire floundered towards disintegration, the eastern Empire prospered, in spite of repeated destruction in the Balkans, since the eastern frontier was quiet and the rich provinces of Asia Minor, Syria and Egypt generated surpluses. Eastern rulers attempted to help the west, especially in the struggle against the Vandals, whose maritime raiding threatened to affect the eastern Mediterranean, but to no avail. Conflict resumed with Persia in 502 when King Kavadh invaded Armenia, capturing

various fortresses and finally, after a fierce siege, Amida. The origins of the outbreak lay much further east in Persian dealings with the Hephthalites of central Asia, who had helped Kavadh regain his throne; they were now demanding subsidies and Kavadh asked the Romans for financial help but the eastern emperor Anastasius refused, perhaps reviving the issue of Persian control of Nisibis or perhaps just reluctant to build up Persian strength.

The Roman response was slow since Bulgar Huns were ravaging the Balkans in 502, but the position slowly stabilised, in spite of dissension between Roman commanders; by 505 Kavadh was distracted by another Hephthalite invasion and agreed a truce for seven years. Anastasius interrogated his generals about their problems, and the lack of a secure base near the frontier was identified as a key. Therefore a site was chosen at Dara and construction of a massive new fortress was undertaken; financial responsibility was entrusted to Bishop Thomas of Amida. By 507 he had raised the walls to a sufficient height to disregard Persian protests that the Romans had breached the agreement to ban new frontier fortifications.

In spite of this tension the truce persisted for a further 20 years, although competition

The southern watergate at Dara showing the full height of the wall (the upper half has now fallen), part of a tower and the arches of a bridge over the stream. (The Bell Collection, University of Newcastle.)

The southern watergate at Dara, from inside the city, showing the two stages of the construction of the circuit wall. The first stage, 30 feet (10 m) high, was constructed by Anastasius, while the thinner arcaded superstructure is Justinianic. (The Bell Collection, University of Newcastle.)

between the two superpowers of the ancient world continued on the fringes of their spheres of influence, in sub-Caucasia and Arabia where religious factors exacerbated tensions. But the occasion for renewed conflict in 527 came from an incident which reflected the continuing strength of the fifth-century traditions of peaceful co-operation: the elderly Kavadh asked Emperor Justin to adopt his son Khusro and so guarantee his succession in a mirror image of Arcadius' appeal to Yazdgard over a century before; Justin was persuaded that full adoption might compromise the Roman succession and so offered Khusro a lesser form of adoption.

The war began badly for the Romans with reverses in Armenia and upper Mesopotamia, but Justinian, who succeeded his uncle in autumn 527, reorganised eastern defences by creating a new military command for Armenia, initiating major defensive works at key sites, and appointed a new general for the eastern command, Belisarius. (Procopius, the main historian for Justinian's wars, joined Belisarius' staff). In 530 the Persians were defeated in Armenia and Belisarius overcame the Persian army outside his base of Dara, but these victories were offset in 531 when Belisarius was defeated at Callinicum on the Euphrates. Justinian's main concern

An example of the international links constructed by Theoderic, who here writes to the Burgundian king to accompany the gift of a clock and urge the benefits of 'civilisation'. (Cassiodorus, Variae *1.46)*

'Therefore I greet you with my usual friendship, and have decided to send you by the bearers of this letter the time-pieces with their operators, to give pleasure to your intelligence ... Possess in your native country what you once saw in Rome. It is proper that your friendship should enjoy my gifts, since it is also joined to me by ties of kinship. Under your rule let Burgundy learn to scrutinise devices of highest ingenuity and to praise the inventions of the ancients. Through you it lays aside its tribal way of life and, in its regard for the wisdom of its king, it properly covets the achievements of the sages.'

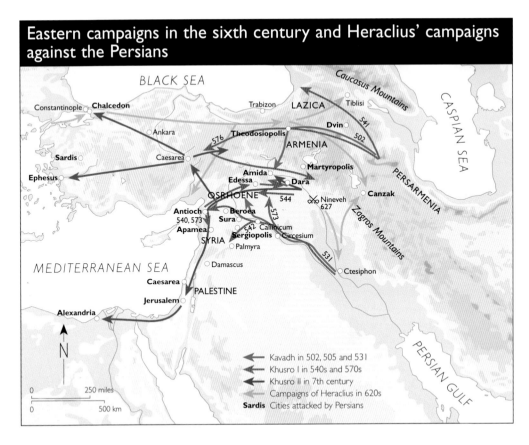

Eastern campaigns in the sixth century and Heraclius' campaigns against the Persians

throughout had been to stabilise the situation on the eastern frontier, and negotiations were now pursued to achieve the Endless Peace to which the new Persian king Khusro agreed in 532: Justinian paid 11,000 pounds of gold, and agreed to withdraw the Roman commander and his troops from Dara.

From the start of his uncle's reign in 518 Justinian had been interested in western affairs and had rapidly rebuilt links between the Eastern Church and the Pope at Rome. This caused strain in Ostrogothic Italy where the Goths, in spite of their heretical status, had sustained good relations with the papacy because of tensions between Rome and Constantinople. The death of Theoderic the Amal in 526 and the struggle of his daughter Amalasuintha to retain the throne for her son Athalaric upset the international balances which had developed in the west during the previous generation. Peace with Persia provided Justinian with the opportunity to advance his grand idea.

The Vandals came first: they were the more obnoxious to eastern Christians because some mutilated refugees from their intermittent persecutions had reached Constantinople. There had been two eastern expeditions against them during the fifth century, and the prospects for diplomacy were better in Ostrogothic Italy. In 533 an expedition sailed in 500 transports escorted by 92 warships and comprised 15,000 Roman soldiers, 1,000 foreign allies and Belisarius' retainers, his *bucellarii*. The Vandal king, Gelimer, was distracted by rebellion on Sardinia whereas Belisarius received help with supplies from the Ostrogoths in Sicily, and the Romans landed without encountering the Vandal fleet. Belisarius advanced on Carthage, defeated a scratch army raised by Gelimer, and captured the city; later that year, when their troops had returned from Sardinia, the Vandals attempted to recapture Carthage but they were heavily defeated just outside the walls.

Justinianic defences at Martyropolis (modern Silvan, Turkey) built when the city became the base for the new general of Armenia. (Author's collection)

Justinian reorganised the province, restoring urban fortifications which the Vandals had slighted, reconstituted frontier defences, and returned property to the Catholic Church. Belisarius sailed to Constantinople with several thousand Vandal captives, who were enrolled in the eastern armies, and was permitted to celebrate a triumph, the first non-imperial triumph for over 500 years.

An opportunity now presented itself in Italy where Athalaric had died and Amalasuintha, imprisoned by her cousin Theodahad, was killed. Justinian protested, and sent expeditions to Dalmatia and Sicily. Negotiations with Theodahad about accepting Roman suzerainty broke down, and Belisarius was ordered to invade Italy, even though he had been sent to Sicily with only 7,000 Roman soldiers, 500 allies and his *bucellarii*: he captured Naples by siege – although some inhabitants supported the Goths – and then marched into Rome from which the garrison had withdrawn. Theodahad had now been replaced by

Vitigis, who moved to besiege Rome in February 537; in spite of shortages of troops and supplies Belisarius defended the massive circuit, and gradually harried the besiegers so that they were suffering as much as the defenders when the siege was ended in winter 537/8. The arrival of reinforcements permitted Belisarius to take the offensive and he secured Liguria, Milan and Rimini, but disagreements between Roman commanders, especially those involving Narses, who did not recognise Belisarius' seniority, led to disaster when an invading army of Burgundians sacked Milan; allegedly 300,000 of its male inhabitants were massacred. Narses was recalled to Constantinople, and in 539 Belisarius drove the Goths out of all Italy south of the Po valley and began to close on Ravenna, whose surrender was negotiated in 540.

So far the reconquest had been a spectacular success since with limited forces the eastern Romans had eliminated two powerful western kingdoms, in spite of the distraction of regular incursions into the Balkans by Bulgars and Slavs, and of problems with mutinies and raiding Moors in Africa. The key was peace in the east, but

The walls at Edessa (Urfa, Turkey) which withstood three Persian sieges during the sixth century. (Author's collection)

in 539 this was breaking down at the time Khusro, perhaps already jealous of Justinian's western victories, received an embassy from Vitigis urging him to act before Justinian became too powerful. A quarrel over grazing rights between allied Arabs gave Khusro an excuse to attack, and in 540 he marched up the Euphrates to seek booty or protection money: cities on his route were stormed or intimidated into buying protection, and Antioch was captured after a fierce siege; it was systematically ransacked to the extent that marbles and mosaics were transported to Persia, while the surviving inhabitants were marched off to found a city of New Antioch near Ctesiphon. During his return to Persia more cities were pillaged or coerced into buying safety. Khusro's successes are often cited as proof that Justinian neglected military matters, but the truth is that, although Roman defences were in a reasonable state, scattered garrisons had no chance of opposing a Persian royal army; there was little to be done except to hold out

in defended cities until mobile units were sent from Constantinople.

In 541 Khusro switched his attention to Lazica in the north, while Belisarius, who had been recalled from Italy to handle the situation, raided into upper Mesopotamia. In 542 Khusro intended to move on Palestine, but was dissuaded by improvements in Belisarius' army. Another factor may have been bubonic plague, which was raging in the Roman Empire. In 543 plague halted Persian moves in the north, but in 544 Khusro returned to Mesopotamia with the specific target of Edessa. Religion appears to have been the main cause, because Edessa was believed to have received a guarantee of protection from Christ in the form of a letter which was engraved over the city gates. Khusro therefore deployed all the resources of Persian siege technology, only to be thwarted, and the story emerged that his great siege mound had been destroyed through the intervention of a miraculous icon of Christ – the start of the fame of the Mandylion of Edessa, the future Shroud of Turin. In 545 Khusro agreed a truce for five years, in return for 5,000 pounds of gold and the provision that operations could continue

The Greek historian Menander records the ratification of peace with Persia in 561/2 (fr.6.1.304–19).

'When these and other matters had been thoroughly debated, the 50-year treaty was recorded in Persian and in Greek, and the Greek was translated into Persian speech and the Persian into Greek. Those of the Romans who ratified the concordats were Peter the Master of Offices and Eusebius and others, while of the Persians Yazdgusnasp the Zikh and Surenas and others. When each side's agreements had been entered in the records they were compared to establish the identity of their contents and wording.

The first clause was written that through the pass at the place called Tzon and the Caspian Gates the Persians should not admit either Huns or Alans or other barbarians to gain access to the Roman realm, and that the Romans should not in that region or in other parts of the Median frontier send an army against the Persians.'

in Lazica; the truce was extended in 551 and again in 557 before a peace agreement for 50 years was signed in 561/2. The treaty contained very detailed provisions about frontier relations, as well as a guarantee from Khusro that he would not persecute his Christian subjects.

In Italy the Roman position soon deteriorated. The Goths believed that Belisarius had tricked them into surrender by appearing to agree to become their ruler and so, although they had lost Ravenna,

they chose a new leader. Totila proved to be a dynamic commander: Roman forces initially outnumbered him, but these were dispersed and their individual commanders failed to co-ordinate their actions. As a result Totila recovered much of southern Italy in 542 and starved Naples into submission in 543. Belisarius returned in

Mosaic of Justinian accompanied by Bishop Maximian, civilian dignitaries and bodyguards. From S. Vitale, Ravenna. (Ancient Art and Architecture)

544 to confront the crisis, with 4,000 new recruits but little money, but he was unable to engage the Goths. Totila captured Rome in 546 and, though Belisarius recaptured it the next year, his lack of resources led him to request a recall. When Totila regained Rome in 550 and threatened Sicily, Justinian was eventually prompted to act. Narses was sent to end the war, having demanded the resources which he deemed necessary. In 552 and 553 he twice defeated the Goths; he then had to deal with a horde of Franks and Alamanni who had taken the opportunity to invade Italy, but in 554 peninsular Italy was firmly under Roman control and at peace. Narses was left in charge of the reorganisation of the country with combined civilian and military authority.

One criticism of Justinian's grand reconquest is that it overstretched east Roman resources, so that his successors struggled to cope with the various challenges of the late sixth century. If hindsight makes this apparent, the contemporary perspective needs to be remembered: Justinian pacified the east to the best of his ability before embarking on his western ambitions and, even though Khusro broke the peace agreement, the frontier was again stabilised after the losses of 540; bubonic plague exacerbated Roman problems, but the prosperity of Africa in the late sixth century illustrates that peace could have brought long-term dividends.

Fortifications at Dara showing main horseshoe towers and smaller intermediate square towers. The citadel is visible in the middle distance. (Author's collection)

Invasion of the Balkans in the sixth century

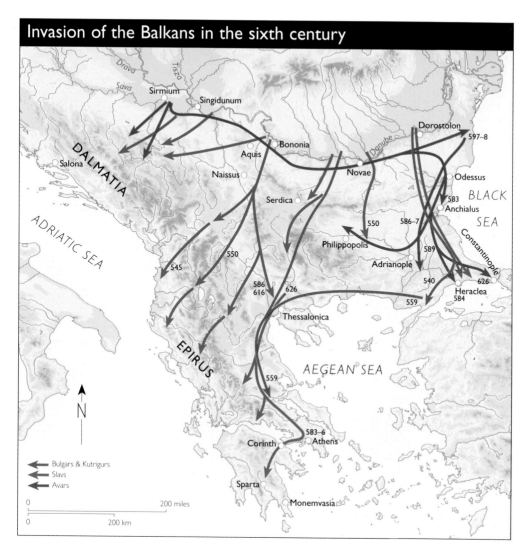

Justinian's successors

Unfortunately a new threat emerged in the late 550s, when Avar envoys contacted the Roman commander in the Caucasus. Like the Huns, the Avars were the former elite of a central Asian federation who had been forced to flee westwards, and they shared the Huns' grand ambitions and ruthless purpose. Once they occupied the Hungarian plain the Balkans, a military backwater under Justinian, became a serious problem again; the threat of Avar domination prompted the Lombards to migrate to Italy where they overran Roman positions in the Po valley. Justin II, who had succeeded his uncle in 565, had grand ideas

about Roman dignity: he dismissed Avar requests for subsidies and then provoked war with Persia. His bellicose behaviour was not complete folly, since he believed that the Turks in central Asia would co-operate by attacking the Persians on their north-eastern frontier, and a revolt of the Christian aristocracy of Persian Armenia suggested that Khusro had further distractions: Justin asserted that he could not abandon his co-believers and refused to make the annual payments agreed under the 50-year peace.

Justin's ambitions were not matched by action and in 573 the Persians captured Dara after a six-month siege: the shock sent Justin mad, and the Romans were compelled to seek a truce. In 576 Khusro campaigned into Armenia, but failed to take any cities and was outmanoeuvred in the mountains; the royal baggage was captured and many Persians were drowned when escaping across the Euphrates. Thereafter the Romans generally contained Persian attacks while ravaging their territories so that Khusro and his successor Hormizd (578–90) were prompted to pursue negotiations. These, however, foundered on the Roman insistence on recovering Dara and peace was only restored in 591: Hormizd was overthrown following disagreements with his leading general Vahram, and his son Khusro II fled to the Romans when Vahram approached Ctesiphon to beg for help. The Romans restored him to power, in return for concessions in the sub-Caucasian principalities and the restoration of Dara and other places captured in the war.

Eastern campaigns traditionally took precedence over other theatres for the Romans, and during the 570s and 580s the Balkans and Italy were neglected: the main impediment to Lombard progress were their own disputes, while in the Balkans Tiberius had few troops with which to repel the Avars when they turned their attentions south in 579. For the next decade the Romans had to rely on increased peace payments and urban defences, which the Avars – like the Huns before – captured. In the early 580s Slav bands pushed south – partly in conjunction with the Avars and partly to escape their domination – ravaging Athens and Corinth, approaching the Long Walls of Constantinople in 584, and attacking Thessalonica in 586.

Maurice, who succeeded Tiberius in 582, could do little until the eastern peace permitted him to transfer troops. Thereafter he embarked on an energetic series of campaigns which gradually stabilised the Danube frontier from the Delta to Singidunum (Belgrade) and permitted the Romans to reassert their authority in the interior. The war was carried north of the river, first in attacks on the Slavs across the lower Danube and then into the Avar

homeland on the Hungarian plains. But constant fighting gradually took its toll, and in 602 the army, already discontented over changes to military pay (which reduced the cost of equipment and horses) mutinied when it was ordered to stay north of the Danube for winter campaigning. A march on Constantinople toppled Maurice and installed the officer Phocas in his place.

Phocas' accession would inevitably have reduced the intensity of Roman activity in the Balkans, but it had more serious consequences: Khusro II seized the excuse provided by the overthrow of his protector, Maurice, to attack the Romans in order to recover the possessions and prestige he had lost in 591. During Phocas' reign (602–10) the Persians gradually captured the Roman positions east of the Euphrates, often after prolonged sieges. In 609/10 Heraclius, the son of the governor of Africa, revolted against Phocas, whose regime in Constantinople had become increasingly unpopular and violent; the distraction of civil war once more proved the Romans' undoing. Heraclius captured Constantinople in 610, but was not fully in control of the east until 611/12, by which time the Persians had pushed on to Antioch and Caesarea (Kayseri) in Cappadocia.

Heraclius was no more successful than Phocas in stemming their advance: in 614 Jerusalem fell to a Persian siege, its inhabitants and the relics of Christ's passion being taken into Babylonian captivity; Egypt was invaded in 616 and captured completely in 619, depriving Constantinople of its food supply and the Empire of its richest province. In 622 Heraclius in desperation 'borrowed' the wealth of the Constantinopolitan Church and embarked on a series of campaigns which assumed the aspect of a crusade: Khusro II, who had flirted with conversion to Christianity in 590/1, now showed himself to be an intelligent enemy of the orthodox, since he favoured the Jews and tolerated heretical and dissident Christian groups. At least Heraclius could legitimately present himself as defender of the faith. Heraclius abandoned attempts to defend Roman territory and instead took the war into Persia, basing himself in Armenia and the sub-Caucasian principalities, ravaging Azerbaijan, and avoiding the Persian armies which attempted to trap him.

War in the east had again led to neglect of the Balkans, and in the first quarter of the seventh century Slavs and Avars took control of much of the north and the centre. Heraclius had no troops to oppose their advance, and he had come close to capture himself in 623 when organising a diplomatic reception for the Avar Chagan near the Sea of Marmara: apparently Heraclius was forced to scamper back to Constantinople with his crown under his arm. Escalating peace payments were the only solution, but these did not work in the face of growing Roman weakness. In 626 the Avars besieged Thessalonica and then turned their attention to Constantinople, which was subjected to fierce bombardment by massed siege engines and waves of Slav attackers. A Persian army encamped on the Bosporus liaised with the Chagan, and an attempt was made to ferry Persian soldiers to reinforce the assault, but their crossing was disrupted by the Roman navy. Roman ships were also instrumental in breaking up a Slav attack across the Golden Horn, and the Avar Chagan was forced to withdraw with his prestige badly dented; stories soon emerged about the divine protection which the Virgin Mary gave the city which housed several of her relics.

Heraclius had declined to return to protect his capital, and his decision to focus on the eastern war was justified. First, with the assistance of Turkish allies he ravaged Persian territory extensively and then, after the Turks withdrew beyond the Caucasus, he defeated the Persians in battle outside Nineveh in December 627. The threat to

This message from Heraclius announcing the overthrow of Khusro II was read out in the Church of S. Sophia at Constantinople (Chronicon Pashale p.728).

'Let all the earth raise a cry to God; serve the Lord in gladness, enter into his presence in exultation, and recognise that God is Lord indeed. It is he who has made us and not we ourselves. We are his people and sheep of his pasture.

And let all we Christians, praising and glorifying, give thanks to the one God, rejoicing with great joy in his holy name. For fallen is the arrogant Chosroes, opponent of God. He is fallen and cast down to the depths of the earth, and his memory is utterly exterminated from earth; he who was exalted and spoke injustice in arrogance and contempt against our Lord Jesus Christ the true God and his undefiled Mother, our blessed Lady, Mother of God and ever-Virgin Mary, perished is the profaner with a resounding noise.'

central Persia led to a palace coup against Khusro, with his son agreeing to peace with Heraclius in return for support. This ushered in a period of extreme instability at the Persian court with a succession of short-lived rulers, including a Christian general in Khusro's service. From this chaos Heraclius extracted the return of Roman territories and the spoils taken from Jerusalem, including the relic of the Holy Cross, which Heraclius reinstalled in its rightful place in a grand ceremony at Easter 630. The Roman world appeared to have been put to rights and a period of consolidation and recovery could begin.

Brothers in arms

Abbinaeus, commander of provincial garrison

Flavius Abbinaeus joined the army in 304/5 and served for 33 years in the contingent of 'Parthian Archers' based in middle Egypt; this was a mounted unit whose name indicates that it was originally raised for service on the eastern frontier, or from captives taken on that frontier, but which was later recruited in the normal way from Roman provincials. In 337/8 Abbinaeus, now a non-commissioned officer, escorted an embassy of Blemmyes (tribesmen from the southern Egyptian border) to Constantinople, where he was promoted to protector by Constantius, a step which included the honour of being allowed to kiss the purple imperial robe. Protectors operated as a group of junior staff officers who undertook a variety of imperial business, and Abbinaeus was detailed to escort the embassy home; after three years among the Blemmyes, Abbinaeus returned to Constantius, who was then in Syria, and received promotion to command the cavalry squadron at Dionysias.

Back in Egypt Abbinaeus faced competition for this position since others also had secured letters of appointment through patronage. Abbinaeus appealed to Constantius and had his post confirmed, but in 344 he was dismissed by the local Count; his position was ratified on appeal. He then remained in office until after 351. The desirability of Abbinaeus' command is revealed by a collection of papyri which illustrate the vicissitudes of his career, the interaction of his troops with the local population, and his soldiers' close involvement in the maintenance of law and order and the extraction of imperial revenues from their district.

Alaric, Roman officer and tribal warlord

Alaric was born in about 370 into the Balthi, a leading family among the Gothic Tervingi. As a youth he probably participated in the Danube crossing of 376 and observed the subsequent encounters with imperial forces; at some stage he became an Arian Christian, the standard creed among the Goths. By the early 390s he had emerged as leader of a warband in the Balkans who opposed Emperor Theodosius, but in 394 he commanded tribal allies in Theodosius' expedition against the western usurper Eugenius. Disenchanted by inadequate recompense for his contribution to victory at the Frigidus River and the heavy casualties suffered by his followers, he proceeded to ravage the central and southern Balkans, taking advantage of tensions between Rome and Constantinople. By 399 he had secured one major wish, the senior Roman command of General of Illyricum, which provided him with salaries and provisions for his followers.

In 401 he invaded Italy and besieged the western emperor Honorius in Milan, but was defeated by the western generalissimo Stilicho; he was forced to withdraw to the Balkans as his men suffered from heat and poor food. He remained in the north-eastern Balkans, attempting to secure a permanent territory, until 407 when he was appointed general by Honorius as part of a western attempt to annex the Balkans. The planned campaign was cancelled, relations between Alaric and Honorius deteriorated, and Alaric invaded Italy again to secure payment for his contracted services. While negotiating with Honorius at Ravenna about territory, alliance, and payments of gold and corn, Alaric besieged Rome. Honorius procrastinated, but in 409 the threat of starvation forced the senate at Rome to agree terms; Alaric had the senator Attalus proclaimed emperor and Attalus appointed Alaric as senior Roman general.

Tensions between Attalus and Alaric, plus further unsuccessful negotiations with Honorius, resulted in Alaric returning to Rome, which was easily captured on 24 August 410. Occupation of the city for three days may have relieved Alaric's frustrations, but did not satisfy his followers' needs for territory. Thereafter he led his forces south, with North Africa as his probable goal, but was thwarted while trying to cross to Sicily; as he withdrew northwards he became ill and died. His brother-in-law Athaulf took over the army, which he led into southern Gaul in 412 where

Theoderic's mausoleum at Ravenna. Constructed from Istrian marble, with the dome formed from a single block weighing 300 tons, this projected Theoderic's ambition to create a lasting regime. (Ancient Art and Architecture)

the Visigothic kingdom was established in Aquitania.

Theoderic, Ostrogothic king

Theoderic was born in the mid-fifth century into the Amal family which led one of the Gothic groups in the northern Balkans. In 461/2 he was sent as hostage to Constantinople, where he remained for 10 years, receiving his education. After succeeding his father in 474, he spent 15 years attempting to establish a base for his people in the Balkans, either through negotiation with or intimidation of the eastern emperor Zeno. Theoderic's successes were marked by appointments as Roman general in 476/8 and again 483–87, when Zeno employed him against other tribesmen

in the Balkans as well as Isaurian rebels in the east. Rebuffs resulted in the sacking of cities, such as Stobi in 479, or the ravaging of provinces, for example Macedonia and Thessaly in 482.

> *Theoderic writes to Emperor Anastasius protesting his loyalty; the letter illustrates a tribal warlord's attachment to the ideal of Rome (Cassiodorus,* Variae *1.1).*
>
> 'Our royalty is an imitation of yours, modelled on your good purpose, a copy of the only Empire; and in so far as we follow you do we excel all other nations. Often you have exhorted me to love the senate, to accept cordially the laws of past emperors, to join together in one all the members of Italy. How can you separate from your august alliance one whose character you thus try to make conformable to your own? There is moreover that noble sentiment, love for the city of Rome, from which two princes, both of whom govern in her name, should never be disjoined.'

The death of his main Gothic rival, Theoderic Strabo, in 481 allowed Theoderic to unite most Balkan Goths under Amal leadership, but he was still unable to achieve his main goal of acquiring a secure and productive territory. In 488 Zeno agreed that Theoderic should move to Italy to attack Odoacer (who had ruled since deposing the last western emperor in 476): if successful, Theoderic could rule on behalf of Zeno. Theoderic forced Odoacer back into Ravenna; after three years of blockade the rivals agreed to share power, but Theoderic soon accused Odoacer of treachery and had him killed. Zeno's death in 491 complicated Theoderic's position, but in 497 Emperor Anastasius recognised him as ruler of Italy; to his Gothic followers Theoderic was king, even sometimes Augustus (emperor), the status to which he clearly aspired, although he was careful to protest his subservience in dealings with Constantinople.

Theoderic's 33-year reign (493–526) came to be regarded as a golden age in Italy, especially in contrast to the fighting of the 540s, and his first two decades were highly successful. Marital diplomacy built links with the main tribal groups in the west, and from 507 brought the Visigothic kingdom in Spain under his control. The senate and Pope at Rome were courted by special treatment and the carefully crafted Roman image of the new regime; religious divisions between Rome and Constantinople facilitated this rapprochement. For Goths Theoderic remained the war leader, but this was now only one facet of his complex public image. Theoderic's last decade was less rosy. The absence of a son, and the early death of his son-in-law raised the issue of succession, while Anastasius' death in 518 brought religious reconciliation between Rome and Constantinople and so made Theoderic more suspicious of leading Romans. Theoderic's death in 526 rapidly brought to the surface the tensions within his kingdom, which Belisarius' invasion was to exploit.

Narses, imperial eunuch and trusted general

The eunuch Narses originated from the Persian part of Armenia but was brought up in the palace at Constantinople in the late fifth century. He advanced through the grades of servants of the Bedchamber, reaching the position of treasurer and senior official in 530/1; in this capacity he provided money to Persarmenian deserters, and travelled to the east to secure valuable booty. In 531/2 he became imperial sword-bearer, and on 18 January 532 his distribution of bribes was crucial in undermining the cohesion of rioters in Constantinople whose violence was threatening to topple Emperor Justinian. In 535 he undertook another delicate mission, this time for Empress Theodora, to reinstate Bishop Theodosius at Alexandria and exile his opponents; for over a year Narses remained in Alexandria, conducting a virtual civil war against Theodosius' opponents.

The Barberini ivory probably showing Emperor Justinian. Above Christ blesses the emperor, who is honoured by a victory to his left while a defeated easterner stands behind his spear and other easterners offer gifts below. To one side a general offers a statue of victory and Earth displays her bounty beneath the horse's hooves. (AKG London/Erich Lessing)

In 538, at nearly 60 years old, Narses embarked on what was to prove a highly successful military career by leading reinforcements to Belisarius in Italy. Narses criticised Belisarius' conduct, and their rivalry led to the loss of Milan. Narses was recalled to Constantinople, to be followed by the allied contingent of Heruls, who refused to remain without him. In 541/2 Narses was again employed on sensitive business, first to spy on an alleged plot that involved Justinian's senior financial minister and then to investigate unrest in Constantinople. In

545 his contacts among the Heruls were exploited to persuade their leaders to enrol for service in Italy.

Narses' big chance came in 551, after Belisarius had failed to stabilise the military position in Italy and Justinian's first choice as replacement (his nephew Germanus) had died. Narses was now appointed supreme commander in Italy, a post he accepted on condition that he was provided with the men and money needed to finish the war. Assembly of troops and other preparations detained Narses in the Balkans, and he did not arrive in Ravenna until 6 June 552 after outmanoeuvring Gothic contingents blocking the main routes. Later that month Narses marched against the Goths' leader Totila, whose various attempts at deception he outwitted and whom he then crushed in battle through intelligent tactics. In July Narses rapidly recaptured Rome before confronting the Goths near Naples. Clever planning again secured victory, although contemporaries also gave credit to Narses' devotion to the Virgin Mary.

For the next decade Narses was occupied in reducing Gothic strongholds in central and northern Italy and defeating Frankish invasions. Meanwhile he was entrusted by Justinian with the massive task of returning Italy to civilian rule, as well as ensuring adherence to the emperor's preferred religious doctrines. By 559 he had received the title of patrician, the Empire's highest honour, and by 565 he had also become honorary consul, a demonstration of his place in the traditional Roman hierarchy. Justinian's death in 565 complicated Narses' last decade, as his relations with Justin II were naturally less close. The migration of Lombards into the Po valley from 568 posed new military challenges, but he remained in post until his death in 573/4, at the age of almost 95.

Shahvaraz, Persian general and usurper

Farrukhan was a Persian Christian, nicknamed Shahvaraz, 'wild boar', by King Khusro II for his energy in attacking the Romans. In 614 he overran Palestine and captured Jerusalem after a bloody siege; he dispatched the surviving Christian population into captivity in Babylonia, along with the relic of the True Cross, although other lesser relics such as the Holy Sponge and Lance were presented to Emperor Heraclius. Over the next three years he organised the capture of Egypt, and then from 622 campaigned in Asia Minor as Heraclius marshalled the Roman counter-offensive. Heraclius had the better of their manoeuvring and engagements, but in 626 Shahvaraz advanced to the Bosporus where he attempted to assist the Avars' attack on Constantinople. Roman naval power prevented him from crossing to Europe, but after the Avar withdrawal he remained at Chalcedon. Apparently Khusro tried to have him assassinated at this time, but the plan was uncovered (allegedly with Heraclius' help) and Shahvaraz refused to commit his army against the Romans.

In 628 Shahvaraz's sons supported the overthrow of Khusro, but in 630 he secured Heraclius' support for a coup against the young Ardashir. Shahvaraz, whose army was still occupying the eastern provinces, agreed to withdraw from Roman territory and return the relic of the Holy Cross. Shahvaraz only survived for two months as king before being murdered. His son Nicetas, whose name suggests an attachment to the family of Heraclius, commanded Roman troops against the Arabs in Syria in the 630s, but was executed by the caliph Umar in 641 after offering to subdue Persia for the Arabs.

Impact of conflict

Administration

Prolonged warfare was not a novelty for the Romans; indeed during their expansion they had almost prided themselves on the regularity of their involvement. But repeated campaigning inside the Roman Empire, with the consequent ravaging of estates, destruction of cities, and death or capture of civilians was unusual: before the frontier problems of the mid-third century, the civil wars of AD 69–70 and 193–97 had been the only serious instances; Hannibal's invasion of Italy in the late third century BC is the nearest parallel for such damage being inflicted by a foreigner. The new situation affected the Empire's organisation, economic and social structures, and systems of belief.

Military need prompted a fundamental change in government, from a single emperor to the collegiate rule which emerged under Diocletian. Subsequent emperors who had the opportunity to rule alone, for example Constantius II and Valentinian I, chose to appoint a colleague to share the burden of command: regional armies and provincial populations had greater confidence when an emperor was on hand. However, having multiple rulers could create tensions, as happened between Constans and Constantius II or Arcadius and Honorius; the most serious case of full-blown conflict between accepted colleagues, after Julian's proclamation in 360, was averted by Constantius' death. Even in the fifth century, when the greater problems and clearer separation of the two halves might have reduced co-operation, the east sent help to the west when possible. Imperial proliferation had administrative consequences: Diocletian's three colleagues,

and then Constantine's three sons, needed their own officials, with the result that the praetorian prefecture split into regional units.

Administrative units were also divided because of pressure from below. In the third century the financial problems caused by repeated invasion and rapid imperial turnover meant that new ways had to be devised to pay and supply the armies. As the value and regularity of traditional sources of tax revenue declined, so it seems that armies were increasingly encouraged to take affairs into their own hands and secure necessary supplies and other resources: instead of monetary taxation being extracted from provinces and delivered to the legions, who would then return much of it to the provinces through purchase of commodities, the armies short-circuited the process by taking what they needed in kind while leaving provincials to offset this against tax liabilities. Under Diocletian the state caught up with this process and acted to institutionalise it.

There had also been a long-term tendency for legions to be divided into smaller operational units whose separate existence gradually solidified as they became accustomed to campaigning and being quartered away from their parent legions. Dispersal of concentrations of legions and the attachment of units to provincial cities also facilitated problems of supply, while this distribution of troops also offered wider security when frontier defences no longer excluded invaders. These developments meant that soldiers had closer and more regular interaction with civilians, while the logistics of the tax system became more cumbersome as agricultural produce had to be gathered and stored.

A law of the early 370s illustrating some of the problems in accounting for official supplies (Theodosian Code *7.4.16*).

'If the military accountants should not deliver at once at the end of a period of 30 days their original requisitions, they shall be compelled to restore from their own property, either to the soldiers themselves or to the fiscal storehouses the supplies which they failed to withdraw from the fiscal stores or which they omitted to issue to the service units whose accounts they kept.'

The traditional system of provincial government, which relied heavily on the participation of local urban elites, could not cope. This was partly because of the complexity of the changes, but more importantly the position of local elites was being undermined by the economic and military developments which surrounded them. Inflation and the decline in value of coinage meant that they had less wealth to spend in their cities, while invasion and civil war might destroy the agricultural prosperity on which aristocrats and cities alike depended; in the worst cases even fortified cities might be sacked. The vitality of cities declined and their elites, who remained wealthy through possession of land, might decide that it was better to withdraw to their estates rather than spend limited resources on sustaining an urban lifestyle. There was an interlocking cycle of urban impoverishment and decay, so that it was harder for cities to play their expected part in imperial government at the very moment when administrative demands were becoming greater.

One result was an increase, approximately twofold under Diocletian, in the number of provinces: if provincial elites could not perform their traditional functions, it was necessary for governors to be more closely involved in supervising tax collection and local justice. This encroachment of imperial governors on customary spheres of operation

for local aristocrats further undermined the latter's authority and contributed to the cycle of decline mentioned above.

Provincial cities – one of the glories of the early Roman Empire whose extensive remains still dominate our perception of the classical Mediterranean world – came under increasing threat as their governing class became less interested in exercising local control. Leading locals could secure more power for themselves by entering the central administration, whose expansion at all levels from the provinces to the imperial courts required more educated participants. Instead of competition for municipal office, service to individual cities often became a chore for local aristocrats whose performance was bolstered by frequent imperial legislation; where this failed, tasks had to be overseen by appointees of the provincial governor, a further extension of central power and erosion of local pride. Ironically one factor which contributed to the continued importance of cities was military insecurity, since urban defences provided refuge for the inhabitants of the surrounding countryside, but this offered only a partial balance. If the threat became too intense or persisted too long, the cities would be in danger of succumbing and the local population, inevitably led by their richest, and hence most mobile members, contemplated flight.

The desertion of parts of the Empire emerged as a problem during the third century when repeated invasions depopulated considerable regions along the Rhine and Danube frontiers. The more fortunate inhabitants would have slipped away southwards, thereby contributing to the increased prosperity in late antiquity of south-western Gaul and the southern Balkans, but the majority either perished or were captured. These developments contributed to the Empire's tax problems, since certain areas produced little or nothing, while it took time to recognise the increased potential of other areas. In theory, the process of regular censuses to update tax registers instituted by Diocletian should have coped with such movements, but the

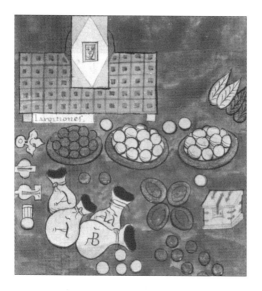

Folio from the *Notitia Dignitatum* showing the office of the *Count of the Sacred Largesses*, displaying, in addition to the standard letter of appointment, different forms of wealth for distribution. (MS Canon Misc. 378, f. 142v, Bodleian Library)

thorough reassessment of even one province was such a major undertaking that the crucial lists could not remain accurate. In practice the easiest way to make up for shortages in revenue was to squeeze accessible producers harder, both through increasing the standard tax demand and by imposing supplementary superindictions.

In some parts of the Empire the tax burden at times was probably excessive, which encouraged people to try to evade their dues. The richest and most powerful could ignore demands, while waiting for an emperor to announce one of the periodic cancellations of arrears. The poor and weak did so either by placing themselves under the protection of a rich neighbour who might (in return for payment or service of some sort) exercise his powers of obstruction for these new clients, or by moving to a new region to escape official notice. These developments prompted imperial legislation that attempted to tie people to their places of work: thus many types of urban craftsmen and shopkeepers became, in legal theory, hereditary

occupations, and in the countryside agricultural tenants were repeatedly decreed to be tied to their estates, although the frequent need for legislation suggests that the process was not all that easy.

Warlords

However complex the economic and administrative problems which protracted warfare caused, the Empire managed to survive the crisis of the third century to flourish for much of the fourth century. In the east this prosperity continued into the sixth century, but the western Empire relapsed into a cycle – ultimately fatal – of shrinking revenues and declining power during the fifth century. Invaders ravaged and depopulated large areas, but this time the damage extended much deeper into the Empire. The inability of the imperial government to repel groups such as the Visigoths led to their settlement, with official agreement, in productive provinces: south-western Gaul, much of Spain and finally, and most crucially, North Africa, passed out of Roman control. In some cases, such as the allocation of south-west Gaul to the Visigoths, the Empire in theory gained a powerful contingent of soldiers; in practice this resource could only be used when it suited the Visigoths themselves, as for example in a series of campaigns into Spain which ultimately benefited the Visigoths, and on other occasions emperors had to act against their nominal allies.

One important consequence of reductions in imperial power, perceived as well as real, was the emergence of local warlords who would control and defend particular areas against external pressures, both central and foreign. On occasions this happened with imperial consent: in the fifth century western emperors relaxed legislation against the carrying of arms by private individuals, an admission that taxation no longer bought safety. The Roman 'withdrawal' from the British Isles in 410 was probably such an incident, with the removal of the last official

Roman troops being accompanied by an exhortation to the Romano-British provincials to attend to their own defence. More often such developments occurred despite imperial wishes. At worst a powerful provincial warlord might come to be regarded as emperor, as was the case with Odaenathus of Palmyra, the separate Gallic emperors of the later third century, and Carausius in Britain; from the perspective of the imperial centre, these men were usurpers who had to be crushed when conditions permitted. When Roman rule was disintegrating similar rulers, such as Syagrius in northern Gaul in the 460s, could be seen as resolute champions of Roman authority.

Most warlords were less powerful and more local than such grand figures. They provide one plausible way of understanding the phenomenon of *bacaudae*, peasant brigands, who are said to have dominated parts of Gaul and Spain for limited periods between the third and fifth centuries. Rather than being class warriors keen to overthrow their landlords and the Roman state, they were probably an alliance of different inhabitants of a particular region ranging from poor tenants to local aristocrats, with the latter providing leadership. Such groups could easily move in and out of formal attachment to the Empire, as illustrated by the Isaurians, inhabitants of the mountains of southern Turkey. In the fourth century they revolted intermittently, probably when the ties binding local Isaurian leaders to the cities of neighbouring regions broke down. In the fifth century Isaurians came to be recognised as a precious military resource, being recruited into imperial service by Zeno, an Isaurian who became consul, senior general and patrician. In the next generation, through their domination of the imperial bodyguard, their leader, another Zeno, became son-in-law of Emperor Leo and eventually his successor. Their fall from favour after Emperor Zeno's death in 491 prompted a return to regional revolt, with even an attempt to proclaim a rival emperor.

Emperors had to strike a balance between tolerating the existence of such powerful local barons and dissipating their own

Charietto came to prominence in the early 350s as a tribal supporter of the western usurper Magnentius, but after the latter's defeat and death he had to sustain himself as a brigand. In 355 Julian, the newly appointed western Caesar, decided it was best to reach an accommodation with him. Charietto became a feared defender of the Rhine frontier, surviving Julian's departure to the east to die in action against invading Alamanni in 365, by which time he held the rank of count.

strength in attempts to discipline them. Many of the most important figures in the Empire had their personal retinues of supporters, most visibly in the form of the *bucellarii* who surrounded leading generals, but also in the monks or other ecclesiastical attendants in the entourage of major bishops and the lance-wielding guards for Anatolian estate owners whose misdeeds Justinian tried to regulate. These developments entailed that emperors did not have a monopoly of violence: a bishop of Alexandria could intimidate a general church council and prevent imperial officers from achieving their wishes, while at home his supporters might dismember a rival bishop and overawe imperial troops attempting to restore order. Legislation was meant to restrict such behaviour, but compromise was often easier; we find estates in Egypt which maintained their own groups of *bucellarii* and had private gaols. It was cheaper to uphold imperial authority in collaboration with such people, even if this effectively reduced the overall supremacy of the individual emperor.

The leaders of tribal groups who established themselves in Roman provinces could be placed in this category of warlords, effective military protectors whose authority gradually came to be accepted by remaining Roman inhabitants, even aristocrats, as well as their tribal followers. Visigothic and Ostrogothic kings had to maintain two contrasting images, as civilised dispensers of

> *In response to the Vandal conquest of Africa, Valentinian relaxed the ban on private individuals carrying weapons (June 440) (Valentinian III, Novel 6.2.3).*
>
> 'As often as the public welfare demands we consider that the solicitude of all must be summoned in aid ... we admonish each and all by this edict that, with confidence in Roman strength, if the occasion should so demand, they shall use those arms which they can, but they shall preserve the public discipline and the moderation of free birth unimpaired.'

laws whose ability to uphold local peace justified their appropriation of properties which had once been Roman and of tax revenues, and as effective war leaders who could still circulate gifts to their entourages. Latin rhetoric, as seen through the writings of Cassiodorus, and Roman law as in the Code of Euric underpinned the former aspect. On the other hand, the continuing importance of military prowess contributed to a militarisation of the Roman elements in their kingdoms: in Merovingian France and Visigothic Spain in the sixth century the surviving Roman cities maintained their own militias which could be quite effective, if small, military units.

Christianity

War fundamentally affected the Empire in a variety of ways, but perhaps the development of greatest long-term significance was its impact on religious beliefs; war and victory underpinned the explosion of Christianity as the Empire's dominant religion. In the third century the traditional Graeco-Roman gods oversaw the salvation of the Empire, aided in accordance with individual preference by a variety of other local or imported deities such as Mithras or the Unconquered Sun. Worship was an important factor in ensuring the allegiance and discipline of the armies, as illustrated by the calendar of religious sacrifices from Dura Europus (the Roman outpost on the Euphrates): the life of military units was organised around a series of sacrifices, in which commemoration of important imperial anniversaries was prominent, while images of the current emperor or emperors were placed between the legionary standards so that they shared the fierce loyalty which the eagles attracted. The major persecutions of Christians in the third century were triggered by imperial demands to sacrifice for the safety of the Empire.

The religious world changed, at least in outward appearance, when Constantine adopted the Christian God as his divine companion and granter of victory, a move justified by successes at the Milvian Bridge and then over Licinius. Thereafter the Christian God assisted his servants, whether in civil war as at Mursa in 351 when Constantius' victory was signalled by the appearance of a cross in the sky at Jerusalem, or in foreign adventures as in Justinian's reconquest of Africa, which was guaranteed by a bishop's dream and Christian omens. Emperors might consult prominent Christians about future campaigns, as when Zeno visited Daniel the Stylite, who had taken up residence on a column near the Bosporus, to ask his advice about an expedition to fight the Vandals. The Church became involved in victory celebrations to the extent that the victorious entry of Justinian to Constantinople in 559 culminated in prayers at the altar of S. Sophia. Imperial warfare might even take on crusading overtones: Constantine's final campaign against Persia was accompanied by propaganda about the liberation of Christians in Mesopotamia, and in the 620s Heraclius mobilised the rump of his Empire to ward off Persians and Avars by presenting the Romans as the beleaguered children of Israel with a mission to crush the heathen and recover the relic of the Holy Cross from Babylon.

In contrast to such successes, non-Christians were spectacularly unsuccessful:

Ankara citadel. (Author's collection)

Julian the apostate led a massive army to disaster in Persia, while his own death in a skirmish was attributed by some to the miraculous intervention of St Mercurius; the pagan usurper Eugenius was overwhelmed by the orthodox Theodosius at the Frigidus River; and Constantinople was delivered from the threat of an alleged Gothic plot by the intervention of an angel. Heretical Christians might be as unsuccessful: Emperor Valens, an opponent of Nicene Christianity, died after the catastrophe of Adrianople.

Everything conspired to demonstrate the power of the true Christian God and the importance of correct worship, an issue which had already exercised Constantine: he urged the importance of Christian unity to achieve efficacious supplications to God and provided support for clergy attached to the correct, orthodox, group. As a result, emperors became closely involved in the agreement and enforcement of what was doctrinally right, and in ecclesiastical discipline, although these areas of belief proved much more resistant to Imperial command than the secular fields in which they usually operated. Within months of his victory at the Milvian Bridge, Constantine was invited to adjudicate in the Donatist dispute – which originated in challenges to the legitimacy of North African clergy who had not stood up to persecution in the third century – and a year after defeating Licinius and acquiring the eastern Empire he presided at the universal council of Nicaea, which attempted to resolve the Arian dispute about the relationship of God the Father and Christ the Son. In each case the dispute was still unresolved a century later.

Emperors used their full military might and political power to uphold their authority over the Church, but it was difficult to achieve the intended results. Justinian had Pope Vigilius brought to Constantinople and then forcibly wrenched from the altar where he had taken refuge to attend a church council in 553, but the Emperor's doctrinal statement which resulted was not widely accepted in the west for over 50 years. In Constantinople occasional tensions between emperor and bishop exacerbated the perennial problems of maintaining order in major conurbations: when Arcadius had Bishop John Chrysostom arrested in 404, the attendant rioting resulted in the burning of S. Sophia and the Senate; Bishop Chrysostom died in exile in 407, but a generation later he was accepted as one of the pillars of the Greek Church.

Alexandria was even more out of control, since the city's bishops financed an enormous clerical establishment, including hundreds of monks in the nearby desert who could be brought into the city and mobilised as needed. Emperors did not regularly keep enough troops in Egypt to confront this potent combination of force, bribery and patronage, and it was easier to come to an accommodation with the preferred leader of the Egyptian Church. Even when emperors resolved to intervene, the authority of their ecclesiastical nominees rarely extended beyond the city of Alexandria, and their opponents were always awaiting the opportunity to strike back: Proterius was sustained as bishop with Emperor Marcian's backing, but on Marcian's death he was dragged from the baptistery of his church and publicly dismembered by supporters of his rival, Timothy the Cat.

Although Christianity often confirmed imperial prestige, the Church could not fail to be involved also in the fragmentation of authority in the Empire. This was partly because of the power of the bishop in local society. The bishop of Alexandria was exceptional in absolute terms, but in most of the Empire's cities the local bishop was a leading property owner and patron, as well as a person of education. As such they were often trusted to represent their cities: in 481 the bishop of Heraclea in Macedonia saved his people by providing food for Theoderic's Goths; during Khusro I's invasion of Syria in 540 bishops attempted to negotiate limits to Persian depredations; and requests to an emperor for tax remission after a natural disaster might well be articulated by the bishop. This authority, however, could also threaten imperial interests: at Thessalonica in 481, the inhabitants rioted at a rumour that Emperor Zeno intended to allow Goths

to settle in the city and removed the keys from the imperial prefect to entrust them to the bishop; in 594 the bishop of Asemus near the Danube prevented the local militia from being conscripted into the mobile army commanded by Emperor Maurice's brother.

Communities might come to look to living saints or relics as well as bishops to protect them in the absence of imperial help. In the fragmenting western Empire of the fifth century, St Genevieve was credited with saving Paris from Attila, while at Clermont Ferrand in the 470s Bishop Sidonius introduced new devotions to sustain local morale during a protracted blockade. The development of the story of Christ's protection for Edessa in Mesopotamia has already been noted (see page 56). Thessalonica is another place where one can see the local church developing its supernatural assistants when imperial protection was lacking. In the early seventh century the city's bishop produced a collection of miracles performed by the city's patron saint Demetrius, which particularly stressed his ability to save his city from capture by Avars and Slavs; the collection was designed for public recitation during a renewed bout of Avar pressure. Later in the century, when the city was virtually cut off from Constantinople and imperial support, the collection was expanded with further examples of Demetrius' miraculous intervention in sieges and blockades. Demetrius was capable of humbling imperial prefects who did not recognise his superior authority or attend to the interests of his city, and of challenging the emperor by redirecting food supplies bound for Constantinople.

As long as the Empire flourished the close connection of Christianity and war strengthened imperial authority, and even the occasions of tension when secular power was fragmenting reflected rather than caused imperial decline. There are, however, ways in which the Church has been criticised for contributing to the Empire's collapse, through the appropriation of

The walls of Nicaea, (modern Iznik, Turkey); the column bases and other reused material at the bases of the towers reflects their rapid construction. (Author's collection)

precious resources and the inculcation of an unwarlike or defeatist spirit.

The Church did require the service of numerous clergy, and the growing monastic

'At the very moment of despair God raised up Ephrem, the Count of the east, to assume every care that the city of Antioch should not lack any necessities. As a consequence the Antiochenes, in admiration, elected him as their priest and he obtained the apostolic see as a reward for his especial support.'

importantly, as a recipient of benefactions individual churches accumulated massive wealth in precious metal. How far these developments drained secular resources depends in part on the costs of religious activities in the period before the triumph of Christianity, but there is likely to have been an increase. In a crisis monks and clergy might be made liable to conscription, and ecclesiastical treasures were often deployed to ransom captives or save cities from being sacked; in the 620s Heraclius financed his campaigns through a compulsory loan of the wealth of the church at Constantinople. This might suggest that these resources were not completely alienated from secular use, but the question must remain as to whether they might have been employed more effectively if they had been available to finance regular military expenditure.

With regard to attitudes towards war it is essential not to impose modern views: for us Christianity might be a religion of peace, but Constantine had chosen the Christians' deity as an Old Testament God of Battles. There was, however, a negative side to Christianity's ability to sustain Roman morale, since the belief that God rewarded his virtuous servants with victory also provided an explanation for defeat in terms of sin or incorrect worship. In the eastern empire during the sixth century a long-running dispute about the composition

movement in the fifth century removed many more from secular activities. As a massive property owner, the Church reduced the area liable to taxation and, more

Walls of Thessalonica, the fourth-century defences of Galerius' capital. (Author's collection)

of Christ, how the divine and human elements were fused within his single being without undermining the integrity of either element, resulted in the alienation from Constantinople of many of the inhabitants of the eastern provinces. Emperors were regarded as heretical, and attempts to coerce unity as persecution. As a result imperial misfortune came to be expected, or at least accepted by the populations of Syria, Egypt and Armenia who did not share the emperor's views. The situation became even more complex in the 630s when Heraclius attempted to impose a doctrinal compromise which most Christians found unacceptable: the emperor's descent into heresy provided the perfect explanation for the contemporary successes of the Arabs. Nothing was likely to be achieved until the emperor turned back to God and worshipped correctly, so nothing should be done.

Notable individuals

Ambrose, Bishop of Milan

Ambrose (bishop 374–97), son of a praetorian prefect, pursued an official career and became governor of the province of Aemilia in 372/3, with his seat at Milan, the western imperial capital. The Church at Milan was dominated by Arians with imperial support when Ambrose got involved, somewhat improperly, in the election of a new bishop for the supporters of the Council of Nicaea. Ambrose was chosen, though he was not yet baptised, so that he progressed to the bishopric one week after formally joining the Church.

Ambrose energetically promoted his brand of Christianity, building churches and discovering relics to underpin their sanctity, promoting female piety, encouraging hymn singing and patronising scholarship. He was an accomplished orator, whose intellectual sermons gained a following among educated imperial officials, people of similar background to him. His secular career gave him the skills to manipulate councils into supporting his views, and the experience to stand up to emperors, first Valentinian II, who demanded a church for Arian worship, then, twice, Theodosius over his attempt to punish zealous Christians in Syria who had destroyed a synagogue and his massacre of civilians in Thessalonica; on the last occasion the emperor performed public penance. Ambrose, however, also used Christianity to uphold imperial power, being responsible for linking the legend of the discovery of the True Cross to Constantine's mother, Helena: Ambrose

Stylised woodcut showing a scene from the life of Ambrose, Bishop of Milan. (Ancient Art and Architecture)

proposed that the incorporation of nails from the Cross into the imperial helmet and bridle symbolised Christianity's support for enduring secular military authority. After his death in 397, Ambrose's reputation was rapidly consolidated through a biography by his secretary, but the bishopric of Milan lost its special importance when the court moved to the greater safety of Ravenna.

Symeon, ascetic and saint

Symeon Stylites (390–459) was one of the most influential of eastern holy men. After a decade in various Syrian monasteries where his fierce asceticism provoked unease, Symeon moved to a hillside near Telneshin where he lived in a small hut; fame brought pilgrims whose attentions prompted Symeon to transfer first to one column, and then to a taller one of about 60 feet (20.4m) where he remained for the last 30 years of his life. The power of his prayers and curses was famous and attracted visitors from the west and beyond the Empire's borders. Symeon berated Emperor Theodosius II for legislating to protect law-abiding pagans and Jews, and Emperor Leo consulted him in 457 about sensitive ecclesiastical issues.

Symeon's death on 2 September 459 provoked competition for his body and relics: his companions feared that local villagers or nomadic Arabs might steal his corpse for their own benefit. Martyrius, patriarch of Antioch, and Ardabur, the senior general in the east, came to the column with Gothic soldiers who escorted the corpse to Antioch, where the inhabitants wanted it as a talisman against earthquakes; Symeon, too, looked after himself by freezing Martyrius' hand when the latter attempted to remove a hair from his beard. Symeon's dirty leather loincloth was offered to Emperor Leo, but ended up in the possession of Symeon's spiritual son, the stylite Daniel, who took up his station on the Bosporus. During the 480s a massive monastic complex was constructed at Qalat Seman around Symeon's empty column, the main church being 328 feet (100m) from east to west and

The historian Evagrius records an occasion in the 580s when the senior general in the east asked to use Symeon's relics (1.13).

'I saw his holy head when Philippicus requested that precious relics be sent for the protection of the eastern armies. And the extraordinary thing was that the hairs which lay upon his head had not been corrupted, but are preserved as if he were alive again. And the skin on his forehead was wrinkled and withered, but still it is intact, as are the majority of his teeth, except for those forcibly removed by the hands of devout men.'

295 feet (90m) from north to south, and the site remained a popular focus for pilgrimage.

John the Lydian, eastern civil servant

John was born in 490 at Philadelphia in Asia Minor, from where he moved to Constantinople to find a post in the palace secretariat. While awaiting an opening he studied philosophy, but then jumped at the opportunity provided by the elevation of a fellow-townsman to the praetorian prefecture in 511. He was allocated a senior position with a substantial income from semi-official fees, and rewarded for a panegyric of his patron with one gold coin per line. John had an excellent knowledge of Latin, which was being used less commonly in the eastern Empire, even though it was the language of law, and for a time he was very busy preparing legal materials in the prefecture while also maintaining an alternative career path by working in the palace. After his patron left office, John's career reverted to a more normal trajectory whereby length of service determined promotion.

John's literary talents continued to attract attention, and he was asked by Justinian to present a panegyric in front of aristocrats from Rome and then to compose a history of the Persian campaigns including the Roman victory at Dara in 530. He secured one of the public professorships in Constantinople, probably in the 540s, and combined this with work in the prefecture until his retirement after 40 years and four months of service in 551/2. He is best known for his work 'On Magistracies', which included a study of the praetorian prefecture that aired his own jaundiced views on administrative innovations and the declining importance of traditional qualities, such as literary ability and skill at Latin.

Cassiodorus, Roman in Ostrogothic service

Three generations of Cassiodori had been important public officials in Italy for Roman and tribal rulers when the young Flavius Magnus Aurelius Cassiodorus Senator was selected by his father, the praetorian prefect, as advisor in 503–07. Thereafter he regularly served the Ostrogoths at Ravenna as legal expert and composer of official correspondence in elegant Latin, along the way securing the honours of a consulship in 514 and the

Folio from the *Notitia Dignitatum* showing the office of the praetorian prefect with ceremonial four-horse carriage, ink stand, candlesticks, and imperial letter of appointment. (MS Canon Misc. 378, f. 90, Bodleian Library)

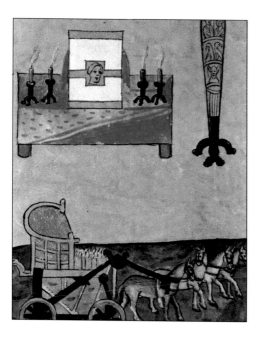

patriciate in the 530s; even after the start of the Justinianic reconquest he continued to serve as praetorian prefect, organising supplies for Ostrogothic forces. With the collapse of the Ostrogothic regime he embraced the religious life, and was in Constantinople in 550, probably as a refugee from the war-torn chaos of Italy. In the mid-550s he returned to found a monastery at Squillace in his native Calabria, where he lived until his death in about 580.

He was a prolific writer. Apart from the 12 volumes of letters which underpin our knowledge of the Ostrogothic kingdom, he composed panegyrics on King Theoderic and his son-in-law, accepted a royal request to write a history of the Goths which proclaimed the antiquity of the Gothic race and the ruling Amal family, and produced several philosophical and religious works. At his monastery he hoped that secular learning could be sustained as an aid to religious understanding; to this end he compiled two books of 'Divine and Human Institutes', works on grammar, etymology and figures of speech, which were intended to assist his monks in their role as scribes, and commentaries on the Psalms and other books of the Bible. In addition he commissioned other works, such as a Latin translation of the main Greek church historians of the fourth and fifth centuries. His monastery scarcely survived his death, but his writings had a profound influence on the direction of western monasticism and its role in the preservation of classical learning.

Antonina, wife of general Belisarius

Antonina was born probably about 484, into a family of entertainers, her father being a charioteer in Constantinople and her mother an actress. She had at least one husband before marrying Belisarius, sometime in the early 520s when he was bodyguard for the future Emperor Justinian; if one believes the historian Procopius (who disliked Antonina) she had previously had several lovers and betrayed Belisarius by pursuing an affair with his godson.

Promotion for Belisarius and friendship with Justinian's wife, Empress Theodora – another product of the entertainment world – brought Antonina considerable influence; at some point she was granted the exalted patrician rank. She accompanied Belisarius on his western campaigns, helping to improve the expedition's water supply on the voyage to Africa in 533, organising a fleet and supplies for Belisarius during the siege of Rome in 537, and allegedly dominating her husband. On behalf of Theodora she helped to oust Pope Silverius in 537, secure the downfall of Justinian's former financial officer John the Cappadocian in 541, and persuade Pope Vigilius to espouse Theodora's theological preferences. When Belisarius was disgraced in 542/3 Antonina worked to recover imperial favour, and then accompanied him on his reappointment to Italy in 544. She returned to Constantinople to plead for reinforcements, but the death of Theodora in 548 persuaded her to press instead for Belisarius' recall; she also terminated the marriage of her daughter to Theodora's grandson to prevent the imperial house from acquiring the family's wealth. She may have outlived Belisarius, who died in 565.

Ravenna mosaic of Theodora, wife of Justinian I, with her entourage. Mosaic from the Basilica of S. Vitale, Ravenna. (Ancient Art and Architecture)

Making new boundaries

Disintegration of the Empire

A period of war lasting four centuries and involving several different regional conflicts is unlikely to have a clear end, but three major developments can legitimately be considered to signal the conclusion of the campaigns of the late Roman period: in the eastern empire and North Africa the sweeping victories of Islamic Arabs; in the Balkans the progressive occupation of territory by Slav tribes, who eventually generated identifiable governing elites; and in the west the consolidation of tribal kingdoms in spite of Justinian's massive effort at reconquest.

In the east while Heraclius had been locked in his desperate struggle with the Persians, events of enormous importance were unfolding in the Arabian peninsula. At Mecca a 40-year-old trader received a divine message from the angel Gabriel. For the next dozen years or so Muhammad stayed in Mecca, receiving more messages, and gradually built up a following, although this success increased tensions with the polytheists who remained the majority community. In 622 Muhammad and his followers moved north to Yathrib (Medina), an event (the *hijra*) which marked the start of the Islamic era.

By Muhammad's death in 632 he had asserted his control over Mecca as well as much of the northern part of the Arabian peninsula, and under his successors the Arabs pushed into Palestine and Syria. In 633 and 634 there was a series of limited victories, which permitted the Arabs to enter Damascus. In 636 a major Roman counter-offensive, commanded by the Emperor Heraclius' brother Theodore who had assembled most of the military resources of the eastern provinces, ended in disaster at the River Yarmuk. Roman resistance was broken and over the next few years the major cities of Palestine and Syria surrendered, while in 640 the Arabs took over Roman Mesopotamia and campaigned into Armenia, Cilicia and Anatolia. In 639 attacks on Egypt began and by 642 this province too was captured; in less than a decade all the richest areas of the Roman Empire had fallen under Arab control.

What is most striking about this achievement – apart from its speed and complete surprise – is that at the same time Arab armies were dismantling the Persian Empire. Admittedly the Sassanid dynasty had been in turmoil since Khusro II's overthrow in 628, but the accession of Khusro's grandson Yazdgard III in 632 had brought some stability; however, Persian armies were unable to withstand this new challenge. By the early 640s Yazdgard had been forced to abandon all the royal cities in lower Mesopotamia and seek refuge in north-eastern Iran; in 651 Yazdgard was under pressure even there when his assassination terminated the Sassanid dynasty and confirmed Muslim rule over the whole of the Middle East.

By 700 the Arabs had wrested all North Africa from Roman control, and had started to conquer the Visigoths in Spain. The one direction in which they failed to make lasting progress was in Anatolia, where Roman resistance gradually hardened. After capturing Alexandria the Arabs developed a powerful navy, which brought control of Cyprus and endangered the southern coastline of Asia Minor and the Aegean islands. On land, repeated raiding impoverished vast tracts of inland Asia Minor, and resulted in the destruction or desertion of many of the major cities: refugees streamed away from the invaders in

Islamic conquests

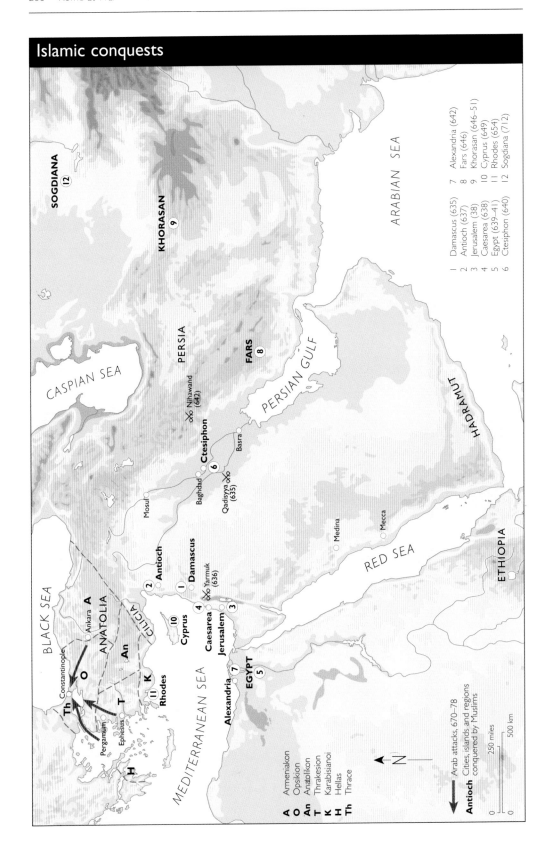

ARABIAN SEA

1 Damascus (635)   7 Alexandria (642)
2 Antioch (637)   8 Fars (646)
3 Jerusalem (38)   9 Khorasan (646–51)
4 Caesarea (638)   10 Cyprus (649)
5 Egypt (639–41)   11 Rhodes (654)
6 Ctesiphon (640)   12 Sogdiana (712)

SOGDIANA ⑫

KHORASAN ⑨

PERSIA

CASPIAN SEA

FARS ⑧

Nihawand (642)

Ctesiphon ⑥

Basra

PERSIAN GULF

Mosul

Baghdad

Qadisiyya (635)

HADRAMUT

Medina

Mecca

BLACK SEA

Antioch ②

Damascus ①

Yarmuk (636)

Ankara A

ANATOLIA

An

CILICIA

Cyprus ⑩

Caesarea ④

Jerusalem ③

Constantinople

O

Th

EGYPT ⑤

Alexandria ⑦

RED SEA

ETHIOPIA

K

T

Rhodes ⑪

H

Ephesus

Pergamum

MEDITERRANEAN SEA

A   Armeniakon
O   Opsikion
An Anatolikon
T   Thrakesion
K   Karabisianoi
H   Hellas
Th Thrace

→ Arab attacks, 670–78

Antioch Cities, islands and regions
         conquered by Muslims

0   250 miles

0   500 km

N

Post-Roman West

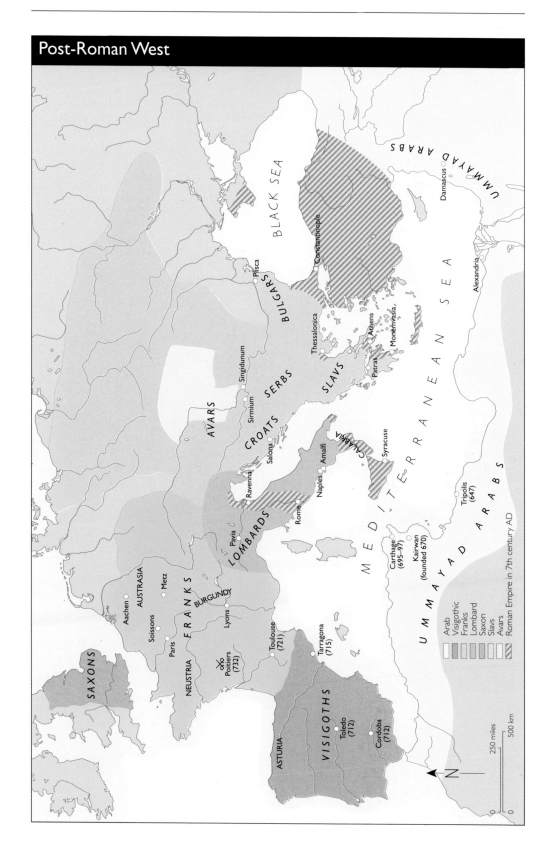

BLACK SEA

UMMAYAD ARABS

Damascus

Constantinople

Alexandria

Pliska

BULGARS

Thessalonica

Athens

Singidunum

SERBS

Patras

Monemvasia

SLAVS

Sirmium

CROATS

Syracuse

Salona

CALABRIA

MEDITERRANEAN SEA

Ravenna

Naples

Amalfi

Tripolis
(647)

AVARS

Rome

LOMBARDS

Pavia

Carthage
(695–97)

Kairwan
(founded 670)

UMMAYAD ARABS

AUSTRASIA

Aachen

Metz

FRANKS

BURGUNDY

Soissons

Paris

Lyons

NEUSTRIA

Toulouse
(721)

Poitiers
(732)

SAXONS

Tarragona
(715)

ASTURIA

VISIGOTHS

Toledo
(712)

Cordoba
(712)

Arab
Visigothic
Franks
Lombard
Saxon
Slavs
Avars
Roman Empire in 7th century AD

250 miles

500 km

N

search of safety in the mountains, while repeated disaster challenged the stability of religious convictions. At Constantinople, however, in the 670s, the Arabs eventually stumbled decisively: the capital's substantial walls and the Roman navy (with its secret weapon of Greek fire) were underpinned by the city's divine defenders, among whom the Virgin was prominent through the relics of her robe and girdle, and the Arabs were compelled to retreat.

Over the next generation a new order was created in Roman territory: the old social system based on the grand provincial cities had been swept away so that villages and rural markets came to the fore, while administrative organisation was directed towards sustaining the military units responsible for frontier defence. Only Constantinople survived as a recognisable city, and even its population had probably shrunk to a tenth of what it had once been. Continued failure to reverse Arab successes contributed to religious upheaval: for much of the eighth century the rump of the eastern Empire was riven by disputes about the validity of images in Christian worship, with iconoclast emperors supporting the Muslim view that images were idolatrous.

In the Balkans the Romans experienced losses which, if less spectacular in terms of military action, were almost as complete as

> *At Pergamum in 716 the defenders resorted to desperate measures, intended to avert an apocalyptic scourge (Theophanes,* Chronographica p.390).
>
> 'Maslamah ben Abd al-Malik came to Pergamum, which he besieged and captured by God's dispensation, through the Devil's machinations. For at a magician's instigation the city's inhabitants procured a pregnant woman and cut her up; after removing the infant and cooking it in a pot, all those about to fight dipped the sleeves of their right arm in the loathsome sacrifice. Accordingly they were delivered to the enemy.'

in the east. We have no detailed knowledge of the sequence of events after Maurice's death in 602, when Roman authority had been superficially restored over much of the peninsula. Phocas and Heraclius both gave precedence to eastern campaigns; troops were progressively removed from the Balkans, which permitted Slav groups to move unhindered across the countryside. The Avars occasionally invaded to extend their authority over the Slavs and surviving Romans, but even their humiliation outside Constantinople in 626 brought no lasting respite. As the Avar federation disintegrated, smaller tribal groups emerged to dominate particular areas, the Bulgars in the north-east, and Croats and Serbs in the north-west. By the latter part of the seventh century only the hinterland of Constantinople and isolated enclaves at Thessalonica, Athens, Corinth and other places accessible by sea remained under Roman authority.

In the western state, the deposition of the last Roman emperor in 476 had brought one sort of end, with Vandals in control of Africa, Visigoths in Spain and southern Gaul, Merovingian Franks in northern Gaul and the Ostrogoths soon to arrive in Italy. Justinian's reconquest threatened to turn back the clock, but in the later sixth century it was the Romans who were being squeezed by the arrival of the Lombards in Italy and the reassertion of Visigothic power in Spain. The west was even lower down the list of imperial priorities than the Balkans, and little could be done to influence events: in 578 Emperor Tiberius had recognised this when he returned the gold which the Roman senate had sent as a gift for his accession with the advice that they should use this to purchase allies among the newly arrived Lombards. By the 590s Roman rule in Italy was confined to Ravenna in the north, which was precariously joined to another area around Rome, and from there to larger enclaves of the extreme south and Sicily. In the seventh century even the visit to Rome of Emperor Constans II did not conclusively re-establish Roman authority. Eventually a

Dome of the Rock, Jerusalem a symbol of Islamic
power at the centre of Christian and Jewish faiths.
(Ancient Art and Architecture)

from the south. These victories were
accompanied by the conversion of their King
Clovis, significantly to Catholic Christianity
rather than the Arian beliefs which other
Germanic tribes espoused; but partitive
inheritance between competing branches of
the family then disrupted the kingdom's
unity. During the sixth century Clovis'
successors had on various occasions
intervened in Italy, on both sides of
the Roman reconquest, contemplated a
grand alliance of tribes to challenge
Constantinople, resisted Avar encroachments
in southern Germany, and weathered
attempts from Constantinople to destabilise
the dynastic balance between different parts
of the kingdom.

> *A graffito scratched by one of the defenders*
> *of Sirmium during its three-year siege by the*
> *Avars in 579–82.*
> 'Lord Christ, help the city and smite
> the Avars and watch over Romania and
> the writer. Amen.'

combination of religious hostility to
iconoclast developments in the east, lack of
respect for the absent and unsuccessful
emperors, and resistance to tax demands
terminated east Roman control over Rome
and Ravenna; the Roman Empire survived in
Sicily and parts of the south, but had ceased
to be a significant element in Italian affairs.

The most important events for the future
of the west occurred in France. By the early
sixth century this had been largely united
under the Merovingian Frankish dynasty
which had first suppressed Roman warlords
in the north and then driven the Visigoths

After the 630s Merovingian rulers wielded
little real power, which increasingly slipped
into the hands of the royal stewards, the
most powerful being the family of Pippin. By
the late seventh century the Pippinids had
effectively displaced the Merovingians and it
was the Pippinid Charles Martel who rolled
back the Islamic invaders at Poitiers in 732.
Thereafter his grandson Charles 'the Great' –
Charlemagne – reunited Frankish Gaul and
conquered the Lombards in Italy.
Charlemagne's visit to Rome in 800 and his
coronation in St Peter's sealed the creation
of the Holy Roman Empire.

Roman legacies

The four centuries of war during which the Roman Empire was torn apart provided the basis for a new political map of Europe, the Middle East and North Africa. Instead of a collection of provinces whose different peoples, cultures and traditions were gradually transformed through contact with Roman power so that acceptance of a central authority was accompanied by a display of some common features, a fragmented world emerged; in different areas diverse elites came to the fore, a process whose results still dominate the modern map.

The Roman Empire did not end, since the rump of the eastern provinces continued to be ruled from Constantinople by emperors who regarded themselves and their people as

Rhomaioi. This beleaguered state, which saw itself as the guardian of the Roman political, religious and cultural inheritance, found the resources to survive the intense Arab pressure of the late seventh and early eighth centuries and then to embark on substantial reconquests in the Balkans and Asia Minor in the tenth. Although the arrival of the Seljuk Turks in the eleventh century curtailed its resources and power again, the fabled wealth of the east attracted Viking mercenaries to travel south through Russia, and then the treacherous Fourth Crusade sacked Constantinople in 1204. But a Roman state survived on the Bosporus until Ottoman artillery blasted its way through the Roman walls of Constantinople in 1453.

In the Middle East, however, a millennium of control by Greeks and Romans terminated and the region changed

The walls of Ankara showing the pentagonal tower. (Ancient Art and Architecture)

Trapian silver, in unreconstructed state.
(National Museum of Scotland)

to leadership by a Semitic race. A visible sign was the reversion of many cities to their pre-Hellenistic local names – Urfa for Edessa, Membij for Hierapolis, Baalbek for Heliopolis, Amman for Philadelphia – the survival of Alexandria and Antioch (Antakya) were exceptional. The centre of gravity of the new power was also significant. For centuries the Romans had faced an eastern rival whose capitals lay in lower Mesopotamia and the Iranian plateau, whereas the new Arab Empire was usually based much closer to the Mediterranean world: in Syria under the Ummayads and Egypt under the Fatimids. Rome's Parthian and Sassanid enemies had rarely had access to the Mediterranean, whereas the Arabs occupied a number of major ports and rapidly developed a powerful navy. The Mediterranean ceased to be our sea, *mare nostrum*, and became an area of conflict and threat.

Arab control of North Africa extended this threat west, and initiated a structural divide between the northern and southern shores of the Mediterranean: whereas Roman Egypt and Africa had been tied closely into the Empire – socially, as the location of lucrative estates for the senatorial elite, and economically, as the major food providers for Rome and Constantinople – the Barbary Coast was a piratical scourge for Christian Europe. In Spain the Arabs remained the most powerful political force for 500 years, an object for crusade by the northern Christian enclaves but also a stimulus for intellectual and cultural fertilisation.

In north-western Europe Roman control ebbed most quickly and decisively. In the British Isles the Saxons gradually pushed the Romano-British into the far west and established their own competing kingdoms in much of England; the process contributed to the creation of popular stories of Arthur and strengthened ties between Cornwall and Brittany, but otherwise helped to confirm that Britain would develop separately from the continent. In France the consolidation of Pippinid or Carolingian control created the first post-Roman supranational political entity, the Holy Roman Empire, an institution which could challenge eastern Rome in terms of religious authority by manipulating the papacy and as true heirs to imperial Rome by the use of Latin and cultivation of Roman practices.

One area for competition between Holy Rome and eastern Rome was the Balkans, which long remained the most chaotic part of former Roman territory. Much had been overrun by groups of Slavs, but these had been slow to generate their own ruling elites. As Constantinople's power gradually revived in the eighth century, it proved possible to expand its authority in peninsular Greece and the south-eastern Balkans from the islands and coastal enclaves still in its possession, but large parts of the northern and north-western interior were ruled by whatever tribal group had managed to dominate the local Slavs and any survivors of the Roman population. The most important units to emerge were the Bulgar kingdom in the north-east, and the Serb and Croat kingdoms in the north-west. In each case the ruling elite developed a complex relationship with Constantinople, eager for the benefits (cultural as well as economic) of Roman recognition, but also wary of too close a dependence upon a potential imperial master. Constantinople's authority waxed and waned, and the best characterisation of the region is as a commonwealth: its members acknowledged strong ties, but there were also rivalries between potential rulers and the ruled, while the existence of alternative sources of support such as Holy Rome ensured that tensions thrived.

Slavs attempt to encourage the Avars to assist in an assault on Thessalonica (Miracles of St Demetrius §197).
   'They said that all the cities and regions in its vicinity had been depopulated by them, and that it alone held out in their midst, while it had received all the refugees from the Danubian regions, and Pannonia, Dacia, Dardania and the remaining provinces and cities.'

Religious divisions

Competition for religious allegiance was one of the disrupting factors in the Balkans as Rome and Constantinople vied to convert different groups, and systems of belief are one of our major inheritances from the period of late-Roman warfare. The emergence of Christianity as a world faith was the first and most obvious, since it was through warfare that Christianity triumphed within the Empire. But the Roman Empire also shaped the nature of Christianity's development and helped to ensure that this universal religion existed in a variety of competing guises.

The struggle to define orthodoxy generated important excluded groups. In the fourth century Christians loosely associated with the views of Arius (that the Son was subordinate to the Father) had converted Germanic tribes north of the Danube. These tribes had remained unaffected by the final triumph within the Empire of Nicene over Arian Christianity in the 380s; as a result the successor kingdoms of Visigoths, Vandals and Ostrogoths all subscribed to Arian views and were regarded as heretical by Catholics.

In the east the identification in the 420s of the Nestorian heresy, over the status of the Virgin Mary and the place of the divine in Christ, had led to a rift: expulsion of Nestorians from the Empire had helped them to consolidate their domination in Sassanid Persia, where they became accepted as the national Church with their own spiritual leader, *catholicus*, whose appointment usually required royal sanction. Nestorian missionaries exploited Sassanid diplomatic and trading networks to make converts in India, central Asia and China. An inter-related dispute about Christ's nature generated the Monophysite schism in the eastern Empire from the mid-fifth century. Attempts at reconciliation failed, partly because doctrinal concessions to eastern Monophysites provoked disagreements with Rome and the western Church, partly because intermittent coercion served to harden attitudes; the textual bases for the arguments became swamped by propaganda, and their precise distinctions vanished because of the difficulty of translating complex arguments accurately between the languages involved – Latin, Greek, Coptic, Syriac, Armenian. In the mid-sixth century a separate Monophysite hierarchy of bishops emerged to control much of Egypt, Syria and Armenia. After the Arab conquests a new division of Christianity crystalised, with the orthodox or Chalcedonians dominant within the Roman Empire, while Nestorians and Monophysites were the main groups in areas ruled by Arabs, where the limited numbers of Chalcedonians came to be known as Melkites, or emperors' men.

Inside the Empire Rome and Constantinople emerged as the two centres of religious power.

Doctrinal dissension almost generated civil war in the 340s, over the exile of Bishop Athanasius of Alexandria, and eastern attempts to resolve the Monophysite issue produced schisms in the late fifth, the mid-sixth, and for much of the seventh century. Successive emperors believed that they had the right to determine what was correct doctrine, and then the duty to see this accepted throughout their realm. Popes, whose independence was encouraged by Rome's decline as an imperial capital, saw themselves as the true guardians of Christian belief and relished occasions when eastern bishops appealed to the west for decisions. Emperors were prepared to use force to secure papal obedience, but this could only work if Rome itself was safely under eastern control. The basis for a split between Greek and Latin Christianity was established in late antiquity.

The church historian Evagrius laments the narrow disagreement between Chalcedonians ('in two natures') and Monopyhsites ('from two') which bitterly divided the Church (2.5).

'The envious and God-hating Devil thus wickedly devised and misinterpreted a change of a single letter, so that, whereas the utterance of one of these absolutely thereby introduces the other, by most people the difference is considered to be great and their meanings to be in outright antithetical opposition and to be exclusive of each other. For he who confesses Christ in two natures openly declares Him to be from two, in that by confessing Christ jointly in Divinity and humanity he declares in confessing that He is composed from Divinity and humanity.'

Christianity's triumph eliminated pagan beliefs at a formal level, but numerous pre-Christian practices were subsumed into the new religion in the process in spite of some condemnation. Christianity's secular power also caused contamination as episcopal office in the right city became a desirable route to power and wealth. The consequent dilution of the Christian message stimulated purists to seek a more authentic response to the Gospel: in different parts of the Empire individuals attempted to pursue a more rigorous regime, and some of these ascetics, or 'trainees', came to be organised into groups of monks. During the fourth century rules of conduct were developed in Egypt, Syria and Asia Minor and these soon spread west, so that by the time the Empire in the west was faltering in the mid-fifth century monasteries were sufficiently established to transmit Roman religious and cultural traditions.

Jews, however, were a victim of Christian zeal. In the pre-Christian Empire, Jews had usually been tolerated as an eccentric but acceptable group whose religious commitment was hallowed by antiquity, whereas for Christians they were the murderers of Christ. In the third-century persecutions, emperors had respected Jewish beliefs and not required sacrifice. In theory Jews continued to be protected by imperial legislation, but in practice this could not be upheld against enthusiastic Christian mobs: synagogues were destroyed, graveyards ransacked and congregations even forcibly converted. Such pressures produced a backlash and on occasions Jews sided with the Empire's enemies, most notoriously after the Persian siege of Jerusalem in 614. Suspicions against Jews increased and popular anti-Semitism came to be reinforced by official tolerance and legislation.

The other great religious change, generated by the wars of late antiquity, was Islam, which spread over the Near East and North Africa through armed conquest. Holy war, *jihad*, spurred expansion, while the privileged position of warriors in the early conquest communities in Iraq, Syria and Egypt, coupled with extra tax burdens on unbelievers, encouraged conversion. The Arab capture of Jerusalem and the Holy Land placed the sacred places of both Christians and Jews under alien authority and created a desire for retaliation. The east–west political rivalry of Sassanids and Romans had now been complicated by a potent religious factor.

Such far-reaching political and religious developments were accompanied by significant social and cultural changes. The corner-stone of the Roman Empire had been

S. Sophia (Hagia Sophia), Istanbul, Turkey. (Ancient Art and Architecture)

the city, which functioned as the centre for diffusing government, the religious focus for an area, and the social magnet for the local elite. In the same way as the growth of imperial prosperity was followed by the spread of urban institutions, so the retreat of Empire was accompanied by their shrinkage or disappearance. During the fourth and fifth centuries rural wealth and urban vitality had contracted away from the northern and western provinces, so that by the sixth century the most thriving cities were located in Asia Minor and Syria. The Arab conquests undermined urban institutions in those areas which remained under Roman control.

Paradoxically perhaps, cities continued to flourish under Arab authority as diverse, commercial social, and intellectual communities. By contrast, in the surviving Empire and the post-Roman west there had been a substantial fall in population levels, due to a combination of warfare, general insecurity, and disease. Bubonic plague had struck the Mediterranean in the 540s, and then returned with regularity for two

centuries. Population centres naturally suffered severely, since plague-bearing fleas needed a reasonable density of hosts in order to flourish; cities were particularly hard hit, but so were armies, and even rural areas such as Palestine (which supported a dense network of villages). For the rich, also, the obligations of urban life had already begun to outweigh the benefits. As a result cities became depopulated. In some areas, such as the north Balkans, there was a vertical move away from exposed lowland sites to the fortified hill-tops used by the pre-Roman inhabitants. Elsewhere the remnants of urban populations clustered around a place of refuge, perhaps a church or monastery, or a fortification built out of one of the massive remains of a Roman city such as a theatre or amphitheatre.

Cultural changes

These shrunken settlements were now dominated by their clergy, and perhaps a few powerful local families, but it was the Church, above all, which gave stability to these societies and determined their priorities. This is particularly evident in the case of education, which had been an important unifying badge for the elite of the Roman world. In the west monasteries became the guardians of knowledge as other sources of learning faded away, while in the east the clerical establishment in Constantinople provided the best opportunities for advanced study within the Empire.

As a result the balance of what was known inevitably shifted, with the priorities of the Church dominating: some aspects of the standard classical education in grammar and rhetoric survived, since clerics still had to participate in debates on doctrine and discipline, but the broad knowledge of the classical literary tradition possessed by leading writers in the fourth century had slipped, and the intellectual speculation encouraged by philosophical study also ceased. Of practical import was the decline in knowledge of languages, which meant that very few in the west outside Byzantine Italy could understand Greek and there were shortages of Latin speakers in the east. The intellectual centre of the Mediterranean world transferred to the lands conquered by Arabs: they ruled Alexandria, the most important university city of the Roman world, there was sufficient wealth in other cities to encourage families to finance the expense of higher education, and there was a curiosity to unlock the secrets of Hellenistic learning. Greek texts, especially of medicine, logic and philosophy, were translated into Arabic and studied, and in some cases it was the Islamic schools in Spain which acted as the conduit for the western rediscovery of this knowledge – Latin translations were made of Arabic versions of the Greek originals.

One aspect of ancient learning that continued to develop was law. In the 430s Theodosius II had presided over a major compilation of imperial law, and a century later Justinian had overhauled the law code and texts for legal education. Organised laws could contribute to the more effective exercise of power, and even the publication of a code bolstered authority. It is noticeable that rulers of post-Roman states in the West saw the advantages in publishing their own codes which combined Roman and Germanic law in differing proportions; this ensured that

important principles of Roman law were transmitted to medieval western kingdoms, and hence to serve as the base for much European law.

Diplomacy was another area of continuing development, driven by practical concerns. In the early Roman Empire there had been no tradition of systematic acquisition and compilation of information about neighbours and possible threats, but this had begun to change as the Empire came under increasing pressure. In the fifth century, when Attila's Huns were threatening the eastern Empire, Constantinople developed a system for regulating relations with Sassanid Persia in an effort to ensure stability, and also appreciated the advantages of detailed knowledge about other neighbours. In the sixth century these practices continued, so that eastern rulers were presented with information about the rulers of Axum in Ethiopia and the Turks in central Asia, all as part of Roman competition with Persia. The ability to play off possible enemies against each other became a hallmark of 'Byzantine' diplomacy, as the progressively weaker Empire relied more on non-military means to secure its survival.

Emperor Theodosius as a lawgiver. Frontispiece from Visigoth recension of the Codex of Theodosianus. (Ancient Art and Architecture)

Further reading

Primary sources

Ammianus Marcellinus, *The Later Roman Empire A.D. 353–378*, ed. W. Hamilton, 1986.
Appian, *The Civil Wars*, tr. J. Carter, 1996.
Blockley, R.C. (ed.), *The Fragmentary Classicising Historians of the Later Roman Empire II*, 1985.
Blockley, R.C. (ed.), *The History of Menander the Guardsman*, 1985.
Caesar, *The Civil War*, tr. J. Gardner, 1967.
Caesar, *The Conquest of Gaul*, tr. J. Gardner, 1982.
Cassius Dio, *The Roman History: The Reign of Augustus*, ed. I. Scott-Kilvert, 1987.
Cicero, *Selected Letters*, tr. D. R. Shackleton-Bailey, 1986.
Lactantius, *De Mortibus Persecutorum*, ed. J.L. Creed, 1984.
Nixon, C.E.V., & Rodgers, B.S. (eds.), *In Praise of Later Roman Emperors: The Panegyrici Latini*, 1994.
Plutarch, *Fall of the Republic*, tr. R. Warner, revised, 1972.
Plutarch, *The Makers of Rome*, tr. I. Scott-Kilvert, 1965.
Procopius, *The Secret History*, tr. G.A. Williamson, 1981.
Suetonius, *The Twelve Caesars*, tr. R. Graves, revised, 2003.

Secondary sources

Adcock, F., *The Roman Art of War under the Republic*, 1940.
Bachrach, B.S., *Merovingian Military Organization 481–751*, 1972.
Barnwell, P.S., *Emperor, Prefects & Kings, the Roman West, 395–565*, 1992.
Barnwell, P.S., *Kings, Courtiers and Imperium. The Barbarian West, AD 565–725*, 1992.

Bishop, M., & Coulston, J., *Roman Military Equipment*, 1993.
Blockley, R.C., *East Roman Foreign Policy, Formation and Conduct from Diocletian to Anastasius*, 1992.
Le Bohec, Y., *The Imperial Roman Army*, 1994.
Bowersock, G.W., Brown, P., and Grabar O. (eds.), *Late Antiquity, A Guide to the Postclassical World*, 1999.
Brown, P.R.L., *The World of Late Antiquity: From Marcus Aurelius to Muhammad*, 1971.
Browning, R., *The Emperor Julian*, 1975.
Brunt, P., *The Fall of the Roman Republic*, 1988.
Burns, T.S., *A History of the Ostrogoths*, 1984.
Bury, J.B., *History of the Later Roman Empire, from the death of Theodosius I to the death of Justinian*, 1923.
Cameron, A., *Circus Factions, Blues and Greens at Rome and Byzantium*, 1976.
Cameron, A., & Long, J., *Barbarians and Politics at the Court of Arcadius*, 1993.
Cameron, A.M., *Procopius and the Sixth Century*, 1985.
Cameron, A.M., *The Later Roman Empire*, 1993.
Cameron, A.M., *The Mediterranean World in Late Antiquity*, 1993.
Cameron, A.M. (ed.), *The Byzantine and Early Islamic Near East III, States, Resources, Armies*, 1995.
Cameron, A.M., & Garnsey, P. (eds.), *The Cambridge Ancient History XIII AD 337–425*, 1997.
Cameron, A.M., Ward-Perkins, B, & Whitby, L.M. (eds.), *The Cambridge Ancient History XIV AD 425–600*, 2000.
Campbell, J.B., *The Emperor and the Roman Army 31 BC–AD 235*, 1984.
Collins, R., *Early Medieval Spain, Unity in Diversity 400–1000*, 1983.
Collins, R., *Early Medieval Europe, 300–1000*, 1991.

Corcoran, S., *The Empire of the Tetrarchs, Imperial Pronouncements and Government AD 284–324*, 1996.

Cormack, R., *Writing in Gold: Byzantine Society and its Icons*, 1985.

Crump, G., *Ammianus Marcellinus as a Military Historian*, 1975.

Dodgeon, M.H., & Lieu, S.N.C., *The Roman Eastern Frontier and the Persian Wars, AD 226–363*, 1991.

Donner, F., *Early Islamic Conquests*, 1981.

Drinkwater, J., *Roman Gaul*, 1983.

Drinkwater, J., & Elton H. (eds.), *Fifth-century Gaul: a Crisis of Identity?*, 1992.

Dupuy, T., *The Military Life of Julius Caesar*, 1969.

Evans, J.A.S., *The Age of Justinian, the Circumstances of Imperial Power*, 1996.

Ferrill, A., *The Fall of the Roman Empire, the Military Explanation*, 1986.

Feugere, M., *Les armes des Romains*, 1993.

Fowden, G., *Empire to Commonwealth, Consequences of Monotheism in Late Antiquity*, 1993.

Frank, R.I., *Scholae Palatinae: the Palace Guards of the Later Roman Empire*, 1969.

Fuller, J., *Julius Caesar: Man, Soldier and Tyrant*, 1965.

Garnsey, P., & Humfress, C., *The Evolution of the Late Antique World*, 2001.

Gelzer, M., *Caesar, Politician and Statesman*, 1968.

Gilliver, C., *The Roman Art of War*, 1999.

Goffart, W., *Barbarians and Romans AD 418–584: The Techniques of Accommodation*, 1980.

Goldsworthy, A., *The Roman Army at War, 100 BC–AD 200*, 1996.

Goldsworthy, A., *Roman Warfare*, 2000.

Goudineau, C., *César et la Gaule*, Paris, 1990.

Greatrex, G., *Rome and Persia at War, 502–532*, 1998.

Greatrex, G., & Lieu, S.N.C., *The Roman Eastern Frontier and the Persian Wars II, AD 363–630*, 2002.

Gruen, E. S., *The Last Generation of the Roman Republic*, 1974.

Haldon, J.F., *Recruitment and Conscription in the Byzantine Army c.550–950*, 1979.

Haldon, J.F., *Byzantium in the Seventh Century, the Transformation of a Culture*, 1990.

Harries, J., *Sidonius Apollinaris and the Fall of Rome*, 1994.

Heather, P.J., *Goths and Romans 332–489*, 1991.

Heather, P.J., *The Goths*, Oxford, 1996.

Holmes, T. Rice, *Caesar's Conquest of Gaul*, 1911.

Holum, K., *Theodosian Empresses: Women and Imperial Dominion in Late Antiquity*, 1982.

Isaac, B., *The Limits of Empire, The Roman Army in the East*, 1990.

James, E., *The Origins of France: from Clovis to the Capetians 500–1000*, 1983.

James, E., *The Franks*, 1988.

Jones, A.H.M., *The Later Roman Empire 284–602, A Social, Economic and Administrative Survey*, 1964.

Jones, A.H.M., Martindale, J.R., & Morris, J. (eds.), *The Prosopography of the Later Roman Empire I*, 1971.

Kaegi, W.E., *Byzantine Military Unrest, 471–843: An Interpretation*, 1981.

Kaegi, W.E., *Byzantium and the Early Islamic Conquests*, 1992.

Keppie, L., *The Making of the Roman Army*, 1984.

King, A.C., *Roman Gaul and Germany*, 1990.

Lee, A.D., *Information and Frontiers, Roman foreign relations in late antiquity*, 1993.

Liebeschuetz, J.H.W.G., *Barbarians and Bishops, Army, Church and State in the Age of Arcadius and John Chrysostom*, 1990.

Luttwak, E.N., *The Grand Strategy of the Roman Empire from the First Century AD to the Third*, 1976.

MacMullen, R., *Soldier and Civilian in the Later Roman Empire*, 1963.

MacMullen, R., *Corruption and the Decline of Rome*, 1988.

McCormick, M., *Eternal Victory, Triumphal Rulership in Late Antiquity, Byzantium and the Early Medieval West*, 1986.

Mango, C.A., *Byzantium: The Empire of New Rome*, 1980.

Martindale, J.R. (ed.), *The Prosopography of the Later Roman Empire II–III*, 1980, 1992.

Matthews, J.F., *Western Aristocracies and Imperial Court AD 364–425*, 1975.

Meier, C., *Caesar*, tr. D. McLintock, 1995.

Millar, F., *The Roman Near East, 31 BC –AD 337*, 1993.

Moorhead, J., *Theoderic in Italy*, 1992.

Nicasie, M.J., *Twilight of Empire: the Roman Army from the Reign of Diocletian until the Battle of Adrianople*, 1998.

Obolensky, D., *The Byzantine Commonwealth*, 1971.

O'Flynn, J.M., *Generalissimos of the Western Roman Empire*, 1983.

Parker, H., *The Roman Legions*, 1928.

Reddé, M., *L'armée Romaine en Gaule*, 1996.

Rich, J., & Shipley, G., *War and Society in the Roman World*, 1993.

Saddington, D., *The Development of the Roman Auxiliary Forces from Caesar to Vespasian*, 1982.

Seager, R., *Pompey, A Political Biography*, 1979.

Southern,P., & Dixon, K.R., *The Late Roman Army*, 1996.

Syme, I., *The Roman Revolution*, 1939.

Thompson, E.A., *Romans and Barbarians, the decline of the Western Empire*, 1982.

Thompson, E.A., *The Huns*, 1995.

Treadgold, W., *The Byzantine Army*, 1995.

Treadgold, W., *A History of the Byzantine State and Society*, 1997.

Van Dam, R., *Leadership and Community in Late Antique Gaul*, 1985.

Watson, A., *Aurelian and the Third Century*, 1999.

Welch, K., & Powell, A. (eds), *Julius Caesar as Artful Reporter. The War Commentaries as Political Instruments*, 1998.

Weinstock, S., *Divus Iulius*, 1971.

Whitby, L.M., *The Emperor Maurice and His Historian, Theophylact Simocatta on Persian and Balkan Warfare*, 1988.

Whittaker, C.R., *Frontiers of the Roman Empire, a Social and Economic Study*, 1994.

Whittow, M., *The Making of Orthodox Byzantium, 600–1025*, 1996.

Wickham, C., *Early Medieval Italy, Central Power and Local Society 400–1000*, 1981.

Williams, S., *Diocletian and the Roman Recovery*, 1985.

Williams, S., & Friell, G., *The Rome That Did Not Fall: the survival of the East in the Fifth Century*, 1999.

Wolfram, H., *History of the Goths*, 1988.

Wood, I.N., *The Merovingian Kingdoms, 450–751*, 1994.

Yavetz, Z., *Julius Caesar and his Public Image*, 1983.

Index